T0114155

Praise for *The Virtue of Prosperity*

"Skillfully illuminate[s] the ethical quandaries of the new prosperity."
—*National Review*

"D'Souza tells us what's right, and what's wrong, with our brave, new, prosperous world. . . . Richly illustrated with fascinating anecdotes."
—*Kirkus Reviews*

"A possible heir to Michael Lewis's role as an insightful chronicler of our times. Delivered in a unique voice and with an unusually light touch."
—*Publishers Weekly*

"D'Souza presents a balanced picture of the current debate between those who applaud technology's achievements and resulting new wealth, and others who deplore the secularization and commodification of human experience that has resulted from our growing dependence on machines and computers."
—Lane Jennings, *The Futurist*

"We have freedom, wealth, and the power to shape a new universe. The last people to find themselves in these circumstances were Adam and Eve. In a great book, D'Souza reminds us: do not log onto www.serpent-chat.com."
—P. J. O'Rourke, author of *Eat the Rich*

"Dinesh D'Souza has done a masterful job of sorting out the explosive issues surrounding today's new wealth and technology. If you want to understand the social and moral implications of the new economy, read this lively and thorough analysis."
—Jim Barksdale, founder of Netscape

"As skillfully as Virgil guiding Dante, Dinesh D'Souza takes you on a breathtaking tour of the new economy. He gives a brilliant and balanced account of the divisions and debates in this new world arising. You will not know during pages of suspense how he will rule, which will keep you flying through this book as fast as a jet."
—Mark Helprin, novelist

"This book shows where the new economy is headed and goes beneath the surface to illuminate the hard choices facing our businesses, our personal lives, and society. It is exactly what we expect from D'Souza—an indispensable book that is also a great read."
—Harvey Golub, chairman and CEO, American Express

"Applying old values to the new economy, Dinesh D'Souza has written a provocative, witty, pertinent, and important book."
—Michael Medved, nationally syndicated talk-radio host

"A fascinating and wonderful book. Even when you disagree with him, D'Souza raises the level of the debate and makes you think. What more could you ask for?"
—John Stossel, ABC News

"In this bracing book, D'Souza neatly inserts himself between the technophiles, who welcome the limitless expansion of technological innovation, and the technophobes, who fear that old values will disappear in this Brave New World. Whatever your politics, read this witty, informative, learned, and lively book."
—Stanley Fish, Dean of Arts & Sciences, University of Illinois, Chicago

Also by Dinesh D'Souza

ILLIBERAL EDUCATION
The Politics of Race and Sex on Campus
(1991)

THE END OF RACISM
Principles for a Multiracial Society
(1995)

RONALD REAGAN
How an Ordinary Man Became
an Extraordinary Leader
(1997)

DINESH D'SOUZA

THE VIRTUE OF PROSPERITY

**FINDING VALUES
IN AN AGE OF
TECHNO-AFFLUENCE**

A TOUCHSTONE BOOK
Published by Simon & Schuster
New York • London • Toronto • Sydney • Singapore

In memory of my father,
Allan D'Souza
1933–2000

TOUCHSTONE
Rockefeller Center
1230 Avenue of the Americas
New York, NY 10020

Copyright © 2000 by Dinesh D'Souza
All rights reserved,
including the right of reproduction
in whole or in part in any form.
First Touchstone Edition 2001
TOUCHSTONE and colophon are trademarks
of Simon & Schuster, Inc.

The excerpt from *Wired* on pages 161–63 is used with permission.

For information about special discounts for bulk purchases,
please contact Simon & Schuster Special Sales:
1-800-456-6798 or business@simonandschuster.com

Manufactured in the United States of America

1 3 5 7 9 10 8 6 4 2

The Library of Congress has cataloged the Free Press edition as follows:
D'Souza, Dinesh, date.
The virtue of prosperity : finding values in an age of techno-affluence / Dinesh D'Souza.
p. cm.
1. Wealth—Moral and ethical aspects—United States.   2. Success—Moral and ethical
aspects—United States.   3. Values—United States.   I. Title.

HC110.W4 D78 2000
174'.4—dc21
00-062313

ISBN: 978-0-684-86815-8

ACKNOWLEDGMENTS

This book would not have been possible without the valuable help of Bruce and Valerie Schooley. Bruce is actually the person who suggested the idea for the book, and he has been involved with it every step of the way. My wife, Dixie, has been a vital source of ideas and suggestions, and has patiently supported me in my labors. My daughter, Danielle, proved to be both an inspiration and, as the reader will discover, an occasional source of research material. My research assistants, Aaron Solomon and Todd Ostroske, were also indispensable. I am very grateful to the American Enterprise Institute for the freedom to pursue projects like this one. Chris DeMuth, president of AEI, is not only the ideal boss but also a very helpful reader. I am pleased to acknowledge the John Olin Foundation, which has provided me with research support over the years. My agent, Rafe Sagalyn, was even more involved than usual in shaping the concept of this book. My editor, Liz Maguire, provided constant encouragement and helpful criticism. While I cannot list all the people I interviewed or whose advice I solicited, I especially wish to thank Larry Arnn and the Claremont Institute, Karlyn Bowman, Robert and LaDorna Eichenberg, David Gerson, Tom Henriksen, Rich Karlgaard, Marvin Kosters, Larry Lindsey, Adam Meyerson, Jim and Mary Nierman, Jim Piereson, John Raisian, Spencer Reiss, Ron Robinson and the Young America's Foundation, and Scott Walter.

CONTENTS

Long is the way and hard,

That out of hell leads up to light.

— Milton, *Paradise Lost*

GEEK CHIC

Anthropologist in a Strange Land

.

You can observe a lot by watching.

—Yogi Berra

To see the new world that is being born, you don't have to go to Silicon Valley. You can see it in Austin, Texas; Boise, Idaho; Boston, Massachusetts; Salt Lake City, Utah; Raleigh-Durham, North Carolina; Reston, Virginia; Champaign, Illinois; or any of the other high-tech cities that dot the map of the United States. You can also find it in Montreal, Canada; Cambridge, England; Dublin, Ireland; Tel Aviv, Israel; Melbourne, Australia; Kuala Lumpur, Malaysia; Taipei, Taiwan; or Bangalore, India. Actually, you don't have to go anywhere. Just turn on your computer and get onto the Internet, that global brain detached from human bodies and powered by hundreds of millions of silicon transistors.

I am in Silicon Valley, however, which is the nerve center of the computer and telecommunications revolution transforming the world economy. Home to an estimated 250,000 millionaires, Silicon Valley has been described as the only place in the world not trying to figure out how to be Silicon Valley. Here, on Sand Hill Road, sit lordly venture capitalists willing to bet millions of dollars on new ideas that promise to wipe out old industries. Here are semiconductor companies that convert sand and oxygen, two of the most abundant materials on earth, into silicon chips, making possible e-mail, e-commerce, e-everything.

Apple Computer is based here, as are Cisco, Intel, Oracle, Sun, Yahoo!, eBay, and E*Trade. Most important, there is a critical mass of brain-power here that rivals that of any other place or time in history. The people of the Valley—many of them scientists or entrepreneurs—are determined to keep astonishing the world and to ensure that the technological revolution unleashed by the silicon chip never stops.

I'm not your typical Silicon Valley guy. Although I use e-mail and do my writing on the computer, I'm a bit of a technopeasant; when my PC misbehaves, I have to call my brother-in-law. I've heard more than I want to about "browsers," "portals," "search engines," and "bandwidth." Fortunately, I am not here to reveal new technological breakthroughs or identify the Next Big Thing. Rather, I want to witness the new culture that has taken shape here, because behind it I sense a powerful new ideology that has already formed a new generation and a new establishment and has staked its claim to lead and liberate the world.

My strategy is to approach the place in the manner of an anthropologist studying a faraway culture. Sure enough, there is a resemblance between the tribal inhabitants of California and New Guinea. Both cultures include lots of half-naked people who worship the sun. Both are heavily into earrings, nose rings, body piercing, and other forms of primitive art. And in both places there is a strong belief in magical contrivances, only in California they go by the name of technology and they actually work.

The event I am attending in October 1999 is called "Inktomi Rocks." Inktomi is a widely used search engine that, in the words of CEO David Peterschmidt, "does a lot of the heavy lifting" for companies that use the Internet. Peterschmidt explains that the strange name refers to a mythical Lakota Indian spider with healing qualities . . . well, suffice it to say that the company was started by two fellows in their twenties who regarded this as a meaningful reference. The party is "your pretty typical Silicon Valley bash," I am assured by Inktomi's attractive vice president for public relations, Shernaz Daver, and besides, "there will be some big names there." The dress code specified on the invitation: "Whatever you wear to climb to the top."

I arrive at the Hotel De Anza in San Jose, where the tribe has already gathered and the music is blaring. Most of the guests are men in their twenties and thirties. Scanning the room, I look to see who's dominating the conversation; I want to locate the alpha males. Just as I suspect, they aren't menacing gorilla types but nerdy little chimps whose bragging rights no doubt derive directly from their bank balances. The only middle-aged face in the room belongs to CEO Dave Peterschmidt, whose green eyes and balding head make him easy to spot. Still, Dave's attire has been fashioned to help him fit into this younger crowd. He's wearing the Steve Jobs look-alike, Silicon Valley uniform: black pants, black T-shirt. As I watch him saunter across the room, his demeanor says: I'm cool.

The room itself has been decorated to look like a dungeon. At one end there is a mountain of rocks that you can climb to the top. There you slip your arms into a contraption that catapults you across the ceiling. Traveling on cable wires, you land at the other end of the room, to the applause and cheers of the natives below. There is plenty of food and drink, most of it going to waste. Conversation is animated, with the only interruption being applause as a human projectile occasionally flies across the ceiling.

A party is a great place to see Silicon Valley at work, because just about everyone at the party is working. The normal purpose of a party—drinking a lot, saying funny things, and meeting members of the opposite sex—seems entirely out of place here. Two young men are eagerly discussing the application of Moore's Law and Metcalfe's Law to the stock market. One guy is arguing that, contrary to the conventional wisdom, Internet companies are grossly undervalued.

Moore's Law, formulated by Intel founder Gordon Moore, states that the amount of computing power on a microchip doubles every eighteen months. This means that the average secretary's desktop now has more computing power than the Manhattan Project, and this is likely to increase by several orders of magnitude before Moore's Law runs into its physical limits: only so many transistors can fit on the tiny surface of a chip.

Metcalfe's Law, first developed by Ethernet inventor and 3Com founder Robert Metcalfe, says that the value of a network increases in proportion to the *square* of its users. If the number of telephone users in a Third World country triples, for example, suddenly more people find they need phones. So the value of that particular network increases ninefold. A quadrupling of e-mail users worldwide means a sixteenfold increase in the value of that network. The Internet is the ultimate network, and its efficiency and use are both predicted to grow exponentially over the next decade. Only by taking into consideration Moore's Law and Metcalfe's Law, the argument goes, can you understand the stock market's heady evaluations of leading Internet companies.

The two men suspend their discussion to admit me into the conversation.

"Nice party," I say, adding, however, that there don't seem to be many women present.

"Correction," replies one of the two, a burly young man in khakis and navy blazer, "there are *no* women present."

This is clearly an exaggeration, so I point to three or four young women milling about the room.

"Oh, those are girls who have been supplied by the PR company that is organizing this event."

"Of course, Shernaz Daver is here," a tall man in black pants, black shirt, and black ponytail says. "And I thought I saw Dave's wife earlier." That would be CEO Dave Peterschmidt.

"But don't you feel odd going to a party without women?"

"Oh, no," the first guy replies casually. "We're not interested in women."

Hm. I pause to digest this answer.

"It's not that," the ponytailed fellow says, eager to correct any false impression. "The reason we're here is to meet people, to make contacts."

Now I understand. These men are possessed by the eros of enterprise. Just about every one of these young tech entrepreneurs has a new idea that he is convinced will revolutionize society, wipe out Ford or General Electric—or, better still, Microsoft—and make him the new Bill Gates or Jeff Bezos. Now they just have to make it work. That's why they're here. Inktomi is part of an extremely influential club—call it the New Boys' Network—and they all want to be insiders, or at least members. Who has time for women when there are millions of dollars to be made and so little time to do it? The only exception is Dave's wife—better be nice to her.

Now that we were on the theme of underrepresentation, I observe that I see only one black face in the room. "High tech," I say, stating the obvious, "doesn't seem to be a very diverse place."

"High tech," the ponytailed fellow responds, in a slightly testy voice, "is more diverse than just about any industry in America. My company is pretty typical, and we have four Russians, three Armenians, a couple of Greeks, several Indians. We just don't have any blacks. Well, we have one black guy, but he's from Africa. Educated at Stanford."

They both give me the same look, as if to say, why are you obsessed with this stuff? I realize that this theme of who is *not* here does not captivate this duo, and so we drop the subject and proceed to discuss the new economy.

"The other day I saw an ad," the burly guy says. "It said, 'We're an Internet company.' Can you believe this bullshit? 'We're an Internet company.' Why? Because you're on the Internet?"

"The old guys just don't get it," the ponytailed fellow chuckles. "I mean, imagine it's 1920 and you're U.S. Steel. The new technology is the telephone. Do you run ads saying: 'U.S. Steel. We're a phone company'? What morons! I mean, duh!"

"When are these people going to realize that in a few years *every* company will be an Internet company?"

"Excuse me," Shernaz Daver breaks in, "but there's someone I want you to meet." Taking my arm, she leads me to Eric Brewer, the thirty-two-year-old cofounder of Inktomi.

"He's a really modest person," Daver whispers to me. "He doesn't live or act like a tycoon at all."

He certainly doesn't look the part. Brewer is a shy, soft-spoken guy with a baby face and a mustache. If I had to guess, I would say that he was completing his air-conditioning repair course at some junior college. In fact, Brewer is chief scientist at Inktomi but is based at the University of California at Berkeley, where he is a tenured professor. Brewer and an even younger man, twenty-seven-year-old Paul Gauthier, founded Inktomi when they figured out a new technology to locate Web sites on the Internet; now each of them is worth around $500 million.

Why, I ask Brewer, is he still at Berkeley and not working full-time at Inktomi? Come to think of it, why is he working at all?

"I don't care about the money," Brewer says with an air of complete sincerity. "My goal is to stay on the cutting edge of technology. I want to look ten years ahead. I can't do that if I retire, and I can't even do it at a company. The outlook at Inktomi is too short-term, too profit-driven. So I prefer to stay at Berkeley."

I make the mistake of asking Brewer what he's currently working on, and he launches into a lecture of such erudition and complexity that

I feel an overwhelming urge to refill my drink. I wonder why Brewer is going into such technical detail, and I finally guess the reason: there are plenty of Asian Indians in high tech, and he naturally assumes I'm one of them. I must keep nodding as Brewer speaks, because he interprets my responses as an invitation to take the discussion to an even more sophisticated plane. Fortunately, a crowd gathers to hear him, the $500 million man himself, and I make my escape, plunging into a group of exuberant techies discussing a topic of considerable interest to me, big-money start-ups.

They are talking about a guy they knew who just launched an initial public offering and saw his net worth go from zero to "two commas," meaning several million dollars.

"He's just bought an eight-thousand-square-foot house," one fellow in his late twenties says. "I asked him how big his previous house was and he said one bedroom. So he's gone from one bedroom to seven bedrooms."

"Are you envious?" I ask.

"No way," the young man replies. "Some people might be because they don't feel there's a lot separating them from him. But my reaction is the complete opposite. I see my friends get rich, and I say, 'I can do that.' They had a good idea. And they stuck with it. They put themselves on the line, and it paid off. So that's where I'm headed."

"But does what these fellows do justify that kind of money?"

"Absolutely," the young man says. "Do you know how hard these guys work? Thirty-six-hour shifts. They go a day and a half without stopping, without sleeping. They eat at their desks, and some of them probably pee into a cup rather than waste time going to the bathroom. But it's worth it, man, because they're in their twenties and they have a chance to do something that very few people get to do. They're changing the way we do business in America. They're the pioneers of a new generation. They're revolutionaries, man. They are opening the doors to a whole new outlook, a new way of life."

"My young friend here is smoking Web heroin," an older guy says. "I know I'm a bit of a skeptic, especially in this crowd. Yes, the Net is making things more efficient, but no, these dot-com companies are not worth their market caps. There's no justification for the net worth of a lot of people in this room, and if they had any sense they'd know it. I see my Qualcomm friends walking around with their chests out. And they tell me, 'I'm worth ten million.' What I'm thinking is, what the hell did you really do? You just did your job. And the stock took off so you lucked out."

"It isn't luck," insists a lanky fellow in glasses who inserts himself into our conversation. He seems very sure of himself. "That's what the losers always say: 'He got a lucky break.'"

This new fellow must be somebody, because there is an awed silence after he speaks. The older guy starts to say something in response, then thinks better of it and shuts up.

Another member of our group says, directly addressing the new guy in an eager-to-please voice, "You're absolutely right, John. Luck has nothing to do with it. By the way, my dad keeps saying the whole Internet economy is a bubble. He keeps predicting it will all come crashing down."

There is a moment of silence, followed by nervous laughter. I take this to mean: ah yes, we've all heard about the Crash. There have been painful market corrections, but the Big One hasn't come yet, has it?

"When I graduated from college, it was the proudest day in his life," the eager-to-please fellow goes on, "but now that he knows what I'm making he's a little pissed, because it's more than he's ever made his whole life. So he's down on the whole thing. He is morally revolted by all this wealth. He needs to believe it's an aberration."

John wears a smug look as if to say, "Dream on, old man!"

I am wondering how he can be so sure of himself when suddenly I recognize the speaker. He is John Little, the founder of Portal Software, based in Cupertino. I haven't met Little before, but a few weeks earlier I published a lead story in *Forbes* about the new tech affluence. The editors titled it "The Billionaire Next Door" and chose a picture of Little, fashionably posed behind his fully loaded speed bike, for the cover of the magazine. *Forbes* noted that Little was worth one billion dollars. In case you haven't guessed, that's an incredible status symbol. *Three* commas.

One might expect that John Little would be feeling pretty good, having a net worth equivalent to the gross domestic product of a small country. He did commend my article, which pleased me until I realized what had impressed him the most: "That was a great photo of me."

"I didn't have anything to do with it," I confess, "but you've had a lot of compliments?"

"The girls tell me that I looked really good," Little says, pushing out his chest. "The guys tell me they liked my bike."

Despite these accolades, something has really been rankling Little, and he proceeds to get it off his mind.

Little explains that he was on a plane a few days ago, and he was reading the issue of *Forbes* with his picture on the cover. (Have I mentioned that modesty is not one of Little's most striking qualities?) Sure enough, the guy sitting next to Little saw his picture and the accompanying headline, "The Billionaire Next Door." Not making the connection between Little and his photograph, the man erupted with indignation, "I'm so sick of these rich Internet brats. What right do those jerks have to make so much money? I'm a smart fellow, I went to a good college, I've got years of experience, I work ten hours a day, and these twenty-five-year-olds make millions overnight while I'm struggling to feed my family."

"How did you respond?" I ask Little in my most casual tone of voice.

"I know what I *should* have said," Little fumes. "The guy undoubtedly thought I got the idea for my company last week and this week I'm worth a billion dollars. Actually, I've been in this business for fourteen years. Fourteen friggin' years. I've worked my butt off, and finally it's come together."

A roar goes up as an Inktomi staffer zips across the ceiling. Little ignores the shouts.

"I don't feel sorry for that guy," Little says. "I've had my time in the wilderness. Show me someone who has been at it as long as I have. Show me somebody who's worked as hard as I have. Show me someone who's taken the risks that I've taken. Then if they haven't seen any rewards, then if they want to complain, I'm willing to listen."

Little is still nursing his grievance, but the night is getting on, and it's time for me to go.

Shernaz Daver catches me on my way out the door. "Are you leaving already?"

"Yes," I say.

She gives me a kind of black power salute. I take it to mean "Long live the silicon revolution."

As I step out of the tech culture into the mundane world of the street, I see two very different societies. One of them is very old, the other is new. But I also see that they are in the process of becoming one. Already our everyday life is being affected by the new technology and the wealth it is creating; very soon it will be transformed. The reason has nothing to do with the extravagant claims made by the twenty-somethings at the Inktomi bash. It is the inexorable logic of Moore's Law and Metcalfe's Law.

Moore's Law predicts that in the next ten years, microprocessor chips will contain 1 billion transistors. That's an increase in computing power of one hundred times. Before Moore's Law reaches its physical limit, computing power is going to expand to at least 1 million times what it is today. Other forms of computing—parallel computing, molecular computing, quantum computing, and DNA computing—promise to continue the exponential growth in this area. There is also a bandwidth revolution under way that is radically increasing our power to transmit digital signals over optical networks, providing the capacity to feed oceans of video, audio, and data at the speed of light into every home and business. Bandwidth is growing even faster than computer power. And as networks become more powerful, Metcalfe's Law dictates that they will also become more indispensable. A company or person who does not work and live in cyberspace will be as out of it as a person today who does not have a telephone.

In 1854, Henry Bessemer, creator of the Bessemer method, described his final test of a new way to produce large-scale steel. He said, "I could now see in my mind's eye the great iron industry of the world crumbling away under the irresistible force of the facts so recently elicited. In that one result the sentence had gone forth, and not all the talent accumulated in the last 150 years . . . nor all the millions that had been invested in carrying out the existing system of manufacture, with all its accompanying great resistance, could reverse that one great fact."[1]

The computer and telecommunications revolutions will have a vastly greater impact. I am thinking not merely about the obsolescence of an industry but about a historic transition from one age to another. This cannot be conceived in just economic terms, as a question of whether Amazon will replace Borders or whether the Nasdaq will surpass the Dow. That's minor stuff. Rather, think about how printing accelerated—some would say caused—the Reformation. More recently, think about how the railroad and the automobile forever changed local communities.

According to management guru Peter Drucker, "The social and political consequences of the information revolution will greatly outweigh its economic and technological consequences."[2] I think he's right. The changes will affect human ways of thinking and living no less dramatically than the shift from an agrarian to an industrial society. The Inktomi event gives a hint of some of the new tensions and challenges that society will face. But the full ramifications of the changes ahead are beginning to press down on me. Surely the new economy will produce a new kind of community. It will dramatically affect our basic political, educational, and religious institutions and reshape our lives. But how? And for better or worse? These are questions we have to figure out.

Of course the skeptics have a point too. There's a lot of hype surrounding computerized gadgets and the Internet. For all the giddiness surrounding them, these are twentieth-century technologies that will soon become part of the infrastructure of our lives, like electricity or the telephone. In the not-too-distant future they will cease to capture our imagination. But that's only because there are other revolutions in store that are so near in their realization but so profound and far-reaching in their implications that they make the computer and the Internet seem like grown-up toys. These revolutions promise to transform our very nature as human beings and possibly introduce a new species into the world, the posthuman. What all this means, and whether we want to go there, are the questions explored in this book.

CHAPTER ONE

A WORLD WITHOUT LIMITS

What's New About the New Economy

We have it in our power to begin the world all over again.

—Thomas Paine

The young people in high tech, who have not learned to talk better, describe it as a "holy shit experience." This is how it works. You are a graduate student living in a group house and paying $375 a month. You have no steady source of income; you are just barely making ends meet. But you have a Big Idea for a company. You've developed software that enables corporate Web sites to handle large volumes of traffic. Or you've figured out a way to use the Net to improve efficiencies in the medical supplies business. Or you've got a new idea for making web sites more interactive. Whatever.

It doesn't matter who you are or where you come from. You are now the founder of a company. You come up with a cool, offbeat name— something techno-sophisticated, like QuantumFour.com, or offbeat like Waitingforgodot.com. You approach investors with your plans for taking over a whole sector of the market. You promise the investors a "ten bagger," an investment that increases tenfold in value. They're skeptical about where your company's profits are going to come from, but you emphasize that at this point "mind share" is really important.

Somehow you manage to convince them that your idea is hot and you are cool. They give you start-up money, and you hire a lawyer and establish a corporate identity. You set up a bank account, find yourself a logo, design some letterhead, and then hire a dozen employees. You've got a bookkeeping guy, a Web guy, a marketing guy, and so on, but you've made it clear to them that there is no strict division of labor, and everyone takes turns taking out the trash. You give these employees options, which at this point are worthless pieces of paper.

You and your team set up shop in a beat-up old office that you've leased for a year at $1,000 a month. It doesn't get too much sun and the landlord had better hope the fire inspector doesn't drop by. Otherwise it serves the purpose. Basically, you move in. You put in eighteen-hour days. Sometimes you fall asleep on the secondhand sofa; soon you start keeping a toothbrush at the office. You dress like a slob and live on Whoppers, Twinkies, and cherry Coke. You rarely read the newspaper, and you don't return phone calls from friends and family. You're totally focused on making your concept work.

Sometimes it doesn't. That's the fear that haunts every start-up. And you know what failure means, because you've seen it happen and you know it ain't pretty. You don't want to default on the rent and have to fire all your employees. You don't want angry investors banging on your door because they got back only eight cents on the dollar. Most of all, you don't want a year and a half of your life to go to waste. But that's the chance you take, as you set your sights on that Wall Street version of Powerball: the initial public offering.

The IPO is the Silicon Valley equivalent of hitting the jackpot. It's even better than being bought by America Online or Yahoo! Either way, forget about moving up the ranks in a traditional company, meticulously putting aside a bit every month, and building up your savings so you can retire with a nest egg, a pension plan, and a gold watch. What you and your friends are after is instant tycoon status. The Big Score. So far things look promising. Your company seems to have people talking; you've got "buzz."

But what will the Big Day bring? You just don't know. So you and your employees sit around the table, and you wait. At first, nothing. The minutes tick by, slow and unforgiving. You get jitters. Then you feel the first nauseous pangs of a panic attack. And then, kaboom! It happens. Your stock price goes up, up, up . . . it isn't stopping . . . it's still going up . . . you can't believe it! By now your employees are cheering and shouting, "Holy shit! Holy shit! This is so insane!" Finally it stops and, almost delirious, you do the math: you are suddenly worth $51 million. Unbelievable! Everyone in the room is a millionaire.

Now you are rich. You can do anything you want with the rest of your life. What a feeling! Now you can afford to fly to Paris for the weekend. You can eat at the Tour d'Argent, and cheerfully pay $3,000 for a bottle of 1982 Château Pétrus to complement your meal. You relish the thought of tossing out a couple of hundred thousand to join that exclusive golf club that your father's boss, the grumpy old fool, still plays at. The there's the Lamborghini you've always wanted. You know you can't do all this right away; after all, your money is tied up in stock. You are, as they say, a multimillionaire "on paper." Even so, it doesn't hurt to plan ahead. What you find most striking is that even in your moment of triumph, you know that neither the French cuisine nor the golf, not even the Lamborghini, will be enough. You're beginning to get the germ of *another* Big Idea. You crave a second Big Score. In short, you have to do it again.

Yes, it's a new economy. If you read the business papers, if you listen to CNBC, you've heard that before. But if we're going to explore the ramifications of it, it is extremely important to understand what precisely is new about today's economy. Some commentators passionately assert that "interest rates don't matter" or that "stock prices have nothing to do with profits" or that "we've repealed the business cycle." That's wishful thinking. Economic logic and historical experience cut the other way. Others point to a more obvious novelty: technology, and specifically the new frontier of cyberspace. But even cyberspace isn't new. Cyberspace is where you are when you talk on the phone. It's been around since Alexander Graham Bell and his pal Watson had a rendezvous there more than a hundred years ago.

Still, the wishful thinkers are responding to something that is real and new, namely, that this is an economy on Viagra, an economy that is rafting on white water, the best economy the world has ever seen. Forget about the Gilded Age or the Roaring Twenties or the Halcyon Fifties and Soaring Sixties; the United States has witnessed an economic juggernaut that got started in 1983 and, with a few bumps and jolts, continues to show its power. We seem to be in possession of a perpetual money machine, and it keeps spitting out silver coins and green notes.

Of course, there's been volatility. Between March 2000 and March 2001, the Nasdaq plunged more than 50 percent. It was motion-sickness time, especially for those who had invested in technology stocks with borrowed money or money they could not afford to risk. For the first time, there were news reports of Internet companies going under, laying people off. It's been a bumpy journey of late. Within a twelve-month period Internet giant Softbank Corporation saw its shares soar from $100 to $1,900 and then go down to $475. The people who say that markets are inherently rational have a lot of explaining to do.

Volatility is here to stay, especially in the Internet sector. The reason is that it is extremely hard to estimate the current value of companies with uncertain future earnings. Even so, let's keep a sense of perspective: we are in an economy where, most of the time, the bulls have been right. The bears have had their moments of vindication, but these moments have been brief. "See, we told you . . ." they say, but soon enough the market has gone back up. In general the momentum has been relentlessly onward and upward. The last twenty years have seen a tripling of the gross domestic product from around $3 trillion in the early 1980s to around $9 trillion now. And don't forget: in 1982 the Dow Jones Industrial Average fell below 800. It tripled in the 1980s, then lost ground for a year or so, then tripled again during the nineties, surpassing the 10,000 mark. Meanwhile, the technology-heavy Nasdaq Composite Index skyrocketed from under 500 in 1991 to 5,000 before pulling back: that's still a five- or sixfold increase in less than a decade.

Throughout this period of prosperity, there have been warnings of disaster. More than once I have heard the story about how Joseph Kennedy, upon hearing a stock tip from a newspaper boy, went straight to his office, sold all his stock, and got out of the market, shortly before the Great Market Crash. It's a good story but useless advice as far as I'm concerned. Everywhere I go I hear stock tips from waiters, office interns, non-English-speaking cabbies, and other extremely unorthodox investors. But I've been hearing from these folks for years, and if I had sold my mutual funds and gone into Treasury bills the first time it happened I would have missed several thousand points on the Dow and a virtual quintupling of the Nasdaq.

This is not to deny that many of the dot coms are grossly overvalued. Buying companies with price-earnings ratios in excess of 100 is not a winning long-term investment strategy. Most of these companies surely won't be around a few years from now. But will the market as a whole crash with them? So far, it hasn't happened. In fact, over the past several years, money managers with bearish investment strategies have been badly pummeled. Boom, boom, boom, the market has shot them down and stampeded over their carcasses. Those who have survived have watched in dismay as complete amateurs have whooped their way to triple-digit returns. The ultimate indignity: many of the surviving bears have been humiliated into joining the bulls. Better we all perish together, the bears now say, rather than going belly-up while the bulls stand around and cheer, smoking cigars made of hundred-dollar bills.

Another novel characteristic of our era is the revival of faith in free-market capitalism. Actually, we're seeing more than faith in the capitalist system; we're seeing a surge of confidence on the part of the average American that the system will benefit him directly. The stock market is a good indicator of this. In 1980, only one in ten American households owned stock; now 50 percent do, either directly or through mutual funds, IRA accounts, or 401(k) plans. Financial columnist James Glassman calls this "the rise of the investor class." More Americans own stock than vote in national elections. Even journalists, who have traditionally spurned such bourgeois pursuits, are now chasing big bucks. "I have decided that I want—I need—to make a million dollars in the stock market this year," writes David Denby in *The New Yorker*.[1] Now we can't wait to read whether he did it. Ten years ago if someone had written that we'd have thought he was joking. O tempora, O mores!

You know the capitalist spirit has penetrated the culture when the *Ladies' Home Journal* features articles about "trader moms" who spend much of their day trying to exploit daily fluctuations in stock prices.[2] *Red Herring* magazine recently featured investment advice from today's breed of stock picker: a cop, a bartender, the chief doorman of the Sir Francis Drake Hotel, and an astrologer who insists that stocks, like people, have birthdays. A stock's birthday, explains "financial astrologer" Yvonne Morabito, is the date of its IPO.[3] In a mass movement of any kind, you get all types.

Indeed, the free market hasn't enjoyed such broad support for more than half a century. In fact, the twentieth century was the era of the welfare state, of big government. That era, which began in America in 1932 with the New Deal, ended in 1989, when the Berlin Wall collapsed. Now we know that capitalism is the only economic system that works and markets are the acknowledged arbiters of production and value. How ridiculous it seems that, as late as the 1980s, leading intellectuals and politicians were calling for blue-ribbon commissions made up of government bureaucrats, university intellectuals, and captains of industry to meet and decide questions such as how many computers should be made each year. They dubbed it "industrial policy" and modeled it on the supposedly invincible Japanese system. Today no one mentions industrial policy, and even though the government continues to chase down monopolies, any suggestion that state-sponsored committees should set timetables for how much and where to invest in high tech would meet with dismissive laughter. The issue is settled: the market will decide.

The triumph of the market has launched us into a new age: the Age of the Entrepreneur. One measure of the zeitgeist is that a number of senior corporate executives have given up their careers in order to take the entrepreneurial plunge. Although market volatility has slowed the trend somewhat, the business press continues to profile traditional gray-suiters jumping ship and joining new-economy companies that give them options. George Shaheen, who used to head Andersen Consulting, is now at Webvan, the Internet grocery service. Heidi Miller, former chief financial officer at Citigroup, is now at Priceline.com. Hey, who cares about being secure and comfortable when there's a chance to get fabulously wealthy? Of course, you're not supposed to *say* you're doing it for the money. Thus you piously intone, "I just felt ready for a new challenge." Liar!

As usual, young people are more candid about their motives. Twenty-six-year-old Magdalena Mik, who works at Priceline.com, recently told *Forbes* that her goal was to be "obscenely wealthy by the time I'm 30."[4] Geoff Cook, a Harvard undergraduate who has set up an Internet editing service, reports, "I will feel like a failure if I am not a millionaire by my twenty-fourth birthday."[5] Naveen Jain, who is already a millionaire, left Microsoft to start his own Internet company, InfoSpace, "to make a billion dollars for myself." Given the number of young capitalists, it makes sense to have young venture capitalists. Joshua Newman, a twenty-year-old student at Yale, runs a $6 million venture capital fund that invests exclusively in student-run businesses.[6] A recent Web poll of two thousand undergraduates at recruitment site jobtrak.com revealed that 25 percent of the respondents intended to start their own companies and be millionaires by the age of thirty; another 25 percent were sure they'd get there by forty.

Another sign of the times: talk to the deans of some of the nation's leading business schools. A quarter to a third of their students who enroll in a two-year MBA program don't come back for the second year. Why not? Because they get a summer job with an Internet company, or they have a friend who wants them to come on board at Yahoo!, or they have an idea for a start-up and they feel they've learned enough to make it work. "We've never had this before, never in our history," confesses Edmund Wilson, dean of students at Northwestern University's Kellogg School of Management. One dean who advised a student to complete his education and then shoot for IPO heaven got this response: "Hey, man, the time to attend school is during a recession! Not when there's this much money to be made." And the dean told me he couldn't argue with the kid. Two of his *professors* are considering leaving teaching to get involved with new-economy companies.

What's new, of course, is not that people want to go into business and make money; what's new is that this impulse is seen as cool. Recall that a few decades ago John F. Kennedy inspired a generation of Americans by saying to them, if you are young, if you are idealistic, you should become a "public servant," you should join the Peace Corps. Millions did. The government worker was regarded as the summit of youthful idealism. By contrast, the businessman was viewed as a selfish bastard.

But the last few decades have witnessed a dramatic switch. The selfless public servant has now metamorphosed into the do-nothing bureaucrat. The term "government worker" now seems like a bit of an oxymoron. Indeed, for the first time in many decades, the government is seen as largely irrelevant to what is really happening in America. And what is happening is the entrepreneurial explosion. The entrepreneur has moved to center stage as the embodiment of American possibility. More parents probably want their children to be like Bill Gates than like Bill Clinton.

Do people still want to work for the Peace Corps? Not many. Recently the magazine *Fast Company* asked young people whether they wanted to join a government agency such as the Peace Corps, work for an old-line, salary-and-bonus company such as General Motors, or join a fast-growing company such as Yahoo!, with a base salary plus options. Four percent opted for the Peace Corps, 30 percent chose the old-line company, and the rest said they would sign up with a fast-growing company with a stock option.[7]

The secret of the rapid-growth sector of the economy is, of course, technology. The new technologies of the Internet and telecommunications—the microcosm and the telecosm—have the unique power to unify the world economy in a single moment of space and time. Never has the global economy previously been integrated to this degree. Earlier technologies, such as the automobile, the airplane, and the telephone, reduced distance barriers and improved communications channels. But there remained powerful physical barriers, such as the time it took to fly from one place to another, or the number of people who could communicate with one another over a phone line. Moreover, there were political barriers that proved difficult, if not insurmountable. Large parts of the world were hostile and closed off to the West.

Now, for the first time, it is meaningful to speak of a single "world economy." We drive cars made in Japan, wear clothes made in Indonesia, use computers assembled in Mexico, and eat fresh fruit grown in Chile. The political walls haven't completely disappeared, but the ones that remain are more porous than ever before. Countries previously inhospitable to capitalism, such as India and Vietnam, are now courting foreign investment and opening their doors to technology. The Internet has made it possible for large numbers of people located anywhere on the planet to communicate with one another simultaneously. Information that was simply unavailable, or that used to require lengthy, time-consuming searches, is now accessible at the click of a mouse. The world is going to become a smaller and much more efficient place.

Even as the world lurches toward the new technology, however, we should not forget that one country is leading the pack. It is not a statement of chauvinism, only of fact, to point out another new feature of our era: it is the era of American dominance. America is the experiment that has produced this technological revolution. Technology has simply consolidated America's military, political, and cultural hegemony worldwide. Here's a single indicator: in 1970, U.S. per capita income was only

10 percent higher than that of other major industrialized nations. Now that gap has widened to 22 percent. For the first time in half a century, America is pulling away from the pack.[8]

American hegemony isn't new; the twentieth century belonged to America in much the same way that the fifteenth century belonged to the Portuguese, the sixteenth to the Spanish, or the nineteenth to the British. But for decades now many people believed that American power had reached its apogee after World War II. After that, America's role in the world was supposed to decline. In 1989, the Yale historian Paul Kennedy published a highly touted book, *The Rise and Fall of the Great Powers.* Had Kennedy warned that the Soviet regime was fragile or that Soviet power was overextended, his book would have proved uncannily prophetic, for that was the year the wall came tumbling down. But, alas, Kennedy's point was that America had run its course, America was on its way out, and Americans should learn to manage their country's diminishing role on the world stage. Never was a book so spectacularly discredited by events.

Today, in Paris and Kuala Lumpur and Addis Ababa, the American influence is everywhere. You can't escape it. There are Burger King and Starbucks coffee on the street corner, Britney Spears on the radio, and Michael Jordan or Tiger Woods on the TV screen. The kids are wearing Gap T-shirts and Nike sneakers, most waiters speak English, and the bellhop is whistling the theme song from *Titanic.* The United States now enjoys unprecedented domination over the political, economic, cultural, and technological life of the world. The Mongols, the Spanish, and the English may have had military control, but none of them enjoyed this kind of comprehensive global superiority. Alexander the Great would be envious. For better or worse, we are living on Planet America.

Not surprising, given the technological edge enjoyed by America, the country is leading the world in the creation of new businesses and new fortunes. Many of these don't just happen to have started in America; they could not have arisen anywhere else. Pierre Omidyar should be thankful that he got the idea for eBay while living in Silicon Valley; if his family had never emigrated to the United States from France, his idea for an Internet auction site would never have taken flight, and he'd be worth a lot less than his current $4.9 billion. French law permits only a small number of certified auctioneers to operate in the country, and .eBay isn't even operational in France. Andy Grove, the famous longtime CEO of Intel, would have kept his real name, Andras Grof, and his obscurity if he had remained in his native Hungary. Only in America could Jerry Yang, an immigrant from Taiwan who came to this country at the age of ten not speaking a word of English, start a company like Yahoo! in his twenties and find himself a boy billionaire. These are uniquely American success stories.

You might have concluded, especially from the cases of Omidyar, Grove, and Yang, that I've been holding out on you. It's true. I have mentioned, but neglected to discuss, the most obvious new aspect of the new economy: money! Being filthy rich is fashionable again. As late as the 1980s, it was okay to have a lot of money as long as you inherited it or built it up over many years. Old money was better than new money. Old money meant that you put numbers at the end of your name (Eli Lilly II, Marshall Field V), belonged to the Woodhill Country Club or the Knickerbocker Club, sat on the board of the art museum, and proved your social worth by tithing to the right causes and charities. If, however, you earned a great deal of money by inventing junk bond financing, like Michael Milken, or taking over unprofitable companies, like Carl Icahn, you were a greedy scoundrel. In fact, the 1980s were dubbed the Era of Greed.

But now prejudice against self-made wealth has completely evaporated. Now new money is better than old money, because it means that you actually earned it. If there's any group that's slightly infra dig today, it's the White Anglo-Saxon Protestants who inherited their wealth and speak with a refined New England accent. The old farts may still belong to the right clubs and call each other "Sport" and "Whizzer," but they are no longer in charge; they know it, and everybody else knows it. Author Louis Auchincloss reports that "the old WASP world is dead and gone."[9] How can we be sure of the triumph of the nouveau riche? Because nobody calls them "nouveau riche" anymore.

New money means that it has to be on display and out in the open, which wasn't the case before. Bob Colacello, who covers the rich and famous for *Vanity Fair*, told me that in New York social circles, until recently, "we knew who the rich people were because they lived on Park Avenue and sent their children to private schools, but we didn't know how much money they had." So discretion was the hallmark of the old affluent class. But now, as Colacello rightly points out, "Rich people have price tags attached to them. Every time people see Michael Dell, they think: 'Twenty billion dollars.'"

Well, perhaps that's not surprising: twenty billion dollars is a lot of money. Yet Dell is hardly alone. Never in the history of the world have so many people made so much money. Many of the richest guys have made it in high tech, but the technology boom has also reverberated in the traditional economy, creating massive fortunes in real estate, financial services, entertainment, even consumer goods retailing. And once again, this degree of affluence is an American phenomenon, although the rest of the world is quickly catching up.

One way of keeping track of all the money made is to observe the lavishness with which it is spent. We've all heard about Bill Gates spending upward of $50 million for his 40,000-square-foot home in Medina, Washington. Apparently he has started a trend among the superrich that might be called "keeping up with the Gateses." Industrialist Ira Rennert recently built a 42,000-square-foot mansion in Sagaponack, Long Island. Herbalife guru Mark Hughes is not impressed; he's spending $75 million for a 50,000-square-foot Italian-style villa overlooking Beverly Hills. If you've dropped in on Oracle CEO Larry Ellison lately, you could update us on his $40 million Woodside, California, home, built in the style of a sixteenth-century Japanese imperial palace. By contrast, the $14 million, 16,000-square-foot home that Gateway head Ted Waitt bought atop Mount Soledad in San Diego seems positively spartan. Entertainment mogul David Geffen apparently wanted a Hollywood landmark worthy of his legendary status and finally contented himself with the enormous Jack Warner estate.[10]

Not long ago, I visited a young tycoon who owned a plantation on the James River in Virginia. When I arrived, I noticed that there were construction crews on the property. I asked if he was doing some new building. No, he said, he was having an old building lifted and relocated to another part of the property so it would give him a more pleasing view of the ducks in the pond. "My architect assures me that this can be done without spilling a single drop of champagne from a glass on the banister," the man enthusiastically informed me. "I've decided to test him on this."

Impressive though these displays are, they are not exactly new. Indeed, William Randolph Hearst's San Simeon is fully comparable to anything being built today, and none of our tycoons has produced anything that could hold a candle to the palace of Blenheim or Versailles. But at no time did Hearst command anything like the resources of today's tycoons. Louis XIV was admittedly in a class by himself, but that's another way of saying there was only one Louis XIV, while today there are hundreds of people living in monarchical residences. What's new is neither affluence or extravagance but rather the number of superrich people today and the amounts of money they possess.

Consider the world's richest man, Bill Gates. Arguably, Bill is not the richest man ever. John D. Rockefeller had around $1 billion in 1913, nearly 2 percent of America's gross domestic product. Bill's net worth is less than 1 percent of the United States' current GDP. Still, Rockefeller at his peak had a net worth of $17 billion in today's money. As of early 2000 Bill's net worth had reached nearly $100 billion. Of course, Bill's net worth has suffered massive fluctuations due to the Microsoft antitrust case. At one point it dipped to $50 billion, making Larry Ellison of Oracle the world's richest man. Fortunately, Melinda Gates did not have to start selling the family china. Bill's second-place humiliation lasted only a day or two. Where he'll be five years from now is anyone's guess. But the wealth that Gates has piled up over the past several years dwarfs anything that any other private individual has been able to accumulate at any time in history.

How much is a hundred billion dollars? The popular magazines know that numbers with a lot of zeros at the end mean nothing to most people, so they try to make it easy for us to understand them. If Bill's entire fortune were made up of one-dollar bills, they explain, they would stretch from the earth to the moon six thousand times. These sorts of explanations inspire great wonder while conveying no real information. Here's a more revealing way to put it: Bill and his descendants could spend $10 million a day in perpetuity and never run out of money.

Here are some comparisons to put Bill's stash into perspective: twenty-six states have a gross domestic product that is less than Bill's net worth.[11] If Bill were a country, he would be number thirty-five in the world rankings. His net worth surpasses the gross domestic products of Hungary, Ireland, Israel, and New Zealand. He ranks just ahead of Finland (GDP $97 billion) and just behind Greece (GDP $106 billion).[12] Indeed, in a single market swing, such as we've seen recently, his net worth can fluctuate more than the GDP of small countries. Moreover, Bill could very well become the world's first trillionaire. If his net worth grows at the double-digit rate the S&P 500 has been averaging for the past several years, he'll be the sole member of the "four comma" club in 2015.[13]

The Man from Microsoft is a bit of a special case, so let's consider some folks a few rungs down the economic ladder. At a net worth of $50 billion, the world's second richest man, Larry Ellison, tops the gross domestic products of Ecuador (GDP $47 billion) and Tunisia (GDP $43 billion). With a net worth of $40 billion, Paul Allen, who is next in line, scores a narrow victory over Guatemala and Kenya (GDP $39 billion each). Warren Buffett's $31 billion puts him safely ahead of Ghana (GDP $27 billion) and the Dominican Republic (GDP $30 billion). At $23 billion, Steve Ballmer compares favorably with North Korea and Bolivia (GDP $21 billion each). Michael Dell's $20 billion lets him surpass Tanzania and Costa Rica (GDP $19 billion each). Gordon Moore, at $15 billion, must content himself with outdoing Honduras (GDP $11 billion) and El Salvador (GDP $12 billion). Craig McCaw's $6.4 billion outperforms Fiji and Iceland (GDP $5 billion each). Even John Doerr, Vinod Khosla, and Sanford Weill, each at a relatively measly $1 billion, get to score symbolic victories over Monaco (GDP $800 million) and Greenland (GDP $892 million).[14]

All of this is very new. As late as 1982, *Forbes* counted only thirteen billionaires in the United States; the richest, shipping magnate Daniel Ludwig, weighed in at $2 billion. The total net worth of all the American billionaires in 1982 was $15 billion.[15] In those days, a mere $100 million was sufficient to qualify as one of *Forbes*'s 400 richest Americans. Today there are at least 267 American billionaires and around 450 billionaires worldwide. The U.S. billionaires alone are collectively worth over a trillion dollars. In 1999, you needed at least $625 million to make the bottom of the *Forbes* list.[16]

Moreover, look at the speed at which many of these tycoons made their fortunes. It took Henry Ford and Andrew Carnegie decades to become centimillionaires; Jeff Bezos managed the feat in just three years. Indeed since Netscape launched the IPO boom following its public offering in August 1995, not just Bezos but several of today's superrich, including David Filo and Jerry Yang of Yahoo!, Jay Walker of

Priceline.com, Rob Glaser of RealNetworks, Joe Ricketts of Ameritrade, Pierre Omidyar and Meg Whitman of eBay, and Steve Case of America Online, have all become billionaires.

It's one thing for a country to produce a small number of superrich people; it's far more spectacular to see affluence extended to tens, even hundreds of thousands of people. This is exactly what has happened in America in the past two decades. Not so long ago there weren't many affluent people; you'd have to go to Beverly Hills to find them, or Manhattan's Upper East Side, or (more recently) to high-tech meccas such as Palo Alto and Seattle. But now the rich have proliferated, and they are everywhere.

Drive through the opulent neighborhoods of Jupiter Island, Florida; Brookville, New York; Saddle River, New Jersey; Weston, Massachussetts; Aspen, Colorado; Hunting Valley, Ohio; Kenilworth, Illinois; Paradise Valley, Arizona; Medina, Washington; and Rancho Santa Fe, California. You will see a collection of exquisite homes surrounded by manicured lawns, set against an Elysian backdrop of tall trees, golf courses, and polo fields. The homes measure 7,000 square feet, 10,000, even 15,000. They have fountains, Jacuzzis, media rooms, guest houses, maids' quarters, swimming pools, and tennis courts. .

The insides of these homes are sumptuous: chandeliers bedazzle, a marble floor adorns the entryway, some sort of art and wine collection is mandatory, hand-painted murals and walk-in playhouses are nice touches for the child's room, and the sheets in the master and guest bedrooms are Egyptian cotton and cost in the range of $2,000 for a set. A little imagination is always appreciated: Limited chairman Leslie Wexner has a dining table that after meals descends into a subterranean kitchen, where the staff can clear the plates. Let's not, however, forget the exterior landscaping. In Rancho Santa Fe, where I live, a typical sight is a man in his fifties, wearing his perky thirty-three-year-old second wife on his arm, supervising the installation in his front yard of full-grown palm trees just flown in from Hawaii. "Paul just couldn't wait all the time that it takes for them to grow," the wife explains.

What's the point of living well if you cannot entertain on an equally opulent scale? The hosts of a recent San Francisco "Arabian Nights" party sent a team to Bangkok, Bali, and New Delhi for ten weeks to find furnishings for Ali Baba's cave—at a cost of $1 million. The party featured costumed genies carrying beaded maharaja umbrellas escorting guests up the carpeted entryway, with carved idols on every table and twelve thousand feet of hand-stitched quilts and coverings. Meanwhile, New York socialite gatherings, already known for extravagance, have now reached limits that flabbergast even social circuit regulars. "It's impossible to hold a real conversation," reports one member of Manhattan's inner circle. "You are too distracted by the wall hangings, the furniture, the china, and the chandeliers. In fact, it's hard to resist the temptation to take home a spoon."

The new rich also believe that there is little point in travel unless it is pursued with indulgence. Dermot Duggan, who manages financial records for Sun Microsystems, feels that his particular choice of vehicle is getting, well, a bit too common. "There are two Ferraris parked in our lot at work every morning," Duggan says. "That doesn't count mine, and that doesn't count the guys who choose not to drive theirs to work."[17] Harvey Vengroff, who owns a bill collection agency, believes it is only reasonable that he drive a different car each day of the week; two of his cars are Rolls-Royces.[18] A frequent business traveler of my acquaintance has some brilliant tips for going light: travel without luggage; buy everything when you get there; and don't bring small items such as socks, underwear, and ties home—throw them out after you use them.

Who are these people whose everyday lifestyle would scandalize much of the world and every previous generation that has gone before them? To answer this question, let's not focus on billionaires; that's still a pretty small club. Rather, let's come down from Mount Olympus and consider Americans whose annual income exceeds $1 million. A hundred years ago, only a few familiar names, such as Carnegie, Mellon, and du Pont, took in that kind of money. By 1980, that number had swelled to 13,500 but remained largely confined to the heads of the biggest corporations, partners of major law firms, highly successful entrepreneurs, world-renowned surgeons, top athletes and entertainers.

Today 144,000 American households—making up close to half a million people—earn seven figures or more each year. That number, which comes from the Internal Revenue Service, dates back to 1997, the latest year for which data are available.[19] Since we all know that Americans routinely seek to minimize their reported incomes, experts are confident that the actual number of households whose annual income tops $1 million is much higher. No longer is this group confined to a tiny elite: it includes many CEOs of small and medium-sized corporations, many successful lawyers and doctors, virtually all major actors and players on major sports teams, and innumerable small-business owners.

Let's look at net worth instead of income. Here too we find some pretty impressive numbers. According to the latest data from the Federal Reserve Board, more than 250,000 American households have a net worth exceeding $10 million, and at least 500,000 American households have a net worth in excess of $5 million. A million American households are worth $3.7 million or more.[20]

Or consider ordinary millionaires, those with a net worth in excess of $1 million. A hundred years ago, according to one study, there were 4,000 millionaires in the United States. In 1989 the number had reached 1,260,000.[21] But today the number of American families whose net worth is at least a million dollars has soared above 5 million. Five million families—that's more than 15 million people! And some analysts predict that over the next decade that number will quadruple.[22] Many Americans (and a fair number of Europeans) have reached a standard of affluence that, in the words of novelist Tom Wolfe, would "make the Sun King blink."[23]

In the past two hundred years the great achievement of the modern West was to create a middle class, allowing the common man to escape poverty and live in relative comfort. Now the United States is ready to perform an even greater feat: it is well on its way to creating the first mass affluent class in world history. A mass affluent class is just starting to emerge in other European countries as well. Call it the overclass. These are the new equivalents of the lords and barons of the Middle Ages. Only today's overclass is already large and growing so fast that perhaps one day it will outnumber the peasants.

The emergence of the overclass has important implications for politics, education, and philanthropy. Already it is dramatically changing the way we think about wealth and opportunity, thus redefining the American Dream. Here let's explore a single implication: the birth of the overclass means that terms like "rich," "middle class," and "poor" don't mean what they used to. Remember reading Tom Wolfe's *Bonfire of the Vanities* in the 1980s? We all chuckled at the woes of Sherman McCoy, who was having trouble making ends meet on a salary of $980,000 a year. McCoy was intended to illustrate the immense wealth and extravagance of the period, but today he would be recognizably *upper middle class.*

Many Americans haven't figured out that wealth in our time has been completely redefined. The premise of the TV hit show *Who Wants to Be a Millionaire?* is that a million dollars makes you rich. The authors of the best-selling book *The Millionaire Next Door* agree: they define "wealthy" as someone whose net worth exceeds $1 million.[24] Sorry, guys, but it's time to redo your calculations: a million just isn't enough anymore. After all, recall that the term "millionaire" became synonymous with "wealthy" and acquired its mystique at a time when the average American was making $10,000 to $12,000 a year.

Indeed, in the old days (around 1980), you were rich if your net worth exceeded $1 million. Even if you had a modest bank account, you were really well off if you earned more than $75,000 a year. After all, a $75,000 salary put you at four times the median annual income of the time and ensured that you could afford the accoutrements of success, such as a four-bedroom house, a new $18,000 car, and a maid to come in and clean once a week. Looking back, these aspirations seem embarrassingly modest. Today $75,000 a year barely qualifies as upper middle class, and in cities such as San Francisco, Los Angeles, and New York it is the starting salary of young professionals, who often think it's scarcely enough to make ends meet.

So let's redraw the lines for the new class structure in America today. Making some allowance for differences in the cost of living, you are poor if your household income is less than $15,000 and your net worth is close to zero. Approximately 20 million households, about a fifth of the population, are poor in this sense.[25]

If you earn between $15,000 and $35,000, you are in the lower middle class. Author Paul Fussell in his book *Class* calls you a "prole," which is short for proletariat. You are one of a nonelite population of 29 million households. Your net worth is less than $72,000, which is the median net worth in the United States today.[26] Virtually none of it is in liquid assets.

Americans who earn between $35,000 and $75,000 are middle

TABLE I

The New Class Structure

	Income	Wealth
Superrich	$10 million+	$100 million+
Rich	$1–$10 million	$10 million+
Upper middle class	$75,000–$1 million	$500,000–$10 million
Middle class	$35,000–$75,000	$50,000–$500,000
Lower middle class	$15,000–$35,000	$10,000–$50,000
Poor	$0–$15,000	$0–$10,000

class. Being middle class does not mean that you are at the midpoint of the income distribution; indeed, the median income in this country, $39,000, comes in at the low end of the new middle class. Interestingly, most Americans think of themselves as middle class, but only 34 million households, about a third of the population, belong to this group. Middle-class people have a net worth between $72,000 and $500,000, most of it in home equity and retirement accounts.

In most parts of the country, an income in excess of $75,000 allows you to claim you are upper middle class. Around 19 million households, just under a fifth of the population, fit into this category. In big cities, full of high-earning peers, the bar should be set somewhat higher. In those areas your earnings should place you in the top 5 percent of the general population to be eligible for upper-middle-class status. That would mean you'd have to make at least $150,000 to qualify.[27]

What about net worth? To reinforce your upper-middle-class credentials, it helps to demonstrate a net worth that is impressive at least to people in the class right below you. For younger people that figure could be as low as $489,000—the level needed to place you in the top 10 percent of wealth owners in this country.[28] If you're near retirement, you need at least $1 million and preferably closer to $5 million to be assured of maintaining an upper-middle-class lifestyle for the rest of your life.

Feel like catering a small party at your apartment, leasing that new

Lexus, or flying first-class to London for your wedding anniversary? Being upper middle class means that you can do these things. But you cannot do them all at the same time. Money remains a constraint. Upper-middle-class people aren't rich, because they can't do whatever they want.

Being rich means being able to do, within reason, whatever you want. In his book *Money*, political scientist Andrew Hacker estimates that to be rich you need an income of at least $1 million a year.[29] That seems about right. In Arkansas and West Virginia $500,000 or even $300,000 a year may be enough. In the places where most rich people want to live, however, a million dollars is the minimum required.

Still, a seven-figure annual income doesn't capture the significance of being rich today. Being rich means you don't have to work. That's why in ancient times the affluent class was the landed aristocracy; they lived off the income generated by their estates. It was considered disreputable to work. Work carries no stigma today, but being rich still should mean being able to maintain a very comfortable standard of living without working. What does it take? If you're a cautious but competent investor, you should be able to earn 5 percent on your portfolio after taxes and allowance for inflation. So a net worth of $10 million can generate around $500,000 in spending money. That's about as good as a $1 million salary and qualifies you as being rich. By this criterion, there are approximately 250,000 rich families in America today.

Even rich folk have their limits, however. They can fly first class, but they cannot own their own Gulfstream V. They can have two homes, typically a permanent home and a vacation cottage, but they cannot maintain homes around the world. They can afford live-in maids but not small platoons of "domestic staff" to manage their various households. They can eat in fine restaurants but they can't, as one Las Vegas tycoon reportedly did, fly in world-famous chef Wolfgang Puck and his staff to cook for a private party. Rich people can get season tickets to the ballpark, but they cannot, as Paul Allen, Wayne Huizenga, and Ted Turner have done, buy a sports team. A well-connected guy can get front-row seats to a Rod Stewart concert. But he can't, as one Santa Barbara multimillionaire recently did, have Rod Stewart himself perform at his wedding.[30] In short, rich people can do whatever they want within reason, but they cannot do whatever they want, period.

That honor belongs to the superrich, a new category that didn't even exist in 1980. To be superrich you need at least $100 million in assets and $10 million in annual income. Probably around 5,000 Americans, and perhaps 10,000 people worldwide, have this kind of money. These levels of wealth and income ensure that money is simply not an issue in the way you live your life. In some cases you may even feel entitled to make your own foreign policy, like investment mogul George Soros, who travels through eastern Europe and boasts of having "one president for breakfast and another for dinner."[31] Despite his megalomaniacal aspirations, Soros isn't really a Master of the Universe, but at the very least superrich people like him are masters of their own destiny.

Don't like the kind of music you hear? Follow author Stephen King's example and buy a radio station. Tired of having to sign up to play golf? Build a nine-hole course on your private estate, as one Long Island Midas recently did. Worried about asteroids flying too close to earth? Pump in a hundred grand, like Infoseek founder Steve Kirsch, to identify and track them. Looking for other similar thrills? Join the few dozen rich and intrepid souls, such as software tycoons Jack Thompson and Richard Garriott, who have paid hefty deposits to sign up for the first commercial rides into space. *Millionaire* magazine even features ads, which do not appear to be a joke, that offer rich people a chance to purchase "an authentic Scottish or French title" in case you feel like calling yourself a duke or a marquis.

In short, being superrich allows you to go totally insane, a fate that has actually befallen more than one American tycoon. No wonder it's hard to keep one's balance when the line between fantasy and reality is erased. Superrich people are limited in what they can do only by their imagination.

The overclass, as I've defined it, doesn't include just wealthy and superwealthy people. It also includes a segment of the upper middle class. Making the usual allowances for how old you are and where you live, in general you are a member of the overclass if you have an annual income in excess of $150,000 and a net worth of at least $1 million. Right now around 5 percent of Americans (5 million to 6 million households) can be counted in this group.

TABLE 2

How Do You Stack Up?

You may be earning well, but are you wealthy? How does your net worth compare with that of Americans in the top tiers? The following table gives the minimum net worth that you need in order to rank in the top 10 percent, the top 1 percent, and the top 0.5 percent of affluent Americans.*

	Wealth Cutoff
Top 10 percent	$489,000
Top 1 percent	$3.7 million
Top 0.5 percent	$5.7 million

*Source: Analysis of Federal Reserve data by Arthur Kennickell.

Perhaps what is most romantic about this group is that increasingly it is made up of young people. Call it the "junior overclass." Its members are frequently found in fields such as telecommunications, financial services, and computer programming. What previous age produced the equivalent of child tycoons such as David Filo and Jerry Yang? Only in the last decade have we seen twenty-eight-year-olds sporting a net worth in excess of $1 billion. The emergence of so many young people with so much money has changed all the rules about affluence in America.

One prominent representative of the junior overclass is Russell Horowitz, who started Go2Net in his late twenties and convinced his mother to pull out $40,000 from her IRA account and invest in his new Internet portal. "If this fails," she warned him, "we're going to be selling T-shirts on the beach." Fortunately for her, Russell did not fail. In March 1999, Paul Allen bought a controlling interest in Go2Net for $750 million. Suddenly Russell was rich, and so was his mom. "I don't know what I did to deserve all this," Sylvia Horowitz says. "All I did was change a few diapers." To which Russell replies, "But you changed the *right* diapers."[32]

Of course, multimillion-dollar portfolios are not typical for young people in their twenties and thirties. But as the rewards of today's technologically driven economy go disproportionately to those who are comfortable with technology and willing to take entrepreneurial risks, they will be. Already six-figure salaries and seven-figure retirement accounts are common among young entrepreneurs and young professionals in major cities. The Census Bureau reports that in 1997, the latest year for which data are available, there were already more than a million people between the ages of fifteen and thirty-five who earned more than $75,000 a year.[33] Today that number is probably closer to 2 million.

Some might say that by today's standards $75,000 is not a lot of money. But that's only because our standards have become so extravagant. For a sense of perspective, reflect on the fact that in 1980 only 11 percent of all households earned an inflation-adjusted equivalent of $75,000 a year. This means that many twenty-somethings are starting out at higher incomes than their parents enjoyed at the height of their earning power. No wonder some of the old boys are feeling a bit peeved.

Of all the new features of today's economy, I have saved the most important for last: the unique power conferred on human beings by the new technologies. Technology today has become not only the primary

TABLE 3

When Eight and a Half Grand Was Enough

What does it take to be in the top 5 percent of income earners in America? In 1950, an annual income of just $8,615 would have put you on the list. Now you need $150,000. What follows is a list of the minimum amount you'd have to have made in each of the given years to make it into the top 5 percent income category for that year.

1950	$8,615
1960	$13,516
1970	$24,250
1980	$55,000
1990	$102,358
2000	$150,000

Source: U.S. Census Bureau.

means of generating wealth but also the most obvious expression of our ability to manipulate our environment. Of course, there is nothing novel about the idea of technology itself. Ever since the earliest cave dweller started to make tools, technology has been man's apprentice, assisting him in shaping his environment to meet his needs. The twentieth century has seen the introduction of important technologies, such as television and the airplane. So what makes today's new technologies any different?

At first glance, it seems that the answer is: nothing. Indeed the computer, the cell phone, and the Internet seem continuous with earlier communications technologies in that they reduce the distance between people and speed up their ability to relate to one another. If this were so, we as individuals and as a society should have no more trouble adjusting to the Internet than we did to the car. This view, which is correct as far as it goes, is a necessary antidote to the Internet hoopla that something radically new has come into the world that requires what author Harry Dent, Jr., calls a "new order of consciousness."[34]

Yet upon reflection the hype turns out to be justified. Something new has come into the world, only it's not the Internet. Rather, it is the *other* technological revolution, the one that is being ignored, or at least downplayed, in all the excitement about the wonders of on-line retailing and e-mail. This other revolution goes by several names: nanotechnology, biotechnology, robotics. Its economic impact is only beginning to be felt, and its social implications are far wider. Basically it involves giving us as a species unprecedented power to control and transform nature, including our own human nature. Biologist E. O. Wilson says we are about to enter "a new epoch of life" based upon "our power to change the essence of our humanity." It is the ability to will our future as a species—a power conferred by these new technologies—that separates our predicament from that of every generation that has come before us.

If the nineteenth century was the century of chemistry and the twentieth century the century of physics, the twenty-first century promises to be the century of biology. Today's biology, however, is no longer restricted to laboratory experiments with test tubes and microscopes; it also involves computerized processing of huge amounts of data, computerized simulations of biological processes, and the sharing, via the Internet, of biological information among experts around the world. Biologists today can perform experiments at much greater speed and much more inexpensively "in silico" than in the laboratory. So biology has become an information science, and the marriage of biology and technology has given rise to a new field: biotechnology.

We think of the effects of biotechnology as confined to producing better crop yields and better vaccines. But the field is crossing a new threshold. In theoretical terms, the threshold was crossed half a century ago with James Watson and Francis Crick's 1953 discovery of the structure of DNA. Practical applications of Watson and Crick's monumental find were slow in coming and were mostly restricted to animals. Most of the excitement over the news in February 1997 that an obscure animal husbandry laboratory in Scotland had cloned a sheep named Dolly was based on the supposition that the next step was going to be the cloning of human beings. Indeed, the knowledge and the means of cloning people already exist; the only question is whether we are going to do it.

But why stop there? Biologists are on the verge of crossing another great barrier with the completion of the work of the Human Genome Project, a multibillion-dollar, multinational collaboration to identify and decipher the 30,000 to 40,000 genes in the human body. Francis Collins, head of the Human Genome Project, has called it the most important scientific project ever undertaken—more important than the Manhattan Project, more important than the moon landing.

The reason is that the human genome is the periodic table of life. Just as the periodic table gave scientists a new understanding of the elements, so the genome project will give biologists a comprehensive view of the genetic code. Once scientists have mastered the workings of genes they will, for the first time, possess a new kind of power. Radical ideologies such as communism and Nazism aspired to power of this sort, but they never attained it. It is nothing short of the power to abolish human nature, the power to create a new kind of human being.

By altering the genes of new embryos, we human beings alive today will have dominion not merely over the succeeding generation but over every generation to follow. Scientists say that within a short time we will have the technology to alter the genetic code of our children. What do you think of the idea of designing and custom-ordering your children? Some people scoff at the idea, convinced that we'll never be able to do that. But this is the same crowd that, without ever setting foot in a lab, declared that scientists would never be able to fertilize embryos in a test tube until they did—and that cloning was science fiction until it happened.

The people who know about these things assure us that "designer children" will soon be a real option for families. James Watson, codiscoverer of the structure of DNA, is enthusiastic about the prospect: "If we could make better human beings by knowing how to add genes, why shouldn't we do it?" Watson isn't talking just about eliminating genetic diseases; he is concerned about what he terms "genetic injustice." Evolution, he remarks, "can be very cruel." He wants to "treat other people in a way that maximizes the common good of the species." So how about a grand project to reform the species itself? Watson adds, "If you could cure what I feel is a very serious disease—that is, stupidity—it would be a great thing for people."[35]

This, right here, is the threshhold. E. O. Wilson told me, "Once we set about remaking not defective but normal genes, then we will have begun the task of remaking man." Then we will be limited almost exclusively by our imagination. It is possible to devise all kinds of ambitious projects for changing our humanity. Biologist Lee Silver envisions the raising of human intelligence to create a new species more advanced than *Homo sapiens,* just as *Homo sapiens* itself emerged from more primitive apelike beings.[36] Alternatively, we could try to eradicate aggression and become a more passive species or to eliminate the genetic differences that lead to inequality.

Some visionaries of the high-tech world have a much more ambitious idea: they think we should choose to relinquish our humanity and merge with our computers. Computer scientist Peter Cochrane, head of research for British Telecom, predicts "a radical symbiosis between humans and machines." He writes, "We will have to allow computer chips to become part of us, and allow ourselves to become part of machines."[37] Scientist and entrepreneur Ray Kurzweil argues that this would simply represent an ongoing evolutionary movement to something higher than ourselves: "Computers started out as extensions of our minds, and they will end up extending our minds. . . . Evolution's grandest creation—human intelligence—is providing the means for the next stage of evolution, which is technology."[38] We can consciously guide this evolutionary process by choosing to enter what cybertheorist Donna Haraway calls "the cyborg era."

To some these will seem like implausible, even wacky ideas, but they are taken very seriously by the best minds in the high-tech world. Already leading scientists are trying to make computers that function like living creatures. This field is called "artificial life." Inventor Danny Hillis, who designs supercomputers, has given himself a challenging project: "I want to build a computer that is proud of me." What kind of talk is this? We know that computers can do many of the things human beings do, such as lift things and count and communicate. Some jobs, such as landing airplanes, guiding cruise missiles, and doing other massively complicated calculations, computers seem to do better. But there are other notable human activities—feeling sorrow, for instance, learning from experience, making babies, or telling right from wrong—that computers seem unable to perform. Many scientists think that these barriers are not invincible, and they are working to produce a computer that can replicate every function of living beings. The premise of this line of research is that we living creatures are, at bottom, mere atoms and molecules, our brains are nothing more than sophisticated electronic circuits, and our genes are fundamentally units of information or code. Biologist Leroy Hood remarks that "our genome may be viewed as the most incredible software program ever written."[39] In this view, we are protein-based computers. So there is no reason in principle that biologists and software programmers cannot replicate by electronic means the complicated material process called life.

Of course, many people doubt that this effort will succeed in practice. Even if scientists are unable to create artificial life, however, they can achieve the same result by inserting living cells into nonliving objects. This is not only possible, it is already being done. And it works. For example, if you take the cells of a glowworm and insert them into a packet of tobacco, the tobacco glows! There is every reason to believe that human cells can be inserted into electronic frames to create "living machines." As we get better at doing this, scientists say, these machines will become more and more "alive" until the distinction between the natural and the artificial is completely abolished.

Of course, "living machines" can also be constructed in another way. Electronic devices can be implanted in our bodies and our brains to turn us into mechanized humanoids, or cyborgs. To some extent this is going on now with retinal implants, cochlear implants, pacemakers, artificial limbs, and so on. Some paraplegics have implants in their legs, arms, chest, and brain. Scientists tell us that silicon implants will monitor many of our body functions in the next several years. Even so, the focus of this enterprise is narrow: to remedy disability. But the concept of disability makes sense only when measured against a widely accepted norm of health, just as the concepts of "subhuman," "inhuman," and "superhuman" are meaningful only when measured against some agreed-upon definition of human nature.

Technology is now giving us the power to get rid of these norms and make of ourselves what we will. By using implants to enhance our physical and mental functions, we can become cyborgs. By becoming cyborgs, we can achieve the superhuman powers that the computers of the future will surely possess. At the same time, our nostalgia over losing our humanity may be overcome by the recognition that we have gotten rid of the sins, follies, and weaknesses that were an intrinsic part of our old "crooked timber." And then the history of our species can be written with the epitaph that we tried out humanity, found it wanting, and opted for something better.

CHAPTER TWO

THE GATHERING STORM

Mass Affluence and Its Discontents

The love of well-being has now become the predominant taste of the

nation; the great current of human passions runs in that channel

and sweeps everything along in its course.

—Tocqueville, *Democracy in America*

A great debate is brewing about the effects of the new economy on our society. On the one side are the pioneers of the new economy. They have a vision for the world, they are making it happen, and they are being hugely rewarded for it. This is the group that champions new companies and new products, that is obsessed with technology, that welcomes the rapid pace of change, that sees ahead a cornucopia of pleasures and possibilities. We could use many different names to refer to this camp: they are economic optimists, cyberspace enthusiasts, techno-utopians. But I have watched this group, and one of its characteristic expressions, usually offered with a signal thrust of the arm, is "Yeah!" Thus I call this group the "Party of Yeah."

It is being fiercely opposed and denounced by another group that is profoundly distressed by the direction in which society is going. This group is passionately convinced that the new economy is a fraud and that unfettered markets and runaway technology, far from bringing us closer to the Promised Land, are destroying our most cherished values. Even if the economy continues to grow, these critics insist, no upsurge in the Dow and the Nasdaq can compensate for the moral and social havoc being wreaked by the new economy. If we do not change course, they warn, we are headed for disaster. This group is ideologically more diverse than the first; it is predominantly made up of cultural pessimists, environmentalists, social conservatives, egalitarians, religious critics of capitalism, and skeptics about technology. I call this group the "Party of Nah."

The clash between the two groups can be seen in the clash over stock market valuations. Speaking for the Party of Nah, economist Robert Schiller warns that we are in "a speculative bubble."[1] This camp likes to recall the Dutch tulip bulb craze of the 1630s or the South Sea Bubble in England in the early eighteenth century. Price-earnings ratios, this group solemnly notes, are even higher than they were in 1929, when the U.S. market crashed. Let's not forget, the naysayers remark, that the Japanese stock market peaked at 40,000; more than a decade later, it hovers below 20,000. When the American market dropped sharply in early 2000, this group got its first chance to gloat. "The bubble has popped," announced Alan Abelson in *Barron's,* which for several years has criticized Internet investing as a form of "Russian roulette."[2] "The dot-com era has ended," proclaimed investment columnist Jim Cramer, whose own company, TheStreet.com, took a steep plunge.[3] The Party of Nah is convinced that there is worse, much worse, to come. Investment analyst Jeremy Grantham says the momentum investors who are driving this market have done well so far, but they are going to be hit by a 50 percent slump in the Dow, a 70 percent decline in the Nasdaq, and an 80 percent liquidation of unprofitable Internet companies.[4]

The Party of Yeah dismisses these warnings and forecasts as ignorant and silly. "This isn't a tulip bulb craze," retorts author and investment writer James Glassman. "The people who say that are basically saying that the computer revolution isn't real, the Internet isn't real." This group dismisses the market skeptics as "fundamentalists," that is, people who look only at traditional measures of value. "Yes, the critics predicted the last correction," concedes *Forbes* publisher Rich Karlgaard. "That makes them right once out of thirty-seven tries." What the bears miss, the Party of Yeah says, is that ideas, knowledge, and information are the new form of capital. The most valuable form of property today is intellectual property. In short, the new economy has new rules that most people still don't understand. "We're still at the dawn of the Internet revolution," writes a columnist in *Business Week*.[5] The Internet, this group contends, will wipe out banks as we know them, travel agencies as we know them, brokerage houses as we know them, publishers as we know them, malls as we know them. "Anyone who would bet a lot of money on a given Internet stock is an idiot," says management guru Tom Peters. "Anyone who would not bet a lot of money on a portfolio that includes Internet stocks is an even bigger idiot."[6] The implication is that the Internet sector will continue to prosper because the profits of the companies that will dominate tomorrow's market are going to be phenomenal. The market may jerk up and down, but the Party of Yeah is convinced that the broader trend is upward. Harry Dent predicts a Dow of 21,500 "and likely higher."[7] Glassman has coauthored a book making the case for a Dow at 36,000.

As this argument illustrates, this is a new debate that cannot be encompassed by our old vocabulary. Indeed, the emerging conflict between the Parties of Yeah and Nah supersedes all the familiar categories: Republican and Democrat, Right and Left, conservative and liberal. Over the next several years, the terms "Left" and "Right," as well as "liberal" and "conservative," will have to be abandoned or reconfigured along the new party lines outlined above. Similarly the major political parties, in the United States and around the world, will fight their major battles over whether the massive social changes wrought by global technological capitalism are a good thing or a bad thing and how we should respond to them.

"It's a war," George Gilder says, placing his arms on my shoulders. "Our enemies are right. It's a religious war. With any technology that's changing the world as deeply as the Internet, religious wars are inevitable. But we are going to win because we have a vision of change and of redemption. Our opponents are reactionaries. They are stuck in the zero-sum assumptions of the premillennial era. They don't understand that creativity is an act of faith. We are the ones who are creative, because we are the ones who have faith."

Although Gilder likes to call for "overthrowing the powers and principalities of the old order," at first glance he doesn't look the part of a revolutionary. He has an absent-minded air about him. His hair is flecked with gray, and he is wearing the typical preppy uniform: light blue button-down shirt, navy blue blazer. That's Gilder's background— he is a New England WASP. Then you notice the piercing eyes. And when Gilder speaks his hands come alive, moving back and forth in unexpected jerky motions. These are the characteristics of a new-economy true believer.

Gilder is well known in the tech world. He didn't start out there; in an earlier life, Gilder wrote books about inner-city decay and the fallacies of feminism. He once described a debate with a misguided European advocate of a certain cell phone technology as "more emotional and irrational than debating Germaine Greer." Gilder's interests are 100 percent tech now, and his annual Telecosm conference attracts techies, entrepreneurs, and venture capitalists looking for the hottest ideas in the industry. His newsletters and technology reports can sharply influence the stock prices of the companies he writes about. The business media call this the "Gilder effect." Gilder is no mere stock analyst, however. He is high-tech capitalism's manic defender, its supreme prophet and visionary. *Forbes ASAP* calls him "the John the Baptist of the Digital Age."[8]

"Imagine gazing at the Web from outer space," Gilder says. "Looking through your spectroscope, what you'll see is a global efflorescence, a sphere of light. *That's* the telecosm. That's it. Ultimately, that radiant light will carry most of the commerce in the world." The Internet, Gilder recently wrote, "is an unstoppable force that will reach into every nook and crevice of the old economy and transform it."[9]

Gilder reminds me of Adam Smith's famous example of the pin factory: "Remember how Smith said that the factory worker is not twice or ten times more productive than the craftsman who makes pins one at a time. He is 5,000 times more productive. Well, he could have been talking about the Net. Only now we're talking about increases in power that amount to a millionfold. Adam Smith couldn't even imagine those numbers." The effect, Gilder argues, is to allow people anywhere on the planet to move capital and information across the world at light speed.

"The Internet transcends geography. The physical costs of new knowledge drop to nearly nothing. Wealth now consists of thoughts, not things." Gilder adds, "The real beneficiaries of this revolution are not in Cambridge or Palo Alto. They are in Santiago, Chile, and

Shanghai, China. Technology and free markets have already brought a billion Asians into the middle class. That's just the beginning. We're going to see prosperity as we've never seen it before, in places where it's never existed before."

Gilder speaks about the future as if it were already here. He gives the impression of a man who's been there. "The era of the personal computer is over," he says. "The most common computer of the next decade will be a digital cellular phone. It will look like a digital cellular phone. It will be as portable as your watch, as personal as your wallet. It will recognize speech, navigate streets, it will collect your mail and your news. It will read it to you. It will open your car door. It will perform banking transactions."

In Gilder's view there is virtually no downside to the proliferation of technological capitalism. "The new age of intelligent machines," he says, "will enhance and empower humanity, making possible new ventures and new insights. It will relieve man of much of his most onerous and unsatisfying work. It will enlarge his freedom. It will diminish despots and exploiters."[10]

Despite these tangible benefits, Gilder says, the Web has no real material existence: "If you turn off your spectroscope, the Web disappears. It's gone. It's as invisible as freedom itself. So many people don't appreciate the importance of what's going on. In a very literal sense, they don't see the light."

Gilder's religious imagery is intentional. He's not interested just in commercial efficiencies. He speaks of the Web as a "redemptive technology" because he is convinced it will prove instrumental in abolishing world poverty, famine, and disease.[11] Indeed, his basic argument for the new tech economy is a moral one. Sounding like an unreconstructed New England transcendentalist, Gilder envisions us in the twenty-first century using the Telecosm to achieve what he terms "the overthrow of matter."

Gilder's enthusiasm for the Web derives from the prospect of people leaving their bodies and indeed all physical limits behind and communicating at the level of pure mind: "We can overcome our alienation from things. We can escape our absorption in the trivialities of subsistence. We can rise to the larger challenges of life, which are the exaltation of mind and spirit. Perhaps we will also discover new pinnacles of vision and new continents of higher truth." In that sense, for

Gilder, the Web is a profoundly spiritual medium. It demonstrates, he says, "the primacy of spirit."[12]

This is what the Party of Yeah sounds like. Not that Gilder is a typical member; he is more literary, more analytical, more theological in his thinking than most of the new breed. At the same time there is a boldness, an ambition, a sweep to Gilder's rhetoric that is entirely in keeping with the spirit of the new age. Everything he says is one part interpretation and two parts exhortation. More than most, Gilder knows history; he knows where we've come from. But like every good new-economy yeahsayer, he has his eyes riveted on the future.

The future is the place where this group really lives. Even as they inhabit the here and now, their minds have already moved there. That shouldn't be surprising: the vast majority of members of the Party of Yeah are young people. Most of these young people live somewhere in the American West, usually in California. This is a group that doesn't have much of a past. For a long time it was a group without a name. Someone christened it Generation X. Not much was expected of it. What can you expect of epicene boys and anorexic girls wearing grungy clothes, weird body attachments, and a forlorn, desperate look? Generation X was portrayed in the media as a confused and listless generation, a generation without a purpose.

Well, the little shits have finally figured out what they want to be: earthshakers! They have done it: they have become the most entrepreneurial generation in American history. And they're just getting started. The net is the Archimedian lever with which they hope to move the world.

This is not a generation of thinkers or social critics. These young people haven't read Plato, Proust, or Max Weber. When they do read, it's more likely to be *Wired* or *Fast Company* or a tech newsletter that some dweeb at Stanford or MIT puts out. Some of them read only Dilbert cartoons. They don't care about Saint Augustine, but they like Gutenberg. They respect Einstein, but Edison was more their kind of guy. That's because Edison wasn't just a thinker, he was a doer. The Party of Yeah admires doers. I saw this point illustrated a couple of years ago, when Michael Dell ascended the dais at his computer company's annual shareholders' meeting. A slide popped up on the huge screen behind him. It showed Dell's stock performance over the past three years, compared with that of other big companies such as Coca-Cola, Microsoft, and rival computer company Compaq. The upward slope of Dell's stock was much steeper than that of the others. A gasp went through the audience. "And that concludes our presentation," Dell said, with a grin. The crowd broke into thunderous applause. What a doer.

As with Dell, most of the heroes admired by the Party of Yeah come from its own culture. Some of these role models we all know, such as Dell and Jerry Yang, but many of them are total unknowns outside the tech world: Linus Torvalds, who invented the Linux system of open-source software; Bill Joy, chief scientist and cofounder of Sun Microsystems; Caltech physicist and inventor Carver Mead; Netscape founder and now start-up investor Marc Andreessen; Hotmail founder Sabeer Bhatia; Morgan Stanley Internet stock analyst Mary Meeker; Tim Berners-Lee, who invented the World Wide Web; Intel cofounder Gordon Moore; Softbank CEO Masayoshi Son; scientist Alan Turing; historian of science Thomas Kuhn; science fiction writer William Gibson; biologist Richard Dawkins; and John Perry Barlow, a former Wyoming rancher and Grateful Dead songwriter who is a founder of something called the Electronic Frontier Foundation.

Notice that I didn't mention Bill Gates; Gates is not a hero to these folk. This was true even before the Microsoft trial. Grudgingly, they will concede Gates's entrepreneurial achievement, but rarely without failing to point out that Gates is "derivative," Gates is a "clone," Gates has never come up with anything original. Some techies even consider him a total fraud, and others do not shrink from terms such as "demon." Envy may be a factor here. Even so, the real hero of the Party of Yeah is clearly not the founder of Microsoft but the founder of Apple Computer, Steve Jobs. "Stevie Wonder," *Fortune* calls him. And at a recent computer trade show Jobs's presentation was interrupted by teenagers cheering and yelling, "Steve rocks."[13]

So what is it about Jobs? Well, first, he has the look. The glasses and chubby cheeks say "nerd," but the aquiline nose suggests refinement and the deep-set eyes convey passionate intensity, but not without a hint of playful cynicism. Jobs has given himself a cool title at Apple: "iCEO." And his trademark black outfits signify that he's a rebel, a misfit, an outlaw. "One of my role models is Bob Dylan," he says.[14] At a re-

cent meeting of Apple stockholders, Jobs spoke at a podium with gigantic posters of Che Guevara and John Lennon behind him. Apple's
current motto, "Think Different," featuring maverick visionaries apparently handpicked by Jobs, strikes exactly the right countercultural
chord. Jobs once made a trip to India to find himself, and his personal
transformation from a kind of 1960s hippiedom to high-tech artist and
sage is regarded as a Buddha-like journey to Nirvana.

Jobs's message is that he is not about money. "When I was twenty-
three," he says, "I was worth a million dollars. When I was twenty-four,
I was worth ten million, and, at twenty five, over a hundred million dollars. But I never really cared about the money." In the good old days,
Jobs says, "I would ride my bicycle to the Stanford artificial intelligence
lab on weekends and hang out. You could feel the magic in the air. I
miss that time. People care more about material things now."[15] Although Jobs is enormously wealthy, he tries to demonstrate his indifference to material things by taking from Apple a dollar a year in salary,
no bonuses, no stock options, no other compensation. From his other
company, Pixar Animation Studios, Jobs draws a comparatively lavish
$50 a year, also without bonus and stock options. The point, if you
haven't gotten it already, is that Jobs isn't just another manufacturer of
machines that compute; he is a technological sculptor. And it must be
said that his products have an almost sensuous appeal. I have seen
techies look at the tangerine-colored iMac with a gaze that borders on
the erotic. Apple doesn't just attract consumers; it attracts suitors.

Moreover, Jobs presents himself as a visionary whose work is intended to serve a larger social purpose. In this sense his cynicism reveals
itself as a veneer. Like Humphrey Bogart in *Casablanca*, Jobs strikes a
sneering pose, but his outward posture conceals the heart of a man who
really cares. Jobs's early slogan for the Apple Macintosh, "Power to the
People," conveyed the impression that he wasn't just about commerce
or marketing; his computers were a veritable catalyst for the leveling of
social hierarchy and the strengthening of the democratic process. Jobs
recruited former Pepsi executive John Sculley to Apple by posing to
him a now-famous question: "Do you want to spend the rest of your life
selling sugar water or do you want a chance to change the world?" The
Party of Yeah rallies to Jobs's manifesto that they should change the
world and empower the masses by following their passion and developing "insanely great products."

The Party of Yeah is generally an inarticulate group. Gilder is an exception to this rule; Dell and Jobs are not. Have you noticed that I've had to excavate a fair amount of Jobs's philosophy from his corporate ads? Even the Party of Yeah's regular columnists, such as management guru Tom Peters and *Forbes* publisher Rich Karlgaard, have a tendency to talk funny. Reading Karlgaard's column is like watching an intelligent but highly wound up guy react in staccato outbursts to the world around him. "Whoa!" "Amen!" and "Huh?" are all characteristic Karlgaard literary expressions. Like Peters, Karlgaard is an aficionado of capital letters, ellipses, one-sentence paragraphs, exclamation points!!! There are a style and a sensibility here—and, contained within them, an ethos.

But the ethos does not fully disclose itself. It has to be teased out. This is a group that is capable of strange actions that don't seem to make a lot of sense. Recently a group of high-tech leaders—including author and inventor Stewart Brand, computer designer Danny Hillis, technology guru Esther Dyson, and entrepeneur Mitch Kapor—rallied behind what seemed to them a truly profound project: they want to build a clock that is eighty feet tall and chimes not once an hour but once a century. So you mean the next time it chimes we will all be dead? Exactly. The clock will even have a cuckoo, but it will come out only once every millennium for the next ten thousand years. Don't wait around. The reason for this bizarre enterprise? "The urgent keeps displacing the important in our daily lives," Brand explains. The so-called Clock of the Long Now is intended to give us all a sense of long-range perspective.

Many people in the Party of Yeah not only do weird things but also use a lingo that can sound, to outsiders, a bit odd. Some of it is youthful argot: "That's cool," "This is awesome," "unreal," "far out," and so on. Some of it is technical mumbo jumbo: "application service providers," "seamless integration," "connectivity," "real-time data feeds." Then there's the e-commerce jargon: "click-and-mortar businesses," "killer apps," "disintermediation," "viral marketing," "first-mover advantage," "Search globally and act locally." There is a fair amount of Darwin-inspired entrepreneurial survivalism—"Don't be Amazoned," "It's e-business or out of business," "You gotta change the DNA of your company," "Today, slow and steady gets creamed"—and a lot of motivational rah-rah stuff: "Failure is not an option," "Always push yourself, even when it hurts," and "Every second counts." Finally, there's a good deal of bumper-sticker philosophy: "The Internet changes everything," "Imagine the future," "Think outside the box," "the courage to change," "Bureaucracy is a state of mind," and so on.

So what do these people really believe? They contend that this is a pivotal moment in history. "A lot of people want to do things the old Newtonian way," Jay Walker, founder of Priceline.com, told me. "We are attempting a quantum approach." *Business Week* says that the Internet revolution is a kind of "Copernican revolution."[16] Jeff Bezos of Amazon.com contends that we are in the middle of the biggest change since the Cambrian period 500 million years ago. Venture capitalist John Doerr wants to go even further back. "We're just after the big bang," he declares. "A new universe has been formed, and its first fundamental laws can be discerned."[17]

Members of the Party of Yeah assert that in previous eras the priest, the intellectual, and the bureaucrat have all tried to lead society, and all have failed miserably. They were unable to solve the problem of scarcity. So all they did was redistribute resources or try to reconcile people to living in degradation. Most of the time, the Party of Yeah alleges, all they did was arrogate power to themselves. Spencer Reiss, a former *Newsweek* correspondent who now edits the investment letter *New Economy Watch*, is outraged by those who resist the spread of technological capitalism around the world. "It's borderline immoral to sit comfortably in Seattle or London and oppose initiatives that bring cheaper food, better products, and universal access to information over the Net." Columnist Virginia Postrel calls these critics "enemies of the future."

Fortunately, in the view of Postrel and other members of the Party of Yeah, the world has changed and the bad guys are no longer in charge. So they had better step out of the way, or they are going to be overrun. In any case, they are becoming irrelevant. Postrel declares, "Few people want to smash their computers, give up off-season fruits and vegetables, turn their backs on modern medicine, move in with their cousins and in-laws, or forgo higher incomes."[18] In this view, change is good because it means progress. One great milestone of progress is our technologically driven economic expansion. Economist Todd Buchholz writes, "The biggest risk to the world economy today is not recession but excessive growth."[19]

The new leaders of society are the businessman and the scientist and, in the view of the Party of Yeah, they have a legitimate claim to be in charge. Never was a group of leaders so ready for the task, so full of animal spirits. As Jeff Arnold of WebMD tells *Fortune*, "I don't like to go to bed at night because I'm so excited about getting up the next day."[20] Mike Saylor, CEO of Microstrategy, is even more emphatic: "I think my software is going to become so ubiquitous, so essential, that if it stops working there will be riots."[21]

These testimonials may sound a bit too gung ho, but in the view of the Party of Yeah, their general message is sound. Today the scientist and the entrepreneur are the only ones who can actually deliver on their promise. This promise, or what cybercowboy John Perry Barlow terms the Great Work, is a spectacular one: to eliminate scarcity, to feed and clothe and heal the world. And, this group says, we are doing it. Dewang Mehta, a leading software entrepreneur in India, told me he believes that the computer industry will realize "Gandhi's dream of wiping a tear from every Indian face." Eventually, the Party of Yeah is convinced, the whole world will be better off because material scarcity will no longer exist. "Unlimited supply at zero cost" is one of the mantras of the Party of Yeah.

But there's more: this group wants to empower the individual. "If I offered you a billion dollars for your right arm, would you sell it to me?" Jay Walker, the founder of Priceline.com, asked me. I replied, "Certainly not." Walker said triumphantly, "Then you have a billion-dollar asset! You're a billionaire!" Walker's point is that there is hidden potential in each person, and the new economy offers each of us a chance to harness it. On the Web, any entrepreneur can set up a Web site and compete directly with the giant corporations. Every worker is now a "free agent" who can put his or her services up for auction. Tech enthusiasts also like to point out that "everyone wired to the Internet owns a printing press." In the Internet age, power is devolving from the corporation to the individual customer, from the state to the individual citizen.

The Party of Yeah believes that new technologies are not just better tools, they "offer us real opportunities for making the world a happier place," in the words of physicist Freeman Dyson. The Internet still has a limited reach, Dyson concedes, but he argues that as it expands, it will become a "truly global Internet" that will be connected to "local networks in every village." Thus people in remote places will be able to buy and sell, learn, contact people, and have immediate access to the rest of the world. "The new Internet will end the cultural isolation of poor countries and poor people."[22] Members of the Party of Yeah promise that cyberspace will bring people together by allowing the formation of "electronic neighborhoods" based not on geography but on shared interests.

These techno-visionaries see a future teeming with exhilarating possibilities. In the short term, they say, we will end poverty and produce global affluence, and we will also empower individuals and build communities. Then we can set about realizing more ambitious projects, such as having virtual-reality experiences that cannot be duplicated in the real world, expanding our minds through electronic enhancements, living longer with the help of antiaging drugs, setting up planetary settlements, or giving our children and future generations genetic modifications that will make them healthier, better looking, smarter, more artistic, perhaps even more caring. "There's no reason death should happen," says Netscape cofounder Marc Andreessen. "There's no reason you shouldn't be able to design exactly the body you want."[23] As we colonize the solar system, predicts George Yeo, Singapore's trade minister, "Planet Earth will become the Old World."[24] Genetic engineering, exults biologist Gregory Stock, "is going to expand our sense of what it means to be human."[25] Thus the Party of Yeah is filled with boundless optimism, because, like Lincoln Steffens, it has seen the future, and it works!

"Bullshit." That is Studs Terkel's one-word response to the rhetoric of the Party of Yeah. "I've heard it," the crusty old author of *Working* says. "I've heard it all. I've seen these young punks in action. And I'll tell you, they scare the crap out of me."

Now in his eighties, his face mapped with wrinkles, Terkel emphasizes that he's not out of it; he's not a Luddite; he doesn't oppose technology. "I believe in refrigerators to cool my martinis," he wrote in a recent article, "and washing machines because I hate to see women smacking their laundry against a rock."[26] At the same time, Terkel fears that "we're losing our humanity, for Christ's sake. I see these guys sitting in little rooms with eighteen computers and a bed. They hire and fire people from those rooms. They hardly speak to anybody, except through their computers. And they're proud of their lifestyle, these pathetic bastards. Look, if they want to live this way, fine. But what pisses me off is what happens to people at the other end of the line. People are struggling to make ends meet in this country. Out there in the world, millions are scrounging for something to eat. Is it right that so many people are starving while these guys have more money than God?"

Terkel permits himself a cynical laugh. "Saving the world, my ass. These rich guys are trying to convince the rest of us that everyone is better off because *they're* better off."

At the other end of the political spectrum, the economic historian Gertrude Himmelfarb sounds a very similar note. She says that in recent years America has witnessed "a revolution in the manners, morals and mores of society." But it is not a revolution she celebrates. "In the name of progress," she told me, "we are destroying much of what gives meaning and purpose to life."

Terkel is an old left-winger; Himmelfarb is a conservative. Terkel speaks in the salty tongue of a man who has hung out a lot with construction workers; Himmelfarb's is the somber, refined tone of the academic. Yet Himmelfarb echoes Terkel's view that the economic and technological gains of America have also been accompanied by steep social and moral costs: "Economically, our society is better off. But in many ways we are a much poorer society than we used to be. There are other forms of poverty than economic poverty, you know."

Himmelfarb illustrates with the example of her own life: "Many of us are doing rather well. My children have a higher standard of living than we could dream of when we were young. And I'm happy for them. But I look at my grandchildren and I see what's going on around me, and I wonder what kind of moral environment are they going to grow up in."

Himmelfarb says, "Look at our divorce rates, our illegitimacy rates, our rates of teen suicide and drug addiction. We have come to accept these as normal because we have become used to them. But they are not normal. They are deeply pathological. But we have become demoralized, and I mean that in both senses. We have lost our will to resist. And even more important, we've lost our ability as a society to tell the difference between right and wrong. Even people who live decently no longer have the confidence to make the case for virtue."

Himmelfarb adds, "We are living in a toxic culture. The sheer volume of incivility, vulgarity, and immorality overwhelms you. There is so much materialism, narcissism, hedonism. We send our children out into the world with fear in our hearts. The environmentalists tell us that the earth is an ecosystem and that its natural balance must be preserved for the ecosystem to flourish. Cultures are ecosystems too, and ours is morally out of balance. Aristotle was right: it is not easy to be a good citizen in a bad society. Even if you want to do what's right as an individual, it becomes very difficult when you have all these social and cultural forces arrayed against you. So what good are our stock market returns when our lives have been diminished in this way?"

She pauses to sip her coffee. "I know what they'll tell you. They'll tell you that all of this is nostalgia, that we've developed this romantic conception of our past. But they are the ones who don't know history. What they're saying is complete nonsense, because we were there, we lived through it. We grew up in the tenements under conditions that simply don't exist today. So I know how hard life was. But it was also a stable life, a coherent life, and a quite satisfying life."

So, I ask Himmelfarb, does Patrick Buchanan have a point when he raises these issues? Himmelfarb doesn't agree with Buchanan on much these days, but she agrees with him that there was an old neighborhood where people had neighbors and helped one another. She also agrees with him when he says that the old neighborhood has gone and that something very important has been lost. "We haven't come up with a good substitute for that old neighborhood," Himmelfarb says, "and please don't tell me that it's going to be 'virtual communities,' because it isn't." Himmelfarb suggests that while the world is more interconnected than ever, the connections among people are becoming weaker.

I sympathize with Himmelfarb's point here: when your cousin is sick or dying, you have to sit by her bedside and console her, you can't do it with e-mail. Himmelfarb comments that e-mail "encourages illiteracy. People don't write in coherent sentences. There is no thought that goes into it." Also, the normal canons of privacy and civility are not respected. There are Web sites where you can watch coeds eat, sleep, even go to the bathroom. Moreover, Himmelfarb points out that "people say things and divulge themselves to strangers in a way they never would in face-to-face conversation or even in a letter."

Himmelfarb concedes that neither technology nor capitalism is the primary cause of the toxic culture she is objecting to. "What I want to emphasize, however, is that they aren't solutions. They are morally neutral. If we as a society want good things, the market supplies them, technology gives us the tools to obtain them. But in the current environment, what markets and technology do is cater to the trivializing and harmful elements of the culture, because that is where the profits are."

Himmelfarb concludes, "People who are trying to live decently have become a dissident culture and, in some ways, a subculture. This doesn't mean they refuse to vote. But in important respects, they have rejected the values of the mainstream culture and set up alternative institutions." She gives the example of parents who have set up "TV-free" homes because they don't want their minds filled with junk. Two million Americans, she writes, practice this form of "cultural abstinence."

Another example: homeschooling. Himmelfarb points out that more than a million children today are homeschooled by their parents. "These aren't all poor evangelical Christians, in case that's what you were thinking. The home school movement may have begun as a religious movement. But now it's much broader than that." Himmelfarb says that many parents from a variety of backgrounds have taken to homeschooling because they realize that the schools—even the private schools—are not giving their children a good educational grounding and a sense of what really matters.

"I don't say any of this easily or cheerfully," Himmelfarb says. "We Jews came to this country, and we have been accepted. We have appreciated mainstream cultural institutions like the public schools because they brought people together into a common culture. So this cultural separation, or partial cultural separation, is something that I regret. Yet more and more people feel that they have to do it. How else is it possible to live a decent life?"

From these conversations we can excavate a left-wing criticism of technological capitalism and a right-wing criticism. The left-wing critique is in the name of nature and inequality. The right-wing critique is in the name of morality. The most significant political development of our time is that these critiques are becoming one. "Nature, community, and decency" will be the rallying cry of the new political movement aimed at resisting the thrust of the new economy. Let us briefly explore what the critics are saying and why their traditional divisions and enmities are likely to dissolve.

First, there is inequality. It cannot be denied that there are staggering inequalities of wealth in the United States and between the West and the Third World. Consider some revealing statistics. The total income of America's 12 million black households is approximately $430 billion a year.[27] The net worth of the 30 richest Americans, according to *Forbes,* equals approximately $440 billion. So thirty people in this country have a net worth that exceeds the collective annual earnings of black-America.

The top 1 percent of the population owns more than one third of the wealth in the United States. The top 10 percent has two thirds. That means the bottom 90 percent of Americans control only about a third of the wealth of the nation. Indeed, nearly half of American households have a net worth below $50,000 and a quarter below $10,000. According to a recent report by the Center on Budget and Policy Priorities, the earnings of the top fifth of the population soared by 15 percent in the past decade or so while the earnings of the bottom fifth remained stagnant.[28] Economist Edward Wolff of New York University, who studies wealth data, estimates that Bill Gates alone has a net worth that surpasses that of 100 million Americans—the bottom 40 percent of the population.

The fifty countries of sub-Saharan Africa, minus South Africa, have a total population of 570 million and a combined gross domestic product of around $200 billion.[29] That equals the net worth of the five richest Americans. A recent U.N. Human Development Report notes that the wealth of the world's billionaires is greater than the combined income of nearly half the world's population.[30] Many Americans and Europeans spend $2 for a bottle of designer water while one third of the world's population lives on less than $2 a day.

Inequality is traditionally a concern of the Left, and not surprisingly, some of the people who have been protesting the inequalities generated by technological capitalism have a left-leaning pedigree. "Progress is more plausibly judged by the reduction of deprivation than by the further enrichment of the opulent," writes economist Amartya Sen, a Nobel laureate.[31] Those who echo Sen's concerns—economist -Laura D'Andrea Tyson, political scientist Bruce Ackerman, philosopher Richard Rorty, journalist Robert Kuttner, and the Reverend Jim Wallis, editor of *Sojourner's* magazine—tend to be old-line leftists. But of late they have been joined by Kevin Phillips, a Republican political strategist, and conservative columnist Arianna Huffington, and I suspect that many more right-wingers will join this unlikely coalition in the next few years.

Why? Because the issue is too important to concede to the Left and because the Left doesn't know what to do with it. We haven't heard much from the Left about inequality lately, in large part because socialism has been resoundingly discredited, and so egalitarian concerns are typically muttered sotto voce or confined to left-wing media outlets. And some on the left cannot resist advancing absurd solutions. Thus Richard Rorty wistfully suggests that "if the intellectuals and the unions could ever get back together again, and could reconstitute the kind of left which existed in the forties and fifties, the first decade of the twenty-first century might conceivably be a Second Progressive Era."[32] A lovely idea, but how practical is it, Rip Van Rorty? Economist Paul Krugman advises the United States to take up "the Swedish model" in which the government consumes 63 percent of the gross national product.[33] Equally implausible, Bruce Ackerman and Anne Alstott argue in a recent book that America should ensure that all citizens have a more equal chance to succeed by handing them $80,000 apiece on their twenty-first birthday.[34]

Conservatives cannot possibly agree with these proposals, yet there are good conservative reasons to care about inequality—not because conservatives are egalitarians who believe that everyone in society should get an equal share but because conservatives care about the merit principle, the notion that hard work brings just reward, and the scale of inequality in today's economy seems to call this whole concept of fair play into question. Think about the old notion of reward in America: you start at the bottom and work your way up, and over a lifetime you hope to build up wealth as a due reward for your efforts. But now if you adopt this approach there is a name for you: sucker. The new formula is one of instant wealth: set up a new company, take it public, and pocket half a billion dollars in two and a half years.

This is a wonderful prospect, except that it destroys the notion of just deserts in a society. Rewards today seem completely detached from any defensible notion of merit; ours feels like a casino economy. Of course, many entrepreneurs have accumulated fortunes by producing very valuable things, but is it fair that their children should inherit multimillion-dollar trust funds while other kids start out so far behind? As economist James Tobin writes, "One generation's inequality of outcomes is the next generation's inequality of opportunity."[35] Then there are the corporate CEOs who leave with multimillion-dollar golden parachutes. These farewell gifts may seem warranted if the CEO has a successful record, but frequently they accrue to failed CEOs who have driven down the profitability and stock price of their companies. Meanwhile, the ordinary working person is given a pink slip and asked to turn in his parking permit. Again, where is the sense of fairness?

In addition to these concerns about merit and justice, another reason conservatives should care about inequality is moral decency. It was the Tory writer Samuel Johnson who said, "A decent provision for the poor is the true test of civilization."[36] Inequality itself may be tolerable, but doesn't the scale of today's inequality raise ethical concerns? How can conservatives who believe that "all men are created equal" complacently acquiesce in a system that permits some people to live like kings while others live like serfs? A further conservative concern is social stability, and when the chasm between people reaches a certain point, it threatens to strain or break the bonds that hold societies together. Alan Greenspan, chairman of the Federal Reserve Board, has warned that if the opportunities of the new economy are restricted to a few, there is a serious danger of social unrest.[37]

Many people across the political spectrum have expressed concerns about the "digital divide," in other words, that technology will exacerbate the already high level of economic and social inequality. Robert Knowling, the CEO of Covad Communications, charges that the exclusion of blacks and other minorities from the tech world constitutes a new form of racism. The lack of access to technology on the part of the poor and minorities is a problem that is taken very seriously in the high-tech world. Intel cofounder Gordon Moore and computer designer Danny Hillis have protested the disenfranchisement of those who are isolated from the knowledge and connections available through the Web. Many high-tech CEOs, such as Bill Gates and Ted Waitt of Gateway, are donating money and equipment to bring computers and Internet access to poor communities and inner-city schools. "People who are not wired are in danger of becoming the new servant class," complains Freeman Dyson. "The gulf between the wired and the unwired is wide and growing wider."[38]

In addition to faulting the new economy for exacerbating inequality, the left-wing critique blames it for environmental devastation. This view holds that technology and capitalism rely for their success and proliferation on an increasing exploitation of nature and natural resources. In its extreme formulation, which goes by the name of "deep ecology," some environmentalists hold that the whole premise of modern technological capitalism, which is to supply the ever-increasing wants of humans, is based on the false premise that the biosphere is ours for the ransacking. In the view of "deep ecologists," technological capitalism is a vicious, predatory enterprise because nature does not belong to us, we belong to nature.

Inverting the usual moral hierarchy, some "deep ecologists" argue that insects, birds, and animals have a higher claim to preservation than human beings because they are part of nature's order and cannot screw it up. Human beings, with our consciousness, reason, and insatiable appetites, pose a direct threat to nature and therefore rank at the bottom of the moral order. Indeed, in this view, our highest moral imperative is to limit our population and our lifestyle so that we cease to contaminate and imperil the biosphere.[39] The radical environmentalist Kirkpatrick Sale says, "Nothing less than a drastic overhaul of this civilization will do anything substantial to halt our path to environmental destruction."

A more moderate version of the environmental critique holds that the natural ecosystem is a complicated and fragile thing, and that as technology and capitalism spread around the world, we are likely to make more and more pressing demands on nature that threaten to destroy the ecosystem's delicate balance. This might be acceptable if we could build a new ecosystem. But the failure of Biosphere 2, an early-1990s experiment in building a functioning ecosystem hermetically sealed off from the earth's supplies, confirmed that we are not very good at playing Mother Nature. If human beings continue to tread on the planet so clumsily, argues biologist David Tilman, who reviewed the Biosphere 2 experiment, "we are heading for a world in which we will have to engineer services we have always received free from nature."[40] This version of environmentalism has been endorsed, indeed promulgated, by the Harvard biologist E. O. Wilson, who is a political conservative and, in general, a booster of capitalism and technology (especially biotechnology).

For years conservatives tended to downplay the claims of nature and to make jokes about the environment, such as Ronald Reagan's quip that "when you've seen one redwood you've seen them all." But conservatism is fundamentally about conserving things, and what is more important for us human beings to conserve than the beauty of our natural world? Teddy Roosevelt was a right-wing environmentalist who loved animals so much that he pursued them with the intensity of a big-game hunter. Perhaps no less paradoxically, right-wingers are moving toward a proenvironmental stance. This does not mean that conservatives are signing up in droves to go tree hugging with the Sierra Club. But conservatives now contend that one of the great benefits of wealth and technology is that they give us the resources and the knowledge to preserve our forests, our rivers, and our wildlife.

The right-wing critique of technological capitalism is a relatively new development. Columnist George Will asserted many years ago that capitalism is problematic for conservatism because it "undermines traditional social structures and values."[41] But in America until recently, this has been an eccentric view. American conservatives, unlike their European counterparts, have in general been champions of technology and capitalism. Reagan, for example, optimistically held that if people are given freedom, if an entrepreneurial climate is encouraged, the market will supply a cornucopia of technological wonders, and people will use these resources and this liberty to craft an American Dream for themselves. In Reagan's view technological capitalism was entirely consistent with what he called "traditional values," because he believed that if people are given freedom they will choose to live virtuously.

It is this Reaganite premise that has, in the view of many conservatives, been discredited by the events of the last two decades. Many conservatives feel they are living in a society where economic capital is rising and moral capital is being depleted, where "wealth accumulates, and men decay." What some conservatives are now saying is that technology and capitalism are partly to blame for this cultural and moral deterioration. Hilton Kramer, the distinguished critic, charges that technology debases and vulgarizes high art and culture by reducing "all mental processes to lower and lower levels of emotional response."[42] The Internet, fumes Richard John Neuhaus, editor of *First Things*, is exacerbating the problem of cultural illiteracy among young people. The people who devote themselves to technology are always in a hurry, but they have no idea where they are going. They are full of opinions, but they are unable to form reflective judgments. Their arrogance, in other words, is utterly unsubstantiated by understanding. In summary, the Internet is producing "a global village of village idiots."[43]

The conservative indictment of capitalism is no less harsh, and it will seem surprising to those who think of the Right as being unabashedly procapitalist. Perhaps that was true twenty years ago, but not now. Some right-wingers charge that capitalism produces affluence and affluence produces moral degeneracy, especially in the children of the affluent. "Decadence is brought to us by the marketplace," remarks conservative activist Don Eberly. A recent issue of *Family Policy*, published by the Family Research Council, blames the rise of sexual promiscuity not on the 1960s but on capitalism, affluence, and social mobility.[44] These views are percolating up to the right-wing leadership. William Bennett recently said, "Unbridled capitalism is a problem. It may not be a problem for production, but it's a problem for human beings. It's a problem for the whole dimension of things we call the realm of values and human relationships."[45]

One right-wing pal of mine puts this argument into perspective. "Look at the so-called greatest generation," he says. "Its virtues were forged in the Depression and in the battlefields of Europe. But the greatest generation couldn't reproduce itself, and why? Because it wanted its children to live well. So in the 1950s, the greatest generation produced the baby boomers. The Clinton generation. And why did this generation become the most self-indulgent in American history? It's simple: too much money."

My friend argues that it's always been this way. Fueled by affluence and the new technology of the time (the automobile), the 1920s produced the rash of hedonism and irresponsibility chronicled by F. Scott Fitzgerald and others. "In moral terms the country was really going downhill," my pal contends, "but we were 'saved' by the Depression. Yes, saved. I know how harsh that sounds, but it's true." If you think that the 1960s were a time of moral confusion and chaos, he insists, wait until the children of the last decade and this one grow up. "We won't be slouching *toward* Gomorrah," my friend says, referring to Robert Bork's book by that name, "we'll have gone there and beyond." The notion that technological capitalism produces a "gale of creative destruction" that uproots traditional institutions and discards extant norms goes back to the economist Joseph Schumpeter in the early part of the twentieth century. In 1976, Daniel Bell updated Schumpeter's argument in his book *The Cultural Contradictions of Capitalism.* Bell argued that capitalist production is based on virtues such as hard work, frugality, and personal responsibility, but the success of capitalism has produced a hedonistic consumer culture that is undermining those virtues. These arguments stirred up a good deal of debate at the time, but they were not in general embraced by conservatives. The ire of the Right was focused on the welfare state, which was blamed for corrupting morality by, for instance, subsidizing illegitimacy. But now many conservatives recognize that out-of-wedlock birthrates have risen dramatically throughout the society, not just among welfare moms. Consequently there is now much greater receptivity on the right to the Schumpeter-Bell thesis that technological capitalism itself is at least partly to blame.

Another surprising turn of events: in the last few years, several traditional liberals have begun to endorse these conservative themes. Among them are political scientist William Galston, a former Clinton aide; feminist scholar Jean Bethke Elshtain; political scientist Richard Sennett; sociologist Robert Bellah; and poet and farmer Wendell Berry. "The invisible hand [of capitalism] no more reliably produces a sound cultural environment than it does a sound natural environment," asserts Galston.[46] What has moved these left-leaning thinkers in this direction? Berry argues that for years he wrote about an ethic of commitment: commitment to the earth, commitment to small, self-sufficient communities. Then suddenly he realized that one of our most fundamental commitments as human beings, the only one that is publicly uttered, is our commitment to our spouse. How reliable are people likely to be in their commitment to nature or to their neighbors if they cannot keep their commitment to their own family?

We will hear more on these subjects later. The point I want to stress here is that the old issues that separated liberals and conservatives, such as how to deal with the Soviet Union or how big the federal government should be, have become less important. The Soviet Union has gone away, and government will continue to consume its current share of around 25 percent of our national product. We will continue to debate the details, and some people will still become very animated about them. But by and large, the political center of gravity has shifted to the social consequences of the new economy and how we as a society should respond to that. On this question, a new coalition is uniting many elements of the Left and Right into a new stance of resistance. This resistance is the intellectual core of the Party of Nah. But the party itself will be much broader, attracting many in the intellectual classes, the clergy, the media, and environmentalists, as well as many parents of young children. Politicians of both major parties will no longer be able to ignore the movement, as they are generally doing now.

We might expect that by now a huge debate would have erupted between the Party of Yeah and the Party of Nah. There have already been skirmishes, to be sure, over the North American Free Trade Agreement, the World Trade Organization, Internet privacy, bioengineered foods, and cloning. The 1999 protests in Seattle and other cities featured a variegated group of environmentalists, union members, intellectuals, aging baby boomers, and college students fuming against globalization and the alleged injustices of open markets. The protesters threw rocks and vandalized stores. "You don't polish the chains of slavery," raged Kevin Danaher, an activist at a human rights group called Global Exchange. "You break them."[47] In France, activist Jose Bove was one of those arrested for trashing the site of a new McDonald's. The open market, Bove charged, "is a planetary dictatorship. If you are not part of the market, you don't exist."[48]

Demonstrations against genetically altered food have showed similar intensity. Like the man surprised to discover he'd been speaking prose all his life, many Americans and an even larger group of Europeans have been shocked to find out that many of the meats, fruits, vegetables, and grains they have been eating all these years have been genetically modified. The National Academy of Sciences, the Food and Drug Administration, and the World Health Organization say these products are safe, and moreover that genetically modified lifestock and crops produce better-quality food and higher yields. But the activists remain recalcitrant: they want "Frankenfood" banned in the United States and Europe. You can imagine what these people think about laboratories working on the manipulation of human genes. There have been some very ugly protests. On a television program I saw, one activist yelled, "Those people are bringing DNA into my neighborhood." She was not a Westinghouse Science Prize winner, I am sure, but her fear and anger were palpable.

These are real debates, but they reflect only small parts of the big picture. Somehow there hasn't been a comprehensive debate over the general direction in which the new technological capitalism is taking our society. The debate is coming, and it will be a furious one. Still, it hasn't really occurred yet. Why not? The reason is that the leading members of the Party of Yeah are scientists and entrepreneurs, while the leading members of the other camp are clergy, politicians, and intellectuals. This professional divide isn't clear cut: there are professors and politicians who champion techno-capitalism, just as there are scientists and entrepreneurs who deplore it. In early 2000, Bill Joy, chief scientist and cofounder of Sun Microsystems, warned that emerging technologies were making available to anyone with access to the Internet the know-how to create self-replicating pathogens and other biological weapons that could do incalculable damage.[49] Joy's article created a big stir because here was a respected scientist who had advanced the frontiers of technology warning that we are approaching a point where the dangers of technology might outweigh the benefits.

Joy is an exceptional case of a technologist who has broad social and political interests. In general, however, there is a harmful segregation between the two camps. Camp Yeah is made up of tech people and entrepreneurs, while Camp Nah is made up of policy wonks, theologians, and academics. Such a professional and social separation between contending sides is quite new in American social policy debate. In the 1980s, for example, there was a lively debate over the role of the welfare state, but that debate was possible because both sides fielded their own teams of intellectuals and policy experts: on the left, Robert Greenstein and Lester Thurow; on the right, Martin Feldstein and Milton Friedman. And the same was true of defense issues. In the current situation, however, the Party of Nah is dominated by wordsmiths while the Party of Yeah is dominated by people like Bill Gates, Steve Case, and Jeff Bezos, who grin a lot but don't really articulate the worldview that lies behind their actions.

Do you doubt the truth of what I am saying? Then ask yourself: When was the last time that any of these guys really defended themselves against public criticism? Look at all the people who have said that Gates is an ogre because he's piling up so much money, he isn't giving enough of it away, he engages in piratical and monopolistic practices, come to think of it there isn't much that separates him from Beelzebub, and so on. Gates could easily answer, "You stupid jerks! I'm the reason you have computers on your desks right now. I'm the reason you can whip off your angry letters to the editor so fast. I didn't inherit my money, I earned it. I've benefited, but so have my employees. I've helped to create ten thousand millionaires. The reason we've done so well is that we have produced something of great value to people. I don't have the power of the government, which is to confiscate wealth through taxation. I have to convince you to go out and buy my products, which you freely do. The reason I have so much market share is that I make better products than everyone else, the test of which is that I can sell my stuff and they can't. And let's not hear any more nonsense about monopoly. What business *doesn't* want to get rid of its competition? The issue is whether you succeed by producing better products or whether you employ goons and thugs to shut down the other guy's store. I don't employ any goons and thugs. So get off my back and let me enjoy my money. I got it the old-fashioned way: I earned it." Correct me if I'm wrong, but in the many interviews that Gates has given he has not said anything like the above. Instead he says a lot of namby-pamby stuff. As I said: the guy does not want to debate.

So we have to wait a while before this argument breaks fully into the open. Gates and his friends will debate when they are forced to debate, just as Gates was forced to make a legal defense when the government filed its antitrust case. Even so, it's wrong to believe that each camp does not feel the force of the other side's position. It does. This is most obvious in the case of the Party of Nah. These naysayers may ferociously oppose where the world is headed, but right now they seem powerless to stop it. The naysayers feel like twigs carried by a current, and the best they can do is thrash around in the surging water. The intellectuals and clergy who proclaim the new economy to be degrading and immoral are worried that no one is listening to them; they are losing influence and becoming irrelevant. They appear to be on the wrong side of history.

It's not enough for them to complain that everyone else wants to get the latest technological stuff and make money; *they* also want to get the latest stuff and make money. This truth was illustrated for me when an editor at a California publishing house told me about one of her authors who has published several books denouncing the rich for selfishness and greed. Even though the latest one has been out for a while now, the author regularly calls the editor to find out how it's selling. Finally she gave him the dismal sales figures, and his response was to curse and say, "Next time I'm really going to slam those greedy bastards."

The conflict in the minds of those who want to criticize the morality of capitalism while enjoying its benefits was illuminated in a recent *Wall Street Journal* article entitled "Even Leftists Have Servants Now." The article profiled several professors earning six-figure incomes who have, ahem, hired gardeners, pool men, cooks, and nannies. Most of these servants are blacks and Mexicans. The contortions these academics go through to justify their behavior make for amusing reading. Political scientist Mark Petracca, who teaches at the University of California at Irvine, says he finally agreed to get a nanny, but he absolutely refuses to hire a gardener even though everybody else in his neighborhood has one. "It reeks of a kind of imperial colonialism one can imagine present in Shanghai in 1920," says Petracca, exhibiting in a single sentence his learning and his hypocrisy.[50]

What is less obvious is that the Party of Yeah is conscious of, and affected by, its critics. By all appearances its leading members seem utterly indifferent to them. For all I know, Michael Dell and Bill Gates don't even know of the existence of culture critics who argue that computers undermine rather than promote literacy. Certainly I don't expect Jeff Bezos to respond to a lengthy critique in *Tikkun* or *Mother Jones* magazine about how on-line book buying lacks the authenticity of going into a used-book store and making serendipitous finds while inhaling a lot of dust. Yet I have spent a lot of time with tech moguls, and I know that they have internalized many of the criticisms. Consequently, they are, despite their outward braggadocio, deeply ambivalent about the social consequences of wealth and technology. They are especially worried about the potentially harmful effects of affluence and technology in their *own lives.*

To understand these concerns, let us begin by noting something very odd and interesting about the style of the new rich. Hang out with these guys, and you will see that, both at work and at social gatherings, they try not to act like rich people. They routinely dress down. They hate to be seen in suits or tuxedos; they love to be seen in torn jeans and baseball caps that they sometimes wear back to front, to show the ad-justo-strap to advantage. Offer them a plate of fancy hors d'oeuvres, and they'll go for the cheese and crackers; give them a choice of beers, and they'll pick Bud. These guys might drive a Lexus or a Porsche in Menlo Park, but they wouldn't be caught dead in a Rolls-Royce. However lavishly they live in private, America's new rich are fanatically determined to appear middle class in public.

This is just as true of many tycoons as it is of the overclass in general. Bill Gates likes to be seen in an oversize sweater. Pierre Omidyar drives the same Volkswagon Jetta he's owned for years. Jeff Bezos, who until recently lived in a rented apartment, still commutes to work in a Volvo station wagon. Warren Buffett frequently reminds people that he still inhabits the modest Omaha house that he bought several decades ago. Instead of the common people aspiring to be billionaires, these billionaires apparently aspire to the style of the commoners.

Hollywood has picked up on all this. A recent film, *Notting Hill,* is a story about a famous actress who falls in love with an obscure and lowly bookseller because she longs for the simple life. Julia Roberts, who starred in the movie, affirmed her identification with the masses by expressing relief that she could slip out of her house and go to the Laundromat without being recognized. Does a woman who makes $20 million for a single movie need to go to the Laundromat? Of course not. But it's clearly very important for Julia Roberts to show America that she's just like everyone else.

Here is a second, equally strange, aspect of the new rich: they are capitalists who have embraced the style of the traditional enemies of capitalism. Virtually all of them solemnly declare that they are not engaged in business for the purpose of making money. "I'm not about that," asserts Tim Koogle, the CEO of Yahoo![51] "What interests me isn't making money per se," remarks Bill Gates.[52] "I never cared much about money," declares Jeff Skoll, vice president of eBay.[53] "It isn't about the money," according to Mary Meeker, investment guru for Morgan Stanley.[54] "I'm not in it for the wealth," comments Larry Ellison.[55] Charles Schwab insists that for him, "It's not about making money."[56] Apparently the new economy—the largest wealth-creation scheme on the planet—is being driven largely by nonprofit motives.

In a recent conversation, I asked Jay Walker, the founder of Priceline.com, about his net worth. How did it feel, I asked, to be worth several billion dollars? With a pained expression, Walker protested that he wasn't *really* worth that much. "Let me put it differently," he said. "I'm not sitting on proven oil reserves. I am trying to change a dimension of the way we do commerce today. My paper wealth is based on a promise to my shareholders that over time I will deliver value corresponding with that wealth. If I don't deliver, that wealth will disappear as quickly as it came." Walker's explanation is a reasonable one, yet his discomfort illustrated for me the embarrassment that many of the new rich feel about the size of their fortunes.

Author David Brooks points out that today's entrepreneurial class is eager to convey the image of being social dissidents, nonconformists, countercultural rebels taking on the establishment. Big corporations such as Microsoft and the Gap cite Gandhi and Jack Kerouac in their advertisements. I recently saw Coretta Scott King featured in an ad for Nortel Networks. Her motto, "To resist injustice, advance human liberation, and build the beloved community," has apparently been taken up by this Internet company. The new affluent class, Brooks remarks, is made up of "cell phone naturalists" who want to be close to nature but cannot leave their high-tech gear behind. Many of them inhabit "latte towns," where the style is bohemian—Jim Morrison on the radio, Colombian throw rugs and African masks for sale, Left Bank–style cafés—but the main subject of discussion, even among the ponytailed set, is commerce and stock prices.[57]

What's going on here? In the past, businessmen were not in the least bit embarrassed about making money. Moreover, once they got it, they were eager to display it. Historically, wealth has been about the accumulation and display of stuff. "Conspicuous consumption," mainly for the purpose of impressing others, defined the behavior of the affluent. In the early part of the twentieth century, for instance, being fat was a way of showing your neighbors that you could afford to consume food in large quantities. In his classic work *The Theory of the Leisure Class*, published in 1899, Thorstein Veblen noted that the distinguishing characteristics of the leisure class were idleness and waste: rich people did nothing productive, and they engaged in futile displays in order to prove how much they had. In Veblen's view the curved driveway that led up to rich people's homes was attractive mainly because it wasted a lot of land and showed a disregard for the principles of economy and efficiency.[58] Throughout history, these were the defining characteristics of the aristocracy.

But not now. Leisure is almost a dirty word in today's tech culture; the prevailing ethic is work, work, work. This is even more unusual when you consider that many of these guys don't have to work another day in their lives. So it's not obvious why they do. Unlike Veblen's soi-disant aristocrats, today's overclass, even in its indulgences, emphasizes the bourgeois virtues of self-discipline and concern for health, longevity, and utility.

Today, if you are thirty pounds overweight, it's a good bet that you are not rich but lower middle class. On the typical bargain cruise to the Bahamas, undoubtedly the vast majority of people in line for the midnight buffet are proles who cannot say no to a free meal. Vacations in general and cruises in particular are ingenious schemes to make middle-class people feel like rich people. The average Joe walks into a hotel where he is overwhelmed by the large hallways and gleaming chandeliers, he is stupefied at being attended and served by white-gloved waiters, he feels like royalty as his every need is catered to. At least for a week or ten days, other people are subservient to him. Then it's back to the real world.

Rich people eat well, but eating is not an obsession for them. For this group being overweight no longer conveys an image of prosperity; rather, it suggests a lack of self-control. Etiquette demands that rich people, especially rich women, be thin. Many in the overclass still have curved driveways, but they like them because of their aesthetic beauty and their beneficial effect in giving visitors a gradually unfolding view of the main house.

As we saw earlier, there's plenty of conspicuous consumption today, but it is more hidden because it is not as fashionable as it was in the 1980s, the 1920s, or the 1890s. The etiquette of consumption is now strictly controlled. According to the new code, it's socially acceptable for tech tycoons to live in beautiful homes, wear really expensive clothes, and drive really expensive cars, as long as they don't seem to be trying to put on a show. In his book *The Road Ahead* Bill Gates is eager to emphasize that his house, costly though it may be, should not be compared to San Simeon, "one of the West Coast's monuments to excess." After giving a detailed account of the ridiculous electronic capabilities of his house—for example, guests can operate remote controls that display their favorite paintings or play their favorite movies on the walls of each room—Gates emphasizes that he's only "experimenting" to prepare the rest of society for the high-tech homes of the future.[59]

So if you are or plan to be a member of the new affluent class, by all means live high on the hog, but do make sure you have mastered the necessary social cues. It's okay to buy that 10,000-square-foot house, but for heaven's sake don't call it a "manor" or "mansion" or "palace." Rather, you should refer to it as "the ranch" or "the cottage." Stretch limos are totally out; today's overclass prefers to be seen in sporty two-seaters or, when toting around the kids, in utility vehicles loaded with features to provide for the greatest possible comfort. If you're going to invest $10,000 or more in a watch, don't buy a diamond-studded Rolex, go for a Patek Philippe and make sure that you wear it with a crumpled shirt and a pair of faded jeans.

Movie producers and tech CEOs like to boast that they wear the jeans and T-shirts and the lawyers and accountants who work for them wear suits. In Silicon Valley today, the tie sends a distinctive message: "I am a waiter." The big boys make it a point to eschew them. "Ties," comments Christos Cotsakos, CEO of E*Trade, "are a rigid symbol of how not to communicate."[60] As author Paul Fussell points out, this is a reversal of the traditional pattern, in which the suit and tie emerged as a crucial badge of distinction between the middle class and the proles.[61] The congruence between the styles of the proles and the superrich means that if you are walking through Hollywood or Silicon Valley and see a man dressed like a bum you don't know whether to shout "Get a job" or "Give me a job."

*   *   *

Of course, it is easy to dismiss the middle-class image of the new rich as rank hypocrisy. Economist Robert Frank, author of *Luxury Fever,* thinks so: "The rich are trying to assure the rest of us that they haven't seceded from the general population." In Frank's view the debauched upper class is seeking popularity by trying to fool people into believing that they share the sentiments of the proletariat. Frank attributes the bohemian style of the new rich as a scheme to co-opt the critics of capitalism. There may be some truth to this, yet true aristocrats have never cared about winning the masses over. Hear the Roman oligarchs address the commoners in Shakespeare's *Julius Caesar:* "you blocks, you stones, you worse-than-senseless things." What a contrast with Bill Gates's, and Julia Roberts's, sniveling flattery of the masses.

As Frank suggests, Gates and Roberts need to pay servile obeisance to popular taste. After all, the hoi polloi are the folks who buy computers and go to movies. But the middle-class yearnings and bohemian style of the new rich are more than a social pose. They reflect a genuine conflict in their psyche. Theirs is not old wealth that has marinated over the generations and has come to seem natural and inevitable to its possessors. Many, like Gates and Bezos, grew up in the middle class. They like hanging out with the guys they went to college with, the people they knew before they hit it big. By applying bourgeois values such as ambition and hard work, they became wealthy. They want to enjoy their affluence, but at the same time they don't want to lose their middle-class self-image.

The conflict in the minds of the overclass isn't merely sociological; it is also moral. The new rich know they're doing well, but they also want to feel as if they're doing good. They want to succeed but without selling out. They want material comforts, even luxuries, but they are eager to show that they have not been consumed by materialism. Moreover, on a practical note, the new rich are terrified of provoking the moral indignation of society. They don't want to be envied by the lower classes; they want to convince people that they are really nice guys. In other words, they want to be accepted on a plane of social equality with the rest of the country. One way the very rich prove their good intentions is by giving lots of money away. Pick up a newspaper, and you'll read of Gates giving a billion here, a billion there to his favorite causes. Philanthropy is now a big issue in the tech world.

All of this seems natural enough in today's culture, but it contrasts markedly with the behavior of the tycoons of the past. Andrew Carnegie and John D. Rockefeller gave away millions, possibly in part to counter their negative portrait as "robber barons." The tycoons of that era didn't worry about envy; they reveled in it. The ones who started out poor or middle class generally sought to escape their humble origins and emulate the European aristocracy; that's why they built English-style country estates and named them Granogue, Winterthur, Longwood, and Bellevue.[62] None curried favor with the masses by cultivating a nice-guy, boy-next-door image. J. P. Morgan disdainfully said, "I owe the public nothing." Then there is Rockefeller's famous retort: "The American people be damned. All I care about is my shareholders." Today's rich would recoil from such insensitive remarks in horror.

The prevailing sentiment among the new rich, especially the tech rich, is that they are not going to leave the bulk of their money to their children, they are going to give it all away. Gates repeatedly affirms that 95 percent of his estate is going to charity. Warren Buffett has pledged to give away 99 percent. Virtually everybody in Silicon Valley says the same thing. And upon reflection it's a very strange thing to say. Throughout history people have saved and accumulated wealth in order to pass it on to their offspring. Indeed, this was considered to be the main reason why people continued to work even after they had provided for their own needs. The old rule was to provide for your family, then for your children, and then (if possible) for their children as well. But no more. Apparently the superrich have no desire to establish dynasties in the way that the Rockefellers, the Fords, the Kennedys, and the du Ponts did.

The reason many wealthy people today are reluctant to bequeath their money to their children is that they fear it would have a corrupting effect. "Leaving children wealth is like leaving them a case of psychological cancer," says broadcasting magnate Jim Rogers.[63] "My children can look after themselves," Jim Barksdale, the former CEO of Netscape, told me. "I know people who are trust fund babies. I don't like them. They work very hard to screw up their lives." Barksdale says he will leave his children "enough to give them security, but not enough for them to sit on their butts and retire."

Wealthy people today talk about "sudden wealth syndrome," the way in which wealth has created new problems in their lives, and about "affluenza," the way in which wealth is messing up the lives of their children. The latter problem is more serious than the former: the overclass is terrified of producing a generation of arrogant, lazy, spoiled brats. The new rich want to raise their kids with the same bourgeois virtues of frugality, persistence, hard work, and responsibility that helped them get where they are. But this, of course, is extremely difficult to do because as a consequence of their success their children live in an entirely different world than their parents did. So today's overclass continues to struggle with this problem and to feel anxiety and anguish about it.

As should be apparent by now, what we are witnessing is not just a clash between techno-optimists and cultural pessimists, or between entrepreneurs and intellectuals. Rather, it is the moral conundrum of success. Many of us have more money than we ever thought we would, but somehow prosperity hasn't made us as happy as we expected. The body is flourishing, but somehow the soul still feels malnourished. Thus we are ·divided between our intentions to prosper and to integrate our prosperity into something higher and more meaningful. We want the material gains that come with wealth, but we do not want to relinquish the goods of the spirit. We want to be rich ourselves, but we are also concerned about not leaving others too far behind, and we want our society's affluence to promote some vision of a civic or common good.

We are similarly divided over technology. We view technology as a vehicle for securing our wants and giving us power over our environment; at the same time, we worry that technology may distract us from the things that matter the most, and at times we fear that technology is betraying our most cherished values of privacy, integrity, and humanity. In short, the moral divide over affluence and technology doesn't just run between ideological camps; it runs through our own hearts. The Party of Nah and the Party of Yeah both dwell, in a sense, within us.

But they don't dwell in harmony. One side says: wealth and technology may make us more successful and powerful, but they don't make us happier, and they corrupt the soul. In this view material accomplishment comes at the price of cultural and moral impoverishment, both for us as individuals and for our society. The other side rebels against this. It is irresistibly drawn to wealth and technology and their capacity to liberate us from necessity. It doesn't want to listen to the critics and the moralizers, who seem incredibly smug and annoying. At the same time, it isn't sure how to answer them. And it is starting to face up to the peculiar dilemmas generated by the new power of wealth and technology.

What follows is an effort to adjudicate this conflict, both within society and within ourselves. My intention is to take both sides seriously and to figure out who is right. But my ultimate goal is not to proclaim an intellectual victor. It is to help heal the social division caused by the new technological capitalism and also to help us reconcile, in our own minds, what place technology and wealth should occupy in our pursuit of the good life.

CHAPTER THREE

CREATED UNEQUAL

Merit and the Ones Left Behind

The protection of different and unequal faculties of acquiring prop-
erty . . . is the first object of government.

—*The Federalist Papers*

If you are pondering the fairness of life in America, you could do worse
than to begin with Jerry Yang. Yang was a graduate student at Stanford
who liked to fool around with the computer. Recognizing that Web
sites were proliferating, Yang posted "Jerry's Guide to the World Wide
Web," a categorized list of sites managed by a search engine. Soon Yang
teamed up with another graduate student, David Filo, who helped him
with programming. "You could call it a hobby," Yang said later, "you
could call it a passion. Call it instinct. But it wasn't really business. We
weren't making money doing it, and we were actually forsaking our
schoolwork to do it." Yang said they just felt "jazzed up" about doing
something on the exciting new medium of the Internet.[1]

But soon the duo realized that their directory had commercial
value. So they started a new company and, in keeping with the irrever-
ent tone of the site, called it Yet Another Hierarchical Officious Oracle!—Yahoo! for short. Today it is one of the most visited sites on the
Web. And Yang, whose title remains Chief Yahoo, is now a billionaire,
one of the richest men in the world. Recently he endowed the Yahoo
Chair at Stanford University. It is now occupied by an extremely bril-

liant older man who draws a salary of around $100,000 a year. That's Christmas spending money for Yang.

Wonderful for Jerry, you say. One lucky dude. But that makes you wonder, as lots of young tech entrepreneurs wonder every day: What does Yang have that I haven't? Sure, Yang is a smart and hardworking guy, but you know lots of people like that, and they don't have a billion dollars. You're like that, and your net worth still has a way to go before you hit nine zeroes. Truth be told, it probably won't. Yang hit the jackpot, and you didn't. It's great this happens in America, but it's not fair that it doesn't happen to you. So is this what America offers its citizens, a one-in-a-million chance to hit Free Market Lotto? Or—a scary thought—is Yang's fortune based upon merit? Perhaps he didn't luck out; perhaps he "made his fortune." And if that is so, if the market has awarded Yang his just deserts, then perhaps you too are precisely where you ought to be. Yang is a winner and you are, well, a bit of an also-ran.

It's easy to feel outrage at the fortunes of those who have scored bigger than you have. Thousands of waiters and waitresses in Los Angeles cannot understand what it is that separates them from Tom Cruise and Gwyneth Paltrow. How come that jerk is riding so high? How did that bitch get where she is? There is more than a molecule of envy in such thoughts. But not just envy. These sentiments also raise the issue of justice, ennobling them and giving their bearers a conviction of justified outrage: you aren't just jealous, you have a *right* to feel this way.

But has it occurred to you that there might be many people in this world who might feel exactly this way about you? You probably live in a nice house. You have lots of stuff. Yet there are many people in America, and countless more in the rest of the world, who are just as talented and determined as you, who work just as hard if not harder, and yet they don't have nearly as much as you do. Some of them have a great deal less. Do they deserve their relative misfortune? Are they too getting their just deserts? Sure, you are outraged at the fortune of the Silicon Valley tycoon. But do you feel a wee bit of guilt that there's a fellow in Dubuque, Iowa, and another in Karachi, Pakistan, and they're every bit as good as you are but they'll never live the way you do?

This chapter is an exploration of the inequalities that exist and have become very large in our society and our world. We accept these inequalities as part of life. They have been delivered to us by the god of the market. Perhaps we believe that they're necessary to make the system run better. But is that really true? Is inequality on the scale that we now see inevitable? Is it just? Do we deserve what we get? Our sense of being fairly treated by our society, and ultimately our cohesiveness as a community, depend on our answers to these questions.

The atmosphere at the American Enterprise Institute on the afternoon of February 9, 2000, is thick with anticipation. In the left corner, facing the audience largely made up of academics and policy experts, sits Edward Wolff, a New York University economist who is one of America's leading experts on wealth and income inequality. In the right corner, straightening out his tie and adjusting his notes, is John Weicher, a former Labor Department official and now a scholar at the Hudson Institute. Sitting in the middle, in a sense playing the role of umpire, is Arthur Kennickell, a senior economist at the Federal Reserve Board.

Conscious that he is in hostile territory—a free-market-oriented think tank—Wolff has come prepared with his research paper densely packed with charts and tables. Adjusting his spectacles, Wolff, a middle-aged man with curly hair and a mustache, methodically begins to outline his data, which appear on a screen behind him. His bottom line is a shocker. In 1983, his numbers show, the median net worth per household in the United States was $55,000. Today it's $54,000. During that same period, according to his data, the net worth of the richest 1 percent of Americans soared from a whopping 34 percent of the country's wealth to a staggering 40 percent. "We've had a rising stock market and a booming economy," Wolff says. "Eighty-five percent of the wealth increase went to the top one percent of wealth holders. And all the rest went to the next nine percent." The bottom 90 percent, Wolff concludes, are no better off today than they were almost two decades ago.[2]

John Weicher's numbers tell a less alarming tale. A round-faced man with a booming voice, Weicher contends that between 1983 and the present, median wealth per household climbed from $57,000 to nearly $72,000, a modest but not insignificant 25 percent increase over a 15-year period. Weicher's data also show the richest 1 percent increasing its take, from 32 percent to 35 percent, but the margin of increase isn't as steep as Wolff would have it. Weicher argues that for most of this century, with some variation depending on whether the economy is doing well or poorly, the richest 1 percent have controlled a third of the national wealth; the next 9 percent, another third; and the bottom 90 percent, the rest. In short, there is substantial inequality, but it isn't really increasing.

Weicher's real point, however, is: Who cares? Inequality per se is not a concern; the real question is whether America is a land of opportunity where people have a chance to become successful. He emphasizes that the vast majority of very rich people today didn't inherit their wealth; they made their own money. "I don't like the products that Microsoft makes and I'm not a big fan of Disneyland, but I have to say that Bill Gates and Michael Eisner have created a lot of value, both for their shareholders and for millions of Americans." So if they've earned what they have and they pay taxes on what they make, where's the problem?

Weicher disputes the popular notion that the way people have become rich over the past two decades is by investing in the stock market. Sure, rich people own a lot of stock, but nearly half of Americans are now in the market, and participation has grown most rapidly for the middle and lower-middle income brackets. Moreover, Weicher argues, the stock gains predominantly enjoyed by the affluent over the past two decades have been paralleled by wealth gains by the middle class due to home appreciation, which is that group's primary source of net worth. Still, the most common path to riches in the United States, Weicher says, is owning your own business. The biggest asset owned by rich people is not their stock portfolio but their legal practice, their medical practice, or their personally run business.[3]

Wolff, who seems to view Weicher's presentation as an apologia for inequality, turns increasingly sarcastic in his rebuttal. He concedes that most of the biggest fortunes, such as those reflected in the *Forbes* 400 "rich list," are self-made. Even so, he says, "A significant part of today's wealth does come from inheritance." As for stock holdings, Wolff points out that the richest 1 percent of Americans own more than half of all stocks and mutual funds; the next richest 9 percent own another 37 percent.[4] "So the top ten percent owns ninety percent of stocks, and the bottom ninety percent holds ten percent." Wolff gazes defiantly at the audience. In *this* group of free-market worshipers, his look implies, I guess that distribution is perceived as wholly fair and reasonable.

In his appearance, Kennickell is the most intriguing of the three panelists. His bow tie, Hercule Poirot mustache, and handkerchief peeping out of his pocket all give him a slightly foppish air. I have been told that Kennickell is an "economist's economist," however, and he proceeds to prove it, giving the audience a lengthy exegesis on statistical technique, sampling errors, weights, and other kinds of methodology. Kennickell's data, which are based on the authoritative Survey of Consumer Finances conducted every three years by the Federal Reserve Board, show that the net worth of the richest 1 percent increased from 30 percent of national wealth in 1989 to 34 percent now; during that period, the bottom 90 percent saw its share decline slightly, from 33 to 31 percent. Kennickell's figures show that while the rich got richer, the ordinary American also saw a measurable boost in net worth: according to new data from the Federal Reserve Board, median household wealth in the United States increased in real terms from $60,000 in 1989 to nearly $72,000 today.[5]

During the discussion, I raise my hand and pose a question to Kennickell. "I need you to adjudicate a dispute," I say. "Mr. Weicher says that wealth inequality hasn't really increased over the past decade and a half; Mr. Wolff says it has increased greatly, and that all the gain in net worth produced by the new economy has gone to the richest ten percent of Americans. Who is right?" Kennickell now faces the dilemma of the man in the middle, but it's a position he seems to have been in before; he tweaks his mustache like Poirot preparing to reveal the identity of the malefactor. "Ah, yes," he says. "Who is right? Well, perhaps that depends on how you perceive the data." With a beaming smile, Kennickell returns to his seat, and the debate is over.

From the perspective of the Party of Nah, that's precisely the problem. The debate is indeed over—or, to put it differently, there is no real national debate about inequality. "It's mystifying," says Michael Walzer, author of *Spheres of Justice*, a critique of social inequality, and leading social scientist at Princeton's Institute for Advanced Studies. "The inequalities in our society continue to get worse, and the public shows no real interest in the subject. Even the people most hurt by inequality appear unwilling or unable to mobilize against it."

Walzer points to several examples of grotesque inequalities of wealth and income. According to a recent study by the Center on Budget and Policy Priorities, the average income of the top 20 percent of U.S. families is now ten times that of the bottom 20 percent of families. That's a much bigger multiple than in the late 1970s, when the richest 20 percent took in "only" seven times the income of the poorest 20 percent.[6] It seems that the most affluent Americans are living like royalty, while for the poorest people the American Dream is, well, just a dream.

These huge differences, Walzer points out, are replicated worldwide. The United Nations recently completed a study showing that the income gap between the wealthiest 20 percent òf the world and the poorest 20 percent, which was thirty to one in 1960 and sixty to one just seven years ago, has now jumped to nearly seventy-five to one.

What this means is that the affluent citizens of the West can spend thousands of dollars on a shopping spree on Madison Avenue or the Champs-Élysées while their less fortunate counterparts in Third World countries must make do on a dollar or two a day.

Recently *Business Week* reported on the compensation of America's top executives, including salary and long-term benefits. Charles Wang of Computer Associates topped the list with a stratospheric $655 million. Dennis Kozlowski of Tyco was second, with $170 million. The list goes on. David Pottruck of Charles Schwab: $127 million. John Chambers of Cisco: $121 million. Stephen Case of America Online: $117 million. Jack Welch of General Electric: $93 million. Sanford Weill of Citigroup: $90 million. At these levels Michael Eisner of Walt Disney ($50 million) and Kenneth Lay of Enron ($49 million) come out as relative pikers. To get a sense of how big today's pay numbers are, it helps to look back only a decade. In 1990 the average big-company CEO pocketed a handsome $2 million. Today the head of a large public company makes an average of $11 million a year. Sure, some of these companies have been extremely profitable. But it can safely be assumed that their employees did not see their annual pay go up fivefold during this period.[7]

Consider how far the wealth of America's tycoons could go toward solving the world's problems. The Census Bureau estimates that there are 13 million children in the United States living in poverty.[8] At $1,000 per child per year, it would cost $13 billion annually to provide for the nation's existing child poverty population in perpetuity. Bill Gates alone should be able to manage that, shouldn't he? On a more modest scale, *Fortune* estimates that if Michael Dell dipped into his portfolio he could purchase a computer for every high school student in the United States for $13.5 billion, leaving him more than $6 billion to spare.[9] If they pooled their resources, the world's richest people could easily feed the starving people of the world, with enough left over for them to live very comfortably.

But there's no reason to hold only the superrich responsible. Consider a paltry $1 million, a figure that hundreds of thousands of Americans could spare without making a dent in their lifestyle. It's interesting to speculate on alternative uses for that money. You could use it to occupy the best suite for 104 days on the cruise ship *Queen Elizabeth II*, or you could send 4,600 inner-city kids to a week at summer camp. You could rent the most expensive penthouse in New York for three months, or you could shelter 10,000 homeless children for a night. You could add a lavish wing to a mansion, or you could build several hundred dwellings in an African, South American, or Indian village.[10]

Walzer speaks in an urbane, clipped tone, but clearly he is outraged by the scale of global inequality. What gives some people the right to so much while others have so little? How can multimillionaires indulge themselves like pigs while others must endure a life that is nasty, brutish, and short? "What we are seeing is the replication of Third World conditions in the United States," Walzer says. "Black men in our inner cities have a life expectancy lower than people in Bangladesh. And the working class is living precariously from paycheck to paycheck. In many cases the family income is only sustained by more people working longer hours. And still they're weighed down by mortgage debt and credit card debt."

The Internet, Walzer predicts, will exacerbate these divisions: "There are the digital haves and have-nots, and this is not likely to change very soon. Some kids grow up in an electronic culture. They are at home in that world. For others, it is completely alien. So we are finding ourselves in a world where some people are locals and some people are globals. The globals are integrated into a huge network of information and opportunity. The locals must inhabit a smaller, more restricted environment. The sadness of their predicament is completely lost in all the celebrations of the new economy."

For Walzer the solution is obvious: some sort of redistribution.

Walzer emphasizes that he's not advocating a simple sharing of wealth. "Every society has to decide what's important. The Athenians thought that theater festivals should be subsidized by the state. In the Middle Ages the cure of souls was socialized, and everyone was in principle eligible for the kingdom of God. Today we must equalize access to basic goods, and that means education, it means health care, it means access to political power."

What he misses, Walzer says, "is any sense that the people who are falling behind are capable of articulating their demands and organizing politically." Since this isn't happening, Walzer is forced to conclude that "they're dropping out. That's why we don't hear from them. They've lost, and they know they're beaten. They've given up on America."

Twirling his pasta at the trendy Il Fornaio restaurant in Palo Alto, my friend Rich Karlgaard, the publisher of *Forbes*, ponders the inequality problem with a look of dismissive amusement. With his navy blue blazer, open shirt, slacks, and tennis shoes, Karlgaard is the epitome of new-economy fashion. And as someone who's known him for a few years, let me assure you that Karlgaard isn't insensitive; he's a really nice guy. He cares as much as the next fellow; he just thinks that when professors such as Walzer get started on their pet peeve of inequality, all we are getting is envy in disguise, statistical hogwash. In short, a load of crap.

"I've heard the entire greed-sin, red-in-tooth-and-claw, orphan-empty-porridge-bowl dreary lecture," Karlgaard says, "and it bores the hell out of me. You know what is really galling these intellectuals? The fact that they have lost power. The fact that no one is listening to them. Not the poor, not the working class, no one cares what they have to say. And you know why? Because they're all at the mall, shopping. Because America's doing too damn well, that's why. People have seen their lifestyles go up with the market. Even the poor are living better, thanks to technology. Inequality is only a problem in the minds of intellectuals."

I wasn't sure I agreed with Karlgaard, and I relayed to him an experience at a recent conference sponsored by his own magazine. During a session devoted to executive salaries, CEO after CEO had stood up to complain about criticism they had received for making too much money. Finally one corporate titan said, "I don't understand the American people at all. They don't begrudge Jerry Seinfeld or Michael Jordan their millions. Why do they care about what I earn?" To this, one of his colleagues retorted, "Because the average Joe turns on his TV, he sees Jerry Seinfeld do his comedy routine and Michael Jordan hit those baskets, and he says, 'I can't do that.' But he thinks he can do what you do."

Karlgaard laughed. "And maybe he's right. I don't begrudge him his arrogance. But he's got to go out and prove it. Don't tell me how smart you are. Go out and start a company. Stop whining about the wealth gap because, when you think about it, the wealth gap is a good thing."

A good thing? "You know who's responsible for the wealth gap?" Karlgaard adds. "I am. I'm responsible. I used to be a poor, unpublished writer. I drove a 1964 Ford Falcon with the trunk tied down by a jump rope. But at least I wasn't contributing to the wealth gap, because I was broke. Now I own a house, two cars, a retirement plan, shares in a few companies, and shoes to fill a closet. I'm a dirty rotten capitalist. I'm the cause of global inequality. You're right—it's unconscionable."

Yes, Karlgaard is on a roll. "I know how we *could* have solved the problem of inequality in America. Maybe Steve Jobs shouldn't have popularized the personal computer. If only Jeff Bezos had stayed in his hedge fund job instead of starting Amazon. Too bad Michael Dell didn't obey his parents and become a doctor. Wouldn't it be great if Ted Waitt had taken up cattle ranching instead of starting Gateway? And who can deny that David Filo and Jerry Yang would have done more for society if they had finished their Ph.D. dissertations! Unfortunately, these things didn't happen, because, if they did, America's wealth gap would be a trifle instead of a cancer."[11] So what now? Karlgaard says there's only one viable solution to inequality: a 98 percent capital gains tax. That, he says, would pretty much take care of the wealth gap.

Karlgaard's point—made in his inimitable style—is that inequality is necessary for markets to flourish efficiently; in this sense, inequality is the natural outcome of a growing economy. In one sense he is right. In 1980 the vast majority of people in the United States earned between $12,000 and $55,000. If you made more than $55,000, you were in the top 5 percent of wage earners. Today the income spread is between $12,000 and . . . what? $200,000? $500,0000? You name it. So, many people who were previously in the lower ranks have ascended rapidly. As they have become well off, they have increased the gap between themselves and the rest of the population. Karlgaard's point is that an excessive focus on inequality carries the implication that this growth and its ensuing affluence are a bad thing, when in fact they are manifestly a good thing.

But is the inequality itself a positive good? Are the current levels of inequality necessary even for the economy to keep up its rapid growth? Karlgaard presumes they must be, because the market created them. The logic of this view is that without the chance of greater rewards people such as Jeff Bezos and Ted Waitt wouldn't have the incentive to do what they're doing. This is true as far as it goes, but it doesn't go very far. The reason is that we don't know how much greater those rewards would have to be to provide an adequate incentive. Would Bezos and Waitt slack off if they made 25 percent less than they do now? Would they work harder if they stood to make even more? The direct testimony of many of these Internet tycoons is that they aren't primarily motivated by money. So it's not obvious that such Himalayan reward structures are necessary to convince them to go to work every day.

For me, Karlgaard's most intriguing point is his suggestion that perhaps the people at the bottom and middle rungs of a society don't mind if inequality increases as long as they too enjoy some of the gains of the new economy. This makes a certain economic sense: Why should I care if the rich pull further ahead if I'm also moving forward? If this is true, however, it requires a revision in our conception of the problem. Traditionally, the debate about inequality has been conducted as if the acquisition of wealth were a zero-sum game. Thorstein Veblen writes, "The accumulation of wealth at the upper end of the pecuniary scale implies privation at the lower end of the scale."[12] This is the old mantra: "The rich are getting richer and the poor are getting poorer." Embedded in it is a big assumption, namely that the rich are getting richer *at the expense of* the poor.

But what if these premises turn out to be false? What if the rich are getting richer because they have created new wealth that didn't exist before? What if we live in a society where the rich are getting richer and the poor are also getting richer, but not at the same pace? If you drive a Mercedes and I have to walk, that's a radical difference of lifestyle that might warrant speculation about first- and second-class citizenship. But is it a big deal if you drive a Mercedes and I drive a

Hyundai? If I have a four-bedroom house, do I have cause to be morally outraged that you have a twelve-bedroom house? These considerations suggest that in order to address the question of inequality, we must examine the significance of the differences in the way that people live today. It turns out that our old categories for examining the issue are largely obsolete. We need a new way of thinking about inequality.

In the past, inequality was largely a synonym for poverty, and moral concern about inequality was simply a different way of voicing concern about poverty. After all, there is no moral force to the protest "I can't believe that Andre Agassi made only $2 million last year, when Evander Holyfield made $20 million." Our reason for caring about how extravagantly some people lived was largely based on the knowledge that others, especially others in America, were struggling to provide their families with the basic necessities of food, clothing, and shelter.

But now, according to champions of the Party of Yeah, poverty in the biblical sense is no longer a problem. "The problem of poverty has been solved," writes Peter Huber, a new-economy enthusiast at the Manhattan Institute. "If history is still being written a thousand years from now, it will record that after countless generations of mortal struggle, humanity finally triumphed over material scarcity, in America, at the close of the twentieth century." This doesn't mean, Huber adds, that we've achieved some egalitarian utopia. "Oh yes, we do still have richer and poorer all about us," he writes, "but that's relative—it's poverty that has ended in our time, not inequality."[13]

Suffice it to say that Huber hasn't been spending a lot of time in Harlem, New York; Anacostia, in Washington, D.C.; or rural West Virginia, for that matter. The homeless man rummaging through a garbage dump looking for a sandwich will surely not be reassured to know that his country has achieved a historic triumph over material scarcity. The clergy and volunteers who serve long lines of people in the soup kitchens across America also have reason to question Huber's smug assertions. Yet it remains to be seen whether, as a general proposition, Huber is right.

The extravagance of everyday life in America is striking enough to support Huber's proposition that the United States has reached the age of plenty. Just go to any airport, any mall, any car dealer, any coffee shop, and you will be surprised to see ordinary people spending money in ways that until recently were considered quite extraordinary. Or open the phone book in your nearest city, and count the number of listings under "Plastic Surgeons." Once restricted to Hollywood stars and aging heiresses, plastic surgery has gone mainstream. Now virtually every pair of bouncy breasts requires a second look, not for prurience but for the purely sociological purpose of ascertaining whether they are real. A couple of years ago, an acquaintance of mine, upon receiving a big bonus, found herself in a peculiar dilemma. "I don't know whether to go in for a piano," she said, "or a nose job."

Another telling social indicator: pet surgery. At animal clinics around the country, such as the Animal Medical Center in New York, dogs, cats, hedgehogs, guinea pigs, rabbits, and even snakes arrive daily: "My snake isn't eating." "My rat has skin problems." "My dog needs a kidney transplant." "My cat needs brain surgery." For sums ranging from a few hundred to several thousand dollars, these animals receive medical treatment as if they were people. I mentioned this to a friend of mine, expecting him to find the whole concept ridiculous. But he didn't: his cat, he explained, was seeing a pet psychiatrist to deal with mood fluctuations. As in my friend's case, the customers who attend the Animal Medical Center aren't rich old ladies toting dainty little poodles with obscure ailments; they are everyday folk who prefer to pay for these treatments rather than accept nature's verdict and make another visit to the pet store.[14]

If these medical examples seem quirky, consider how ordinary Americans live today, compared with the way their parents lived a generation ago. The real story in real estate isn't the McMansions and "starter castles" of the nouveau riche; it is the fact that the average house built in the United States today is nearly double the size of its counterpart of the 1950s. In Levittown, New York, the archetypal 1950s suburban development, the average home was 1,100 square feet; today's homes average 2,150 square feet. And most of our homes are fully loaded; they have dishwashers, two-car garages, multiple color TV sets, full indoor plumbing, and central heating and air-conditioning, which relatively few homes in the 1950s had, as well as microwave ovens, personal computers, videocassette recorders, CD players, cell phones, and answering machines that nobody in earlier generations had because they didn't exist.[15]

The average price of a new car sold in the United States today is $22,000, up more than 75 percent from a decade ago.[16] When I came to this country in 1978, air travel was still considered a luxury; most Americans on vacation drove or took public transportation to where they were going. Now air travel has become the Amtrak of the skies, just as cruise ships are becoming the Greyhound of the seas. Americans now take approximately 700 million airline flights each year, an average of three flights per person.[17] For Americans, going to Europe has become commonplace. A couple of decades ago, if you took the family to Europe, you could upon your return assemble the neighbors to show them your slides of Buckingham Palace and the Eiffel Tower; if you tried that today, you would be regarded as an intolerable bore.

I once asked the novelist Tom Wolfe if he was awed at the levels of opulence that he observed in New York society. "What I find even more remarkable," Wolfe said, "is that at this very moment, your plumber or my electrician is vacationing with his third wife in St. Kitts. I can see him sunning himself and lazily fondling the gold chain on his chest. Soon they will take a walk along the shore, sipping glasses of designer water and getting ready to sample the local cuisine." And guess who employs servants these days? Maria America, a southern California agency that places housekeepers, nannies, and other domestic help, reports that its recent clients included a plumber, a Pizza Hut manager, and a cashier at Costco.[18] Admittedly, some of these clients are two-wage earners who need additional help at home; even so, in the past hiring help was a luxury that the lower middle class could not possibly afford. As for the servants, even they don't make out too badly: I contacted the agency and was informed that they earn around $80 for a day's work.

Given the ascendancy of ordinary Americans into a lifestyle once reserved for the affluent, the rich have been compelled to react in the only two ways they know how: by raising their own level of extravagance and by running away. Now that it's not a big deal to have a gold American Express card, the rich go in for the platinum card; it's the only one with any snob appeal left. When every Tom, Dick, and Harry shows up for your flight—sometimes even sitting next to you in first class, courtesy of his frequent-flyer miles—what's a self-respecting rich guy to do but charter his own plane or buy part ownership in a jet? When your nanny's kid wears a Tommy Hilfiger jacket and your gardener shows up for work in a Polo shirt, it's time for the truly well heeled to go for custom-made clothing, such as a hand-tailored Kiton suit, which runs between $3,000 and $5,000. And with run-of-the-mill types showing up at all the familiar vacation spots and engaging in all the usual tourist routines, the rich have to flee to remote and little-known places where they can participate in truly exotic activities: quail hunting on Bray's Island, Georgia; lemur spotting on Madagascar; antiques shopping in Kathmandu; playing golf along the ocean at the Teeth of the Dog course in the Dominican Republic; doing yoga at a spa resort in the Himalayas. The duke of Bedford once said that the upper classes expect only one thing from the common man: that he should remain common. The rich today are forced to take extreme measures because so many Americans are ignoring the advice of the duke of Bedford.

The comforts of the ordinary American do not, of course, disprove the existence of poverty. Indeed, the U.S. Bureau of the Census claims that more than 30 million Americans, or 12 to 13 percent of the population, are poor. But what does "poor" in this context really mean? Does it mean that millions of Americans are starving or don't have clothes to wear or a roof to sleep under? It does not. I cannot help but recall the saying of a school friend in Bombay. "I am going to move to America," he vowed, "I want to live in a country where the poor people are fat."

Today's poor people in the United States spend less than half their income on basic necessities. Some people may be surprised to learn that 50 percent of Americans defined by the government as "poor" have air-conditioning, 60 percent have microwave ovens and VCRs, 70 percent have one or more cars, 72 percent have washing machines, 77 percent have telephones, 93 percent have at least one color television, and 98 percent have a refrigerator. Not only are poor Americans today better housed, better clothed, and better fed than average Americans were half a century ago; in many respects they live better than the average western European does today.[19]

How is this possible if poor people make so little money? One reason is that the Census Bureau does not take into account government benefits such as welfare, food stamps, unemployment provision, and rent subsidies, all of which supplement the earned income of the poor. A second reason is that poor people often grossly underreport their incomes, no doubt to maintain their eligibility for federal programs. We know this because the average poor person reports a standard of living—measured in terms of consumption—that considerably exceeds his earning capacity. Finally the census counts as poor many elderly people who are fairly well off but earn little income, as well as young people who live comfortably on parental assistance but whose incomes are small because they are just starting out in life.

The good news is that the Census Bureau is aware that its poverty numbers are inadequate. The bad news is that instead of downsizing them to correspond with a more mainstream understanding of poverty, the bureau wants to revise them upward in an apparent effort not just to maintain but to multiply the number of Americans officially classified as poor. Recently the *New York Times* reported that census bureaucrats want to raise the poverty threshold from $16,600 for a family of four to $19,500, a move that would immediately plunge more than 10 million Americans into poverty, even though their standard of living would remain unchanged. Rebecca Blank, dean of the School of Public Policy at the University of Michigan, explains that the Census Bureau's new definition would go beyond life's necessities to define poor people as those lacking "a socially acceptable standard of living."[20]

Using statistical legerdemain, the Census Bureau seeks to guarantee the biblical assertion that "the poor you will always have with you." But by any absolute or historical standard, Huber is right. Poverty, understood as the absence of food, clothing, and shelter, is no longer a significant problem in America. What remains is relative inequality and the question, does that continue to matter?

Robert Frank, a political scientist at Cornell University and author of *Luxury Fever*, thinks it does. The equality principle of the Declaration of Independence, he points out, doesn't say anything about poverty. It simply says that we are all created equal. Jefferson wrote that this doctrine was based on "the palpable truth that the mass of mankind has not been born with saddles on their backs, nor a favored few booted and spurred, ready to ride them legitimately, by the grace of God."[21]

What Jefferson was concerned about was not merely poverty but aristocracy. He didn't want social differences between people to become so large that a favored few could lord it over the rest of us. Frank argues that since money is the predominant measure of social value in our society, big differences in socioeconomic status raise precisely the problem that Jefferson had in mind. Despite his warm-and-fuzzy sweater, isn't Bill Gates really a baron and isn't the guy who mows his lawn a serf? In today's America, Frank worries, all men are created equal, but some are more equal than others.

Many scholars have argued that gross and enduring inequality is harmful because it threatens the principle of equal opportunity and at the same time imperils social stability. How can the children of barons and serfs have any expectation that they have an equal chance to succeed? Barons and serfs can coexist in a society but they cannot live together as free citizens. The cohesiveness of a democratic society depends upon people, those at the top as well as those at the bottom, feeling a certain kinship with one another. Otherwise society is fractured into two camps, the blessed and the damned. And the damned can be expected to look for ways, some involving the ballot box, others involving breaking into houses, to seize the possessions that are otherwise denied to them.

Frank argues that people's conception of dignity, and of their place in society, does not depend upon some absolute measure of material well-being; rather, it is forged in relationship to how their fellow citizens, or more precisely the people in their relevant community, are doing. "In principle," Frank concedes, " it shouldn't make much difference if you drive a Honda Civic and I drive a BMW. But it all depends on the situation. If you're a film producer and you drive a Honda Civic, it might matter very much to you. In fact, you might have to park around the corner."

I told Frank that while I didn't doubt the genuineness of the embarrassment that relative inequality might impose, I wasn't sure why this was a matter of public concern. As a society, why should we care if a film producer has to park around the corner? "In that case it probably doesn't matter," Frank concedes, "but in other cases it might."

Frank gives another example, his own: "When I got out of college, I worked as a Peace Corps volunteer in Nepal. I lived in a one-room house without heat or indoor plumbing. We didn't even have electricity or running water. It took me a while to get used to that, but after a while I did. It felt normal to me. Actually, I even felt rich, because my $40 monthly stipend gave me spending money that few other people had. So I was content.

"But can you imagine how I would have felt if I lived in those conditions in Europe or the United States? I would be totally crushed. Every single day I would feel how little I had compared with everyone else. And that's just the point, isn't it? It is natural for us to evaluate our circumstances relative to those around us. The problem is not one of absolute but relative deprivation. But that doesn't make it any less real."

To illustrate the kind of inequality that has serious social consequences, Frank cited the case of Wendy Williams, who lives in a trailer park in Dixon, Illinois. Williams has never known grinding poverty. Her father earns $9 an hour as a welder; her mother works part-time as a cook. Williams's problem is that her public school is largely made up of the sons and daughters of doctors, lawyers, and business executives. These parents think nothing of taking their children on expensive vacations or buying them designer clothes and the latest toys. "Wendy goes to school around these rich kids," her mother says, "and wonders why she can't have things like they do."

What Williams suffers is not the physical hardship of going hungry but the psychological suffering of everyday humiliation. Some of the children call her "trailer girl." She compliments another student on a stylish outfit, asking where she got it, and the girl replies, "Why would you want to know?" Williams speaks with her lips pursed because she is aware of her protruding front teeth. Her new nickname at school is "Rabbit." She hates it and is constantly begging her parents to send her to an orthodontist. Her parents ask her to be patient, but they know that they might never have enough money to pay for her to get her teeth fixed.[22]

In a rich country, where the body is secure from the depredations of extreme deprivation, the spirit is nevertheless vulnerable to a different kind of torment: the feeling of inferiority. It is hard not to sympathize with the plight of a little girl who, through no fault of her own, feels like a second-class citizen. Frank's argument is that the social gap between Wendy Williams and her classmates constitutes a kind of offense against the equality provision of the Declaration of Independence. Aren't this young girl's woes precisely what Jefferson was concerned about when he articulated the principles that Frank appeals to, principles that have shaped the American understanding of the role of government?

Actually, no. Jefferson's doctrine that all men are created equal was a statement of metaphysical equality. We are all equal, not in every respect but in the eyes of our Creator. This equality has practical implications: it means that we have certain inalienable rights to life, liberty, and the pursuit of happiness. But in his discussion of the "natural aristocracy," Jefferson introduces a seemingly contradictory concept. "There is a natural aristocracy among men," he says, and goes on to assert that he favors the idea: "The natural aristocracy I consider as the most precious gift of nature."

Jefferson's defense of aristocracy seems surprising, because like most of the American founders Jefferson was a fierce enemy of the aristocracies of Europe. But Jefferson emphasized that he opposed these hierarchies because they were based on birth and blood. He called the European system "an artificial aristocracy" and a "tinsel aristocracy" because its claims to excellence were spurious. Jefferson *supported* social hierarchies that were based not on such arbitrary characteristics but on individual merit. The best government, he wrote, is the one that elevates the natural aristocracy, separating "the wheat from the chaff."[23] For Jefferson the Declaration of Independence does not mean that we are equal in endowments, only in rights.

If Jefferson were alive today, I am quite sure he would have sympathized with young Wendy Williams's plight. But private concern for an individual does not translate into a public responsibility involving the federal government. Jefferson had a clear sense of the government's role: not to undo all harms, not to secure equal sympathy for everyone, but to secure equal rights. In Jefferson's view, what we make of these rights, what social status we obtain as a result of our efforts is not a subject of public concern; it is entirely up to us.

Before we determine how we should evaluate relative inequality, therefore, let us explore the reasons for such inequality. Does inequality in our society exist because of arbitrary factors such as inheritance and nepotism, or is it largely a function of individual merit?

Fortunately, there is a general consensus among critics and defenders of inequality about why inequalities have grown so large in America today. One reason, emphasized by Robert Frank, is "winner-take-all markets."[24] Such markets have long existed in such fields as sports and entertainment. A hundred years ago, for example, many people made a decent living as dancers performing in local halls or singers performing in local opera houses. Today who wants to buy concert tickets to listen to a local tenor when, for a few dollars, we can get Luciano Pavarotti on a compact disc? Why spend an evening watching a homegrown lad prance around in tights when you can watch Mikhail Baryshnikov on cable TV? What this means is that local dancers and tenors are going to have trouble finding work and Pavarotti and Baryshnikov are going to make millions of dollars a year.

Now the winner-take-all phenomenon has spread to other fields. Everyone is, in a sense, a free agent competing in a reward structure that pays fantastic dividends at the very top. People in the high-tech world tell me that an outstanding computer programmer can be five or even ten times as productive as a mediocre programmer. In the old economy this difference might not have mattered very much; both programmers would have worked for a salary, and the better programmer could have expected little more than a year-end bonus in recognition of his superior skills. But in a highly competitive market, where skills go to the highest bidder, there is no reason why the superior programmer should not be paid five or ten times more than his mediocre counterpart. In a truly free economy, everyone is paid what his skills are worth in the global market.

A second reason for inequality, pointed out by critics such as Laura D'Andrea Tyson and Robert Kuttner, is that there are large differences of education and training among workers. Thirty years ago people with a high school education or less who worked with their hands made roughly the same kind of money as people who worked with their heads. A plumber who dropped out of school in the eighth grade had a standard of living similar to that of a medical researcher with many years of college and graduate education. Today, however, a high school education doesn't count for much. Jobs in the highest-paying sectors of the economy, such as technology, call for at least a college degree and preferably some graduate training on top of that. Moreover, menial work now has two forms of competition: automation and immigrants. Machines and immigrants tend to do more work for less money than native-born Americans. Consequently, many critics of inequality worry that the new global economy has literally rendered a whole generation of working people superfluous and obsolete.

A third reason for inequality is differences of age and family structure. Young people on average earn a lot less than middle-aged people because they haven't been in the workforce very long and don't have much experience. Similarly, families with several wage earners generally do a lot better than families with one wage earner or none. A majority of affluent families have at least two earners. An increasing number of middle-class families do as well. Meanwhile, low-income families typically have one earner. In many cases the poor are single mothers whose obligations to their children make it difficult for them to work at all.[25]

Another important cause of inequality is that poor and middle-class people are working less while the affluent are working more. Here it is the behavior of the ordinary American that makes sense and that of the rich person that is anomalous. Adam Smith expected that as families and nations became more successful they would increasingly trade work for leisure. The reason is simple: work is not its own justification. We do it to get paid, to give us the means to support ourselves and have fun. We work in order to buy things, and also to buy time so that we don't have to work. For most working Americans, that means living for the weekend, looking forward to vacations, and building up savings in order to be able to retire in comfort. Smith expected that capitalism would increasingly allow people to work less and enjoy more leisure.

This in fact is what Americans have been doing for the past several decades, but especially since the end of World War II. In a recent study, economist Dora Costa documented the huge rise in leisure in American society. Many poor people, of course, are for various reasons accustomed to not working. But Costa shows that—contrary to all the humbug about "the overworked American"—most Americans today work vastly less than their predecessors.

Early in the twentieth century the typical worker put in a twelve-hour day; now eight hours is the norm, and that often includes an hour for lunch. To be sure, women are much more likely to be in the workforce today. But that's partly because housework, which was previously a full-time job, can now be performed relatively quickly. Thanks to mechanization—vacuum cleaners, washers and dryers, microwave ovens—women are now free to work outside the home in a way they couldn't before. All the evidence shows that women today work fewer hours per day than their mothers and grandmothers did.

In times past, most young people started working between the ages of twelve and sixteen; now young people typically enter the full-time workforce in their late teens or early twenties. It is not uncommon for college graduates to take a year off and bum around before getting their first real job. And while earlier generations worked until a few years before they died, today's Americans expect to quit at age sixty-five and enjoy fifteen or twenty years of retirement. In summary, earlier generations of Americans worked for virtually their entire waking lives, while only about half of our waking hours today are devoted to work.[26]

Costa points out that there is one exception to this rule of trading work for leisure: the rich. The rich are today the hardest-working people in society, and they refuse to follow Adam Smith and work less or stop working, even if they can easily afford to. We've heard about the ungodly hours that technology entrepreneurs put in. Senior executives in old-line companies are also known for working six or seven days a week. The overclass in general is a hard-driving group. Even when these people take vacations, their work frequently goes with them. Some don't even plan to quit in old age, insisting, as media magnate Rupert Murdoch put it recently, that "my retirement plan is to be carried out of here."[27]

Economists have an interesting explanation for this. We think of leisure as "not working," but in the economic literature leisure is more precisely defined as "doing what you want to do." Rich people frequently find their jobs challenging and interesting, and so they would prefer to put in overtime at the office rather than sit on a beach sipping margaritas. If you're a welder or a longshoreman, sitting on a beach seems like a wonderful respite from the grime and ardor of your everyday existence; but if you're a scientist or an inventor pursuing a new discovery, an entrepreneur building a new business, an acclaimed singer or athlete, or a successful author completing a magnum opus, lounging on the sand in the middle of nowhere can seem like an awful waste of time.

Our examination of some of the primary causes of inequality leads to a surprising conclusion: the prime culprit in causing contemporary social inequality seems to be merit. Today it is differences in skills, effort, and earning capacity, and not arbitrary factors such as inheritance or favoritism, that appear to be responsible for producing large differences in earnings and wealth. The guy who is worth little has probably produced little of value. By the same token, the guy who's earning twice as much as you is most likely—perish the thought—twice as good as you are. This brings us back to the question we started with: Are inequalities not merely efficient but also justified, in the sense that they correspond with what we produce and what we truly deserve? In the next chapter we explore more closely whether this is really so and the implications that follow if it is.

CHAPTER FOUR

THE LOTTERY OF SUCCESS

Who Wins, Who Loses

In a free system it is neither desirable nor practicable that material rewards should be made generally to correspond to what men recognize as merit.

—Friedrich Hayek, *The Constitution of Liberty*

"Merit is a very funny word," remarks Eric Schmidt, the CEO of the software company Novell. "I'm not sure I entirely understand what it means." Formerly the chief technical officer at Sun Microsystems, where he helped develop the Java programming language, the gawkish, bespectacled Schmidt is widely regarded as one of the most thoughtful men in the high-tech world. We are eating lunch at the Ritz-Carlton hotel in Atlanta. Sitting in on the conversation is our intermediary, the dapper, bow-tied Raymond Nasr, who works for Schmidt and set up this meeting for me.

"Who said that life is fair?" asks Schmidt. "Who says that we get what we deserve? I can't say I have a moral right to this wealth. In a sense, it's a complete accident in my life. And if it went away that would be okay too."

Schmidt's annual salary is $1.2 million, which just qualifies him as "rich," but when you factor in his total compensation package, it adds up to a cool $7 million.

I'm intrigued by the professed indifference to wealth that is part of the Silicon Valley manifesto. What difference, I ask Schmidt, does money make in your life? Does wealth matter? "Sure it does," Schmidt says. "Everyone I know is well paid. No one is struggling with mortgage payments or medical bills. That's a nice feeling." Schmidt adds, "I'm told that most husbands and wives fight over money. That's not a problem in my family."

At the same time, Schmidt stresses that when wealth is geographically concentrated, as in the tech cities, it does little more than bid up the price of real estate. "I know a couple who is looking at a house in Menlo Park. Three bedroms, fourteen hundred square feet. Do you know the asking price? Five hundred and seventy thousand. Do you know what this couple bid? Six hundred and ninety. Do you know what the house sold for? Seven hundred and twenty."

Schmidt cites another example of a friend seeking to buy a home in Woodside, California. It was a beautiful house, Schmidt says, 8,000 square feet on a nice lot. "But the asking price was $5.2 million. Five million bucks! And it sold for $6.45 million, all cash! The guy I know could have bought it, he has the money, but he couldn't bring himself to do it. And I agree with him. It's completely crazy."

Schmidt stresses that desirable real estate, unlike a consumer good such as a Lexus or Mercedes, is a scarcity that money cannot abolish. If the number of rich people in the country doubles, car companies can make twice as many luxury cars, but the number of coveted ocean-view lots in America will remain exactly the same: only now there will be more rich people bidding for them.

Schmidt carries this point further. Like real estate, he says, "life is defined by scarcity. Money removes certain scarcities, but it cannot eliminate others. I'm acutely aware that my body is aging, for example. I'm conscious of my mortality. I can let doctors play around with my face, I suppose, but no amount of money can stop me from growing older or from slowly approaching death."

If he has enough money, I ask Schmidt, why keep working? "I've seen people quit," he replies. "They take their money and disappear. Then they get bored and come back. But by this time they're out of it. No one listens to them. They've lost their platform. A few of them will tell me that they've never been happier. But they're not. You can see it in their face."

So is the pursuit of wealth merely a means of warding off boredom?

Not really, Schmidt says. "Wealth by itself only buys stuff, but great wealth brings with it fame. Fame is intoxicating. It gives people a thrill to be in your presence." The superrich, Schmidt suggests, are part of a wealth sweepstakes, with celebrity as its ultimate reward.

What about the allure of beautiful women? I ask delicately. After all, Veblen in *The Theory of the Leisure Class* suggests that "the seizure of female captives" is one of the biggest prizes of the alpha males in any society.[1] At this point Schmidt's associate, Raymond Nasr, is giggling, but Schmidt looks shocked. "I keep hearing about these beautiful women," Schmidt says. "Where are they? I have yet to meet them."

Call me naïve, but I believe him. The culture of Silicon Valley, and high tech in general, is much less profligate than that of Hollywood or Wall Street. Of course, there are exceptions. I know nothing of suave Raymond Nasr's personal habits, but I'm not sure I'd want him taking my daughter to the prom.

Schmidt concludes that, for him, "money is an important source of validation. It means that my ideas are being listened to. In that sense, my company's stock price is a measure of my self-worth. My life has a report card, and this is it."

I bring Schmidt back to the issue of merit, or just deserts. In what sense, I ask, can tech millionaires be said to deserve their fortunes? "It is undoubtedly true that the vast majority of people in the high-tech world have made their own money," Schmidt says. " Inherited wealth is simply irrelevant. We're talking about wealth that didn't even exist a decade ago, in some cases five years ago.

"Another factor that's a lot less important is discrimination. By discrimination I mean the notion that you don't get the job because of the color of your skin. I'm not saying that doesn't exist, but it's rare. The most important question is not who you are or what you look like but what you can do. That's what matters. And that seems to be a big change from a few decades ago, when the world was a wonderful place as long as you were white and male."

But what about the people who are being left out of the high-tech universe? Schmidt says he's concerned about the "digital divide"—rich people can take advantage of the Internet better than poor people; whites can use it to increase their lead over blacks. These are group differences, but there are, of course, large differences in computer literacy among individuals as well. The problem isn't access, Schmidt admits, it's that "some people know what to do with the technology and others don't. So the Internet may end up increasing inequality because the skills that are needed to take advantage of it are unequally distributed."

I ask Schmidt about another group that seems to be excluded from the new prosperity—the hard-working guys who play by the rules and feel shut out of the kind of money that high-tech twenty-five-year-olds make. What does Schmidt have to say to him? "Sorry, buddy," Schmidt answers, "but you played by the *wrong* rules."

Schmidt argues that the new economy is heavily biased in favor of technology and that success in that fast-growing sector requires a set of specific technical skills. That doesn't mean the old virtues—general intelligence, drive, hard work, reliability, and so on—don't matter. But they aren't sufficient.

"Intelligence and drive have always been basic requirements for success in this country," Schmidt says. "What's different today is that it's getting harder to succeed if you are not extremely well educated, if you don't have the right degrees and preferably from the right universities."

Why the right universities? "Because colleges like Harvard and MIT and Stanford are part of a social network. You can be a brilliant entrepreneur, but if you go to a no-name school you don't have access to these networks. Take my word for it, the networks count for a lot in this industry. I keep reading in the business magazines that anybody can raise venture capital for an Internet company. Yeah, right. Anybody can raise capital for an Internet company if they know the same guys that I do."

Schmidt dips into his seafood salad, while Nasr wears a roguish grin on his face, as if to say, "see, I told you that Eric's an iconoclast; he doesn't buy into the standard Silicon Valley best-product's-gonna-succeed, anybody-with-a-good-idea-can-make-it propaganda."

I ask Schmidt whether he can justify the gigantic rewards the tech tycoons have won in the past few years. "Of course not," he says. "I don't feel too bad about it, because I didn't set out to make money. I got into this business because I liked it, and the money showed up afterward. It's crazy. Suddenly I woke up and said, 'Wow, I'm not middle class anymore.'

"But hey, I realize that I don't have all this because I'm so brilliant. Luck had a lot to do with it."

*　　*　　*

Although Schmidt is considered a new-economy enthusiast, a member in good standing of the Party of Yeah, it's clear from his comments that he is also a skeptic who is willing to challenge libertarian nostrums of "equal opportunity," "equal access," and the market as a dispenser of "just deserts." Indeed, Schmidt's arguments threw our discussion wide open, and I will return to them at various points throughout this chapter.

At the outset, he compels us to reexamine more carefully the concept of merit. Amy Dean, who is business manager of the Silicon Valley office of the AFL-CIO, recently told *Forbes* that much of the new tech wealth was the result of "a bunch of young white guys being in the right place and winning the lottery."[2] This has always been the claim of old-line leftists such as Lester Thurow and Christopher Jencks. In their view rich people don't deserve their wealth; they just luck out. But is this really true?

Schmidt seems ambivalent on this point. He points out that most successful Americans today earn, rather than inherit, their fortunes. That's not just true in high tech; it's true of very rich people generally. Even those who don't do it all by themselves typically inherit a small amount of money and go on, through their own efforts, to turn it into a very large amount of money. The American publisher Walter Annenberg, real estate speculator Donald Trump, and Australian-born media tycoon Rupert Murdoch all came from wealthy families. But they multiplied their wealth many times over through their own deal making and entrepreneurial savvy.

One way to see this is to review the annual *Forbes* 400 "rich list." Lots of commentators observe that each year the rich get richer, but they fail to notice that from year to year the list has a different lineup of people. New faces appear every year, and lots of people move up and down or drop off the list. In fact, many of the old dynasties—the Fords, the Morgans, the Kennedys, the Astors, the Vanderbilts—no longer make the *Forbes* list. Others, such as the Rockefellers and the du Ponts, still make the cut, but they've fallen to the bottom of the ranks. Of the ten richest Americans listed in the first *Forbes* ranking in 1982, only two remained in the top ten a decade later, and by 1997 those two were gone as well. All this is very good news, because it means that even at the top levels America remains a mobile society without a hereditary upper caste.

Today's richest Americans—Bill Gates, Larry Ellison, Paul Allen, Warren Buffett, Steve Ballmer, and Michael Dell—all made their own money. In 1982, approximately eighty-five people on the "rich list" got there through inheritance; by 1999, that figure was down to thirty-five. Indeed, *Forbes* calculates that 251 out of the 400 richest Americans in 1999 are "entirely self-made."[3] Fairly typical is the case of E*Trade founder Christos Cotsakos, who grew up in a Greek immigrant neighborhood where his father was a store clerk and his mother a cook. And being self-made isn't a peculiarity of the *Forbes* list. Millionaires in general are even more likely to have earned their own money than the superrich. Thomas Stanley and William Danko, authors of *The Millionaire Next Door*, estimate that more than 80 percent of millionaires in the United States are "ordinary people who have accumulated their wealth in one generation."[4]

So not many of today's affluent got that way by "choosing their parents carefully." The very richest Americans do seem to have chosen their businesses very carefully. While a hundred years ago the biggest fortunes were made in oil, railroads, mining, and automobiles, today they are in the fields of computers, software, and telecommunications. Still, the typical rich person in this country is not a software magnate. He is much more likely to be a sixty-two-year-old white male from Flint, Michigan, or Tucson, Arizona, who owns a car dealership or a mobile home park, or runs a welding, contracting, or pest control business.[5] As John Weicher pointed out in the previous chapter, most wealthy people in this country got that way not by playing the stock market but by running a successful business or professional practice. Moreover, the typical business or professional practice that is successful is one that supplies the everyday needs of ordinary people.

A second characteristic of successful people today that is especially evident in the high-tech world is that they come from diverse ethnic backgrounds. I have attended several high-tech conferences around the country and hung out in the restaurants and cafés of high-tech cities. Everywhere I am startled at the variety of accents: eastern European accents, Japanese and Chinese accents, German accents, British accents, East Indian and Pakistani accents. Everyone is trying to speak English, the lingua franca of modern technology, but the success rate is moderate at best. At companies like Microsoft and America Online, there are now caucus groups and cafeteria sections not just for Asian

Indians but for Gujaratis, Bengalis, and Keralites. Each group speaks a different native language and savors a different cuisine. Economist Gary Becker reports that more than a third of the 1 million people employed in Silicon Valley are foreign-born.[6]

Schmidt pays lip service to discrimination as an enduring reality, but there is no evidence that it plays any significant role in entrepreneurial success in America today. When Carly Fiorina was named head of Hewlett-Packard, one of her first comments was that "at companies competing hard to win every day, there is not a glass ceiling."[7] Women are underrepresented in the tech world, concedes Kim Polese of Marimba, but she adds that this is because females tend to view technology as "something that is not engaging and fun but complicated and hard and scary."[8] Fiorina and Polese could be wrong, of course, but it's significant that two of the most successful female entrepreneurs in America feel this way. Moreover, Fiorina's claim is supported by the data that compare the representation of women and minorities in the upper ranks of high tech with the qualified pool of candidates from those groups.

It has often been pointed out, for instance, that African Americans make up a tiny percentage of senior personnel in the computer and telecommunications industries. But that is directly attributable to the fact that blacks, who make up 12 percent of the U.S. population, earn between 2 and 3 percent of the Ph.D.s in relevant fields such as engineering, physics, mathematics, and computer science. Women, who are also underrepresented, are much less likely to get graduate degrees in these fields than men.[9]

Social networks, of course, are a reality in high tech as in other fields. Venture capitalist Andy Rachleff acknowledges that his firm, Benchmark Capital, has "never invested in a company that wasn't referred to us or that came from someone we didn't know or know of."[10] Still, what is striking about the computer and telecommunications fields is how successfully nonwhite immigrant groups have established networks of their own. When Sabeer Bhatia, a native of India, first came up with the idea for Hotmail, he met with rejection from a series of venture capitalists. As a "person of color," he naturally felt he was a victim of discrimination. But, he says, "I quickly realized that being foreign-born was no barrier, it was only a barrier in my mind." Now East Indian entrepreneurs such as Bhatia are so successful that they have set up their own "curry network," complete with regular deal-generating powwows, an annual conference, a magazine, and a Web site. Indian-born venture capitalist Vinod Khosla, a partner at Kleiner Perkins Caufield & Byers, remarks that in Silicon Valley "it's almost reverse discrimination. People almost assume that if you're Indian or Chinese you're smarter, and you get the benefit of the doubt."[11]

Even outside the high-tech sphere, ethnic groups do not start new businesses at the same rate. Whether restaurants, cab companies, souvenir stores, or small motels, some groups are more likely to start and run these operations than others. Koreans, Japanese, Chinese, Asian Indians, and Cubans all have high rates of business formation. About 10 to 15 percent of members of these groups are self-employed. African Americans, Filipinos, Mexicans, and Puerto Ricans start relatively few businesses for themselves. The self-employment rate in these groups is around 3 percent. Whites fall somewhere in the middle; their self-employment rate is around 7 percent. Not surprisingly, the most entrepreneurial groups also have the highest per capita incomes in the United States, and the least entrepreneurial groups, the lowest.[12]

What about Schmidt's concerns—echoed by Michael Walzer and several tech entrepreneurs—about the "digital divide"? They bemoan the fact that not all individuals and ethnic groups have equal access to the cornucopia of information and opportunity provided by the Internet. Walzer fretted about the prospect of "digital haves" and "digital have-nots." Civil rights leaders have called for special efforts to promote diversity on what they contemptuously term the World *White* Web. And some have called for the government to provide "info-stamps," the high-tech equivalent of food stamps, to enable the digitally deprived to buy access to computers and the Web.

It is certainly true that not everyone uses the Internet equally. Surveys show that around 60 percent of whites and Asian Americans surf the Internet, compared with 50 percent of Hispanics and African Americans. The discrepancy is more pronounced along economic than along racial lines. Among the poor and lower middle class, only 20 percent of people use the Internet; among the upper middle class and wealthy, more than 70 percent do.[13] *Fast Company* informs us that "a child in a low-income white family is three times as likely to have Internet access as a child in a comparable black family."[14] These are worrisome statistics, but do they really reflect a problem of "access"?

After all, Internet access today seems about as serious a problem in the United States as "telephone access" or "automobile access." When computers cost $2,500 five years ago, it made sense to worry that only families with surplus income could afford them. Now a secondhand computer doesn't cost any more than a TV set, and some companies are virtually giving away PCs. Internet use ranges in price from $20 a month to free. Obviously just about anyone who wants access can have it. Even if the person doesn't have the money, he or she can use the computer at school or work or, in the worst case, go to the local public library.

There is a "digital divide," but it is not about gaining access to computers or the Internet. The real digital divide is that some people and some groups know how to use these tools to get information and put it to use, and others are not as adept in doing so. In the United States, the information and knowledge are available; the problem is one of teaching people the value of knowledge, how to obtain it, and what to do with it. Abroad, especially in the Third World, the situation is different. There, access is a genuine problem. Today only about 10 percent of the world's population has access to the Internet. But network and storage capacities are increasing at a rapid rate, and costs are decreasing. We can assume that access to information will soon cost pennies or nothing. Even in the villages of Asia, Africa, and Latin America, the issue of Internet access will become irrelevant in the not-too-distant future. The world's biggest library and the world's biggest marketplace will both be available essentially free to anyone, anywhere in the world.

Still, Schmidt insists, luck is a big factor in entrepreneurial success. To understand what he means by luck and whether he is right, we need to examine what it is that entrepreneurs do. What skills do they possess that have the potential to produce such an avalanche of financial rewards?

If intelligence is measured in the Ivy League sense, it must be conceded that entrepreneurs are not, in general, very smart people. I don't just mean that they say unsophisticated things or that they don't know the century in which the French Revolution occurred or that Max Weber's last name is pronounced with a "V." Ivy League graduates, to be sure, rarely make such gaffes. What I mean, rather, is that the mode of thinking, the ensemble of traits and skills, that many of us associate with intelligence—a broad background knowledge of the world, a curiosity about one's place in space and in time, an ability to formulate ideas and arguments, a capacity to anticipate and understand objections, and a facility for articulating positions and responding to criticism—is seldom found even among top business leaders.

A couple of years ago, my wife and I were at a *Forbes* dinner, and seated right between us was a computer tycoon whose name you would recognize. At the time I was writing a book about President Reagan, and I posed to this man the following question: Why did the silicon revolution erupt in the 1980s? Why wasn't it launched in the 1970s? The tycoon gave me a funny look, which indicated that he didn't see what I was getting at. So I elaborated. In 1980, I said, not many Americans had a personal computer. Did the technological explosion of the 1980s occur because the physics just happened to work at that point, or were Reagan's policies—tax cuts, privatization, deregulation, the celebration of the entrepreneur—a catalyst for providing venture capital as well as a social context in which the silicon revolution could flourish? The tycoon hemmed, hawed, and mumbled. "It is, as you say, an interesting issue," he said. "I suppose how you think about it determines how you come out on it." After some irrelevancies the man finally concluded, "So, yes, I think you are right. The issue is an important one, and your question is, indeed, a question."

At this point my eyes met my wife's across the tycoon's shoulders and we were both thinking the same thing: this is Mister Ten Billion Dollars? How could we square his public reputation as a Genius of the New Economy with this private display of glossolalia? Samuel Johnson's line came to mind: "He was dull in a new way, and that made many people think him great." But surely these assessments were too severe. As my wife and I talked about this later, we concluded that although our interlocutor did not appear to be smart in the way that we defined the term, he must have a high "entrepreneurial IQ." Judged by his success, he is undoubtedly very good at what he does, but what he does is apparently not captured by our definition of intelligence.

I have been reading a lot of what leading entrepreneurs have to say, and a fair amount of it is risibly inane. "I'm a deep thinker," Ted Turner says. "I have traveled all over. I have more access to information than anyone on the planet." In addition to non sequiturs, Turner also shows a facility for broad claims unsubstantiated by evidence. Discussing global warming on the Larry King show, Turner resorted to everyday experience to prove his point: "Haven't you been outside lately? It's hotter than hell out there. The polar ice caps are melting. I got an island and I know the ocean is rising because I watched my beach get washed away."[15] Poorly paid logicians are tearing out their hair while Turner basks in fame and riches.

Bill Gates is routinely described in various articles as a genius, yet outside the field of software, when has the man said a single thing that is interesting, insightful, or provokes the reaction "I wish I had thought of that"? Gates himself acknowledges that the only topic he is an expert on is "making great software," yet people are always pressing him for wisdom on other topics.[16] The moral of the story is that tech tycoons, like athletes and film stars, should be regarded as authorities only in their particular sphere of expertise.

So what is it that people such as Bill Gates and Ted Turner do that the rest of us don't? What is this thing called "entrepreneurial IQ"? It's not synonymous with regular IQ. Some entrepreneurs, to be sure, have plenty of both. Venture capitalist Vinod Khosla says he got the idea for making big investments in telecommunications start-ups in the mid-nineties: "I remember being on vacation in April 1995, lying on the beach in Hawaii, reading about the physics of optical communications."[17] An odd fellow. But no doubt a high-IQ one.

Still, Khosla isn't typical. Henry Rosovsky, longtime dean of the college at Harvard, liked to say that Harvard's policy was to keep its A students to get graduate degrees and become professors; its B students it would send back to the business world to run the nation's enterprises. I have no doubt that professors with Ph.D.s have, on average, higher IQs than entrepreneurs. Indeed, one reason so many of them resent entrepreneurs is that they know they are smarter and yet they must manage on $80,000 salaries while some fat Rotarian with a gold chain on his chest pulls in $1.4 million a year selling term life insurance. This doesn't mean that academic hostility to capitalism is purely the product of envy. It also springs from a wounded sense that capitalism produces a society in which the most deserving, that is, the most intelligent, don't get the biggest rewards.

The people who get the biggest rewards seem to operate with a very different set of skills from academics. They move fast, while in the academic world speed is considered a sign of superficiality. "It took me just three months to write my book on the French Revolution." To professors, that sounds like a book not worth reading. Entrepreneurs take a lot of risk, looking to the prospect of gain, while academics are famously cautious, calculating what they stand to lose. Finally, entrepreneurs are gregarious and typically have the capacity to build teams and motivate others. These qualities are rare in the academic world, where achievement is usually the result of individual excellence.

But if there is a single trait that most distinguishes entrepreneurs from others, it is this: they have an uncanny ability to anticipate and supply what large numbers of people want. For them, opportunities aren't given, they are created. Indeed if there is a central entrepreneurial skill, it is the ability to see a problem where other people see only inevitability or one of life's necessary inconveniences. As inventor and entrepreneur David Levy described his modus operandi to *The New Yorker*, "When I lie in bed, I try to think of things that suck."[18]

Akio Morita, the legendary founder of Sony, once told me how he had gotten his idea for the Sony Walkman. He would go to the beach with his children, and the kids and their friends would listen to loud music from boom boxes from morning to evening. Teenagers are a cultural plague that we must all endure, you say. But not Morita. He asked himself, "Why should I have to listen to this ghastly music?" And further, "Why should they have to carry those cumbersome boom boxes?" Morita asked his engineers to figure out a way to build a small radio and cassette player that would sound like a high-quality car stereo and yet could be attached to a person's head: that way people could take their music with them, they could listen to it without annoying others, and they could ride bikes and do other things with their hands while listening to music. The Sony staff was dubious, but Morita insisted, and the rest is entrepreneurial history: the Sony Walkman stormed the market and almost instantly become a regular feature of teenage and even adult life.

Morita illustrates the "supply side" truth that truly novel ideas never emerge as a direct response to consumer demand. No one was asking for little radios that they could attach to their heads. Morita intuited that something like that would be useful and desirable, and he produced it. Then he found out that his intuition was right. His offering was eagerly seized by millions of consumers. This is where the entrepreneurial payoff comes in. The skill is to anticipate the want and produce a product that addresses it; the reward is to see your idea vindicated as consumers embrace your product.

The intelligence of the entrepreneur mainly reveals itself as insight into what consumers are likely to want in the future and how those wants can best be supplied. In the mid-1980s, Scott McNealy, Bill Joy, and a team of computer scientists at Sun Microsystems came up with the slogan "The network is the computer." No one, not even forward-looking computer geeks, had any idea what they were talking about. The insight of the Sun team was that a single computer on a desk is a mere word-processing, number-crunching machine. But when computers throughout a society can communicate with one another, forming a single network, then we have a transformational technology on our hands. The Internet, which became a mainstream phenomenon only in 1995, vindicated the Sun team's insight. The company suddenly found itself at the epicenter of the Internet revolution. The enormous rewards that McNealy and others at Sun have harvested are directly attributable to figuring out where the computer was really going to make a difference in people's lives and in building products that made that vision a reality.

Frederick Smith proposed the idea of an overnight mail delivery service in a paper that he wrote as an undergraduate at Yale University. His professor thought it was a fairly stupid idea, and Smith got a C. No doubt the professor was convinced, as the conventional wisdom had it at the time, that if government didn't deliver the mail, no one would. But Smith thought differently, and in 1971 he founded a new company, Federal Express. Before this, he says, "overnight delivery didn't exist on a national scale."[19] Smith drew on techniques used in the banking and telecommunications industries to set up a national clearinghouse to ensure that he could deliver on his promise: "Absolutely, positively overnight." Thus did one man accelerate the pace of doing business in America.

Mark Cuban and Todd Wagner, the cofounders of Broadcast.com, got their concept for a company at Indiana University. The two basketball fans figured out that the Internet would be a great way to listen to games all over the country, since radio typically aired local games. So they founded a company called Audionet and then renamed it Broadcast.com when on-line video made it possible not only to hear but also to watch sports events all over the country. Today Broadcast.com enables viewers to use the Internet to watch virtually every college and pro team play various sports on hundreds of TV stations and cable networks. Although Sun, Federal Express, and Broadcast.com are supplying very practical efficiencies and comforts, it should be emphasized that the wants satisfied by entrepreneurs can be quite arbitrary. They bear no necessary relationship to basic needs or even reasonable aspirations. In- deed, the question of why people want things, and whether they are right to want them, is of no interest to entrepreneurs or to capitalism generally. Consider an extreme example: let's say I can throw sharp objects into the air and catch them between my teeth. Ordinarily this talent would make me eligible to be a barroom curiosity. In a capitalist society, however, I could put my skills up for public consumption. If for some reason millions of people are fascinated by my skill—and, even more important, if they are willing to pay to watch me—then my peculiar talent suddenly becomes marketable. Now it has the potential to make me very rich. Here, as in all cases, the verdict lies with the consumer. It all depends on what people vote for, using ballots that are otherwise known as dollar bills.

What does luck have to do with all this? Is the woman from the AFL-CIO correct that success in today's new economy is not much different from "winning the lottery"? Consider what Richard Santulli does for a living. A graduate of the Polytechnic Institute of Brooklyn and a former math teacher, Santulli says he spent lots of time in his formative years playing around with math problems: "All my friends would spend hours on history and philosophy. To me, I hate to say it, math was the easy way out." Santulli got a job at Goldman Sachs and put his math skills to use doing computer analysis of companies. Then he became interested in airplanes. He knew that owning a jet made no financial sense for most people unless they flew hundreds of hours a year. Yet he guessed that lots of corporate executives and other busy and well-off people would love to have their own plane to fly around when they wanted. There was the dilemma: How to supply them with a plane just at the time they wanted one? Using his math skills, Santulli figured out how fractional ownership could work. "I knew that if we could come up with a way to share the cost and at the same time guarantee service, we would hit a home run." And he did. In 1986, Santulli launched his company, Executive Jet, which was subsequently acquired by Warren Buffett's Berkshire Hathaway company, making Santulli a centimillionaire.[20]

Is luck a factor here? Arguably, yes. Entrepreneurs such as Santulli come up with ideas and offer them to the market. The market sometimes embraces and sometimes repudiates these ideas. Even ideas that sound wonderful, that seem guaranteed to work, often don't. One such idea was Cybercash. A few years ago, the concept of digital money that would replace dollar bills and credit cards seemed like a no-lose idea for the electronic age. The only problem was that, for some reason, nobody wanted it. When people shopped on-line, they preferred to pay with American Express and Visa. So the companies that got into the digital cash business failed. Bad luck. Now a few companies are trying to revive the idea. I wish them good luck, because if they succeed, that's going to be part of the reason.

In Santulli's case, one cannot put down the market's favorable reception of his fractional jet ownership concept to mere luck. Santulli deserves credit for anticipating and then figuring out an ingenious way to meet the wants of a small but high-end group of consumers. Still, Santulli describes himself as a very lucky man, as do many successful entrepreneurs. "I am the right man in the right place at the right time," remarks media magnate Ted Turner.[21] Perhaps Turner's comment can be put down to posturing self-deprecation. Yet others not given to similar showmanship say the same thing. Asked to explain his extraordinary success, John Chambers, CEO of Cisco, says, "There's no substitute for being in the right industry at the right time."[22] Jeff Bezos recently said that luck had been a "huge" factor in the success of Amazon.com.[23]

Here's why these men are being truthful. Imagine a Richard Santulli figure in the year 1910. He has incredible math skills. He can perform amazing gymnastics with numbers. But what can he do with that skill? In 1910, virtually nothing. He can impress his friends by calculating probabilities on a gambling spree, perhaps. But not much else. So our math whiz becomes a high school teacher in his hometown. Today, however, those same math skills are in incredible demand. Suddenly a talent that was once nearly worthless becomes, in the electronic era, very valuable to high-growth companies. Now if you can figure out a way, like Santulli, to put your math skills to work, you too can become a centimillionaire.

The comedian Jerry Seinfeld recently made the same point: "I just had the good fortune of being in this culture when there was a market for nice, funny guys."[24] Notice that Seinfeld is not saying that he isn't talented. No doubt he finds himself extremely amusing. His point, however, is that in another cultural context there might have been a very limited demand for his brand of humor. In a different milieu, say the frat boy culture of an earlier era, it is easy to see the prevailing ethic as one not of applauding but of beating the crap out of guys like Jerry Seinfeld. So Seinfeld's luck is to possess a skill that happens to be highly appreciated at this particular time and place.

In a broader context, investment guru Warren Buffett applies this concept of luck to himself. Buffett says he just happens to have a set of skills "that pays off huge in this society." If he had been born in prehistoric times, Buffett confesses, he would have been some animal's lunch. If he had grown up in Paris in the Middle Ages, Buffett knows, he would not have made a very good theologian; I don't see him providing much competition for Thomas Aquinas. Even as a twentieth-century man, would Buffett have enjoyed his legendary success if he had been born and raised in, say, Uruguay or the Seychelles? It's doubtful, and Buffett knows it. He recognizes that he had the fantastic good fortune of being born and living in the United States of America, and of "being wired in a particular way that I thrive in a big capitalist economy with a lot of action."[25]

In several public statements, Buffett has outlined his mechanism for designing a fair and equitable society: "Let's say that it was 24 hours before you were born, and a genie appeared and said, 'What I'm going to do is let you set the rules of the society into which you will be born. You can set the economic rules and the social rules, and whatever rules you set will apply during your lifetime and your children's lifetimes.' And you'll say, 'Well, that's nice, but what's the catch?' And the genie says, 'Here's the catch. You don't know if you're going to be born rich or poor, white or black, male or female, able-bodied or infirm, intelligent or retarded.'

"Now," Buffett asked his audience, "what rules do you want to have?"[26]

It may seem as if the sage of Omaha has been doing some truly hard thinking about our social problems—calling into question my low estimation of the intellectual sophistication of entrepreneurs—until I inform you that he has lifted his paradigm directly from the philosopher John Rawls. (But let's at least give Buffett credit for reading Rawls.) In his classic treatise *A Theory of Justice,* first published in 1971, Rawls asks us to construct the rules for a just society by standing, as it were, behind a "veil of ignorance." Rawls's conditions are pretty much the same as Buffett's, but his argument is much more deeply conceived, so it is to his analysis that I now turn. The radical premise of Rawls's thought—the reason we are even talking about genies and veils of ignorance—is that he considers all the qualities that are normally described as merit actually to be the product of pure luck.

What does he mean by this? Consider two examples, Tiger Woods and Albert Einstein. Woods has marvelous athletic talents, to be sure. But how did he get them? He inherited his basic physique, thus prevailing in the genetic lottery. No doubt he works hard and practices a lot, but what is the source of his skills? Probably they were socialized into him at an early age. So in this analysis Woods deserves no personal credit for his work ethic; those habits too are part of his social inheritance. The same applies to Einstein, who had the good fortune to be born intellectually gifted and curious.

Rawls holds that all success is the product of "accidents of natural endowment and the contingencies of social circumstance" and that these are "arbitrary from a moral point of view." From this premise Rawls concludes that people have no automatic right to the fame or money generated by their labor. In this view, markets may be efficient, but they are profoundly unfair. So the free society is, for Rawls, an unjust society. Rawls does not, however, call for absolute egalitarianism, a division of social resources into precisely equal shares, because he recognizes that such a measure would inhibit growth and make everyone worse off. So what is Rawls's solution? He argues that since some people have greater abilities, the fruits of those abilities should be used for the common advantage. Choosing from behind the "veil of ignorance," Rawls contends that the basic structure of society should be designed in such a way that inequalities of wealth are permitted only when they serve the interests of the disadvantaged members of the population.[27]

Stated abstractly, Rawls's argument is ingenious, even in some sense unanswerable. The problem with it is that it defines luck so broadly that we cannot make valid distinctions between the ways in which people acquire wealth. For example, the vast majority of today's tech entrepreneurs used their creativity and skills to produce products for which they have been amply rewarded. Yet their children will acquire their vast fortunes without having contributed a single ounce of effort. Clearly the moral case for allowing an entrepreneur to keep his money is vastly stronger than that for allowing his offspring to inherit it. Rawls, however, makes no such distinction. He assumes that both are equally undeserving, just as he assumes that all poor people, no matter how lazy, irresponsible, or unreliable they are, do not deserve their fate.

Historically, wealth has been obtained in one of three ways: by coercion or confiscation; by luck or lottery; and by earning or wealth creation. Surely we can all agree that wealth obtained by coercion, looting, or confiscation—in short, wealth obtained without the consent of the person parting with it—is generally a crime and a monstrosity. What this says about our tax system will have to be reserved for another discussion.

But what about luck? Rawls assumes that people have no right to the fruits of luck, but this remains to be demonstrated. Consider the most obvious example of luck, the lottery. Every participant invests a dollar, and one guy ends up with $100 million. Who says that life is fair? But hardly anyone jumps up and says, "Hey, I don't have the lucky number, but that guy has a moral duty to share his winnings with me. After all, what did he do to earn the money?" Most people accept that even if the winner did absolutely nothing to deserve the money, he or she is still entitled to it. Sure, it was luck, but the losers are consoled by the hope that if they keep buying tickets maybe one day luck will rain money on *their* heads.

Or let's assume that you and I are taking a walk through the forest. I happen to glance down, and I find a $100 bill. I pick it up and put it in my pocket. You give me dirty looks. "What?" I ask. "Nothing," you reply. But you sulk all the way home. If I am a nice guy, I may offer to use the money to take you to dinner. But do you have a moral right to share the money with me? And why limit it to you, who just happened to be on the scene? Must I share my winnings with the entire society on the grounds that this money isn't mine and therefore everyone has an equal right to it?

This is utterly absurd. The money didn't belong to me, to be sure, but I found it, and absent any prospect of locating the original owner, the money is rightfully mine. Yes, it's fortune, but fortune happened to be winking in my direction that day. I may not have a moral right to the funds, but even less do you have any moral claim upon them. Therefore, for all practical purposes, the money does and should belong to me, and the question of whether I should share it depends entirely on my goodwill. Even if I have no interest in sharing, perhaps I don't want you to be a pain in the butt for the rest of the day, and so I give you some of the money, say $30, as a consolation prize. That would seem to be a humane solution. Everyone is better off, and, equally important, all parties are reasonably content.

So Rawls is wrong about luck; it does not give the unlucky a license to claim or seize the possessions of those who do well. It seems fair to conclude that wealth obtained by confiscation is bad and should be deplored; wealth obtained by luck or lottery is morally indifferent and should be tolerated; and wealth that is earned rightfully belongs to the wealth creator. But there is a deeper truth to Rawls's argument. What he is saying is that we have to try to design a social system in which winners and losers can live together. The winners can't win so big, and the losers lose so much, that the latter group gives up on the system or conspires to destroy it.[28] How, then, do the winners obtain the consent of the losers to a system in which they come out so far ahead? To ask this is to move the question from the traditional "left-wing" concern about egalitarianism to the traditional "right-wing" concern about social stability.

Although there is a lot of inequality in America and the world today, differences of income do not seem to have produced serious instability or conflict in any capitalist society. Modern capitalist countries are divided over ethnicity, nationality, language, religion, and other such factors, but they are seldom torn apart by class warfare between the rich and the poor. Why not? The main reason, I believe, is that contrary to the assumption of Rawls and many others, technological capitalism is a powerful catalyst of enduring equality among citizens. Rawls's criterion for a just society—that it should be fundamentally oriented to allow inequality to work for the benefit of those at the bottom—seems an impossible one. I think I can show, however, that it is fundamentally satisfied by technological capitalism. Certainly this system does a better job in achieving Rawls's goals than any other existing society, or any other society we can practically envision.

The key to understanding this is to take a long-term view. Rawls himself encourages this. "The appropriate expectation" for his vision of social justice, he writes, is "that of the long-term prospects of the least favored extending over future generations."[29] Seen from this historically enlarged perspective, the effects of technological capitalism appear in a new light. Consider a few examples. A century ago a rich man traveled by horse and carriage, while the poor man traveled by foot. Today the rich man might drive a Jaguar, and his poorer counterpart a Toyota Camry. A Jaguar is faster and more luxurious than a Camry, but still, there has been an enormous leveling of difference between the rich man and the poor man in terms of getting from here to there. Another example: in the early twentieth century the rich could escape the bitter cold of winter by going to homes in warmer climates and the sweltering heat of summer by going to cooler retreats. Meanwhile, the common man had to endure the elements. Today most homes, offices, and cars are temperature-controlled, and the benefits are enjoyed by rich and poor alike.

These examples could be multiplied, but here is the most telling one of all: a hundred years ago the life expectancy of the average American was around forty-seven years. The gap between rich and poor Americans was considerable: about ten years. It was not uncommon for a wealthy person to live into his late sixties or seventies but quite rare for a poor man or woman to do so. A similar gap separated the United States from poorer countries such as China and India. Today the average life expectancy in the United States is around seventy-six years. Not only have the poor made absolute advances in terms of life span, but they have gained ground enormously against the rich. Today the life expectancy gap between the affluent and the indigent in the United States is negligible: two to three years. This increase in longevity has occurred in the poorer nations as well. At the beginning of this century, a typical child born into a poor family in India had only a 50 percent chance of making it to adulthood. The odds were great that he or she would die at birth or in the early years. Now the vast majority of children conceived in Asia, Africa, and Latin America have the chance to live through the full range of human experience from infancy to old age. Indeed, life expectancy in the Third World today has more than doubled to nearly seventy years. That's six years behind the American average, but still, who can deny that the doubling of the life span is not only an immense achievement but also an egalitarian achievement?

Technological capitalism deserves the main credit for this achievement, because it has produced advances in medicine and food production, as well as countless other amenities, making them available to ordinary citizens. (Let's be fair: government policies have also helped, by providing adequate nutrition and medical care for the poor.) Economist Joseph Schumpeter made this point in a general way when he wrote, "Queen Elizabeth owned silk stockings. The capitalist achievement does not typically consist in providing more silk stockings for queens but in bringing them within the reach of factory girls in return for steadily decreasing amounts of effort."[30] Two strong advocates of free markets, economist Michael Cox and business journalist Richard Alm, go further: they argue that it is the rich who have subsidized the provision of new technologies that have brought the greatest benefit to the life of the common man.

Cox and Alm point out, for example, that when Henry Ford first introduced the Model T in 1908, its price was $850, a sum that amounted to two years of pay for a factory worker. Not surprisingly, Ford sold only 2,500 of those automobiles that year, mainly to more affluent buyers. Critics dismissed the automobile as a "rich man's toy." But not for long. Another example: In 1915, it cost $20 to make a long-distance phone call from New York to San Francisco. No ordinary citizen could afford that, yet someone had to make phone calls at that price, or else there would have been no market for telephone service. In footing the initially high bill, the rich paid the fixed cost of bringing long-distance service to the masses. Today a three-minute, coast-to-coast phone call costs almost nothing. In 1984, it cost $3,995 to buy an IBM personal computer and $4,195 for a cellular car phone. Ridiculous prices. But Cox and Alm argue that by buying computers and cellular phones at those rates, the rich invested the resources that could then be deployed into making those products better and cheaper, so that ordinary citizens and even the poor can now afford them.[31] The same is true with new medical technologies, which are at first outrageously expensive, so that only the affluent are able to pay for them. This seems horribly unfair, because the rich have earlier access than others to medical benefits, but what is often forgotten is that by paying the heavy initial freight the rich are carrying the burden of research and development that enables those same treatments to cost much less and reach a mass market over a period of time.

Time, then, is our problem. The egalitarian benefits of technological capitalism are achieved only in the long run; in the short term, we must contend with large and in some cases rising inequality. Some Party of Yeah enthusiasts downplay the significance of inequality, implying that having more money is no big deal, and some Party of Nah critics, who recognize that it is a big deal, nevertheless hope that the influence of money can be contained. Philosopher Michael Walzer, a member of the latter group, concedes that "it just doesn't matter that you have a yacht and I don't, or that the sound system of her hi-fi set is greatly superior to his, or that we buy our rugs from Sears and they get theirs from the Orient." What does matter, he writes, is that citizens have equal access to certain basic goods and that the power of money should be abolished "outside its sphere." In a democracy, for instance, rich people should not be able to buy better legal representation or more political power than poor people.[32]

Walzer's list of basic goods is fairly extensive; it includes food, medical care, security in old age, and a chance to pursue one's interests and grow emotionally and spiritually. No country supplies Walzer's full list of desiderata, but in most Western countries there is basic provision for citizens in terms of food, shelter, and (at least) emergency medical care. But Walzer's second goal—to establish clear parameters for what money can and cannot buy—turns out to be utterly unfeasible. The reason is that money is simply a medium of exchange, and there is virtually nothing in a capitalist society that money cannot buy. Try as one might to limit the advantages that money buys, one cannot fundamentally alter them.

So what does money buy? I was provoked to think about this question recently upon witnessing an exchange between my friend David McCourt, who heads the telecommunications company RCN, and Professor Paul Argenti of Dartmouth's Amos Tuck School of Business. "You know, Paul," McCourt said, "I didn't go to an Ivy League school.

I don't have a Ph.D. But if I want the word 'doctor' before my name I can buy that, can't I?" Like the French policeman in *Casablanca,* the wily Argenti feigned shock. "Dartmouth is not for sale," he declared. Then he offered a second opinion: "Ten million. For ten million dollars I guarantee it." He added, "If you get it from Georgetown it'll cost a bit less." McCourt decided to test a lower bid. "What if I only want to spend thirty grand? What will thirty grand get me?" Without missing a beat Argenti replied, "Two football tickets and a parking pass."

So the amount of money you're willing to spend matters. But if you're willing to spend enough, is there anything apart from eternal salvation that money cannot purchase? Think about it: money buys safety, because it allows you to move from a dangerous neighborhood to a relatively secure one. More broadly, it buys emotional security, because rich people don't have to worry about how they are going to make their mortgage payments or pay for their children's college education. Money buys beauty, so that rich men can not only possess lovely objects such as fountains and vases but also win the allegiance of beautiful women. It works the other way too: wealth enables an older woman to get a young stud. In South America people use the phrase "money whitens," not only because a dark-skinned rich man can find many light-skinned women who want to marry him but also because, by thus producing lighter-skinned children, he can literally bleach his family line.

Vast wealth also buys fame, as Eric Schmidt pointed out earlier, and it commands the admiration and attention of virtually everyone in society, including politicians. As the Yiddish proverb has it, "With money in your pocket, you are wise, you are handsome, and you sing well too." What Henry Kissinger said of the celebrity is true of the very wealthy person generally: when he or she is boring, people think it's *their* fault. Money buys serenity and time, because rich people can minimize hassles, waits, and inconveniences that attend most people's everyday life. If you are ever in trouble with the law, money buys top legal counsel, so that you have the best chance of getting off. Money even buys influence with the church: Want an annulment, Mr. Kennedy? Perhaps most important, money gives independence to the affluent; they are not beholden to others, and they can be architects of their own destiny. Affluence creates for the rich the space to pursue higher things, while the poor remain captive to the consuming struggle over necessities.

This inequality of access to "spiritual resources," as economist Robert Fogel calls it, is probably the most significant form of inequality in America and the West today.[33]

The good news for egalitarians such as Walzer is that while money produces enormous benefits for the person moving from the bottom to the top—from the underclass to the overclass—it produces rapidly diminishing marginal returns after that point. William K. Vanderbilt, who was worth close to $200 million, liked to say that the fellow who had $1 million lived just as well as he did. Apart from fame, it is hard to see a very big difference today between people who are worth $10 million, $50 million, and $500 million. "I have two big things that you don't have," one tech tycoon recently told me. "I have domestic staff, and I have a plane. Those are nice things, but other than that, there is not much difference in our standard of living." At first I had difficulty believing him. But in general I think he is right. Once you can afford to dress well, live in a large and lovely home, eat in good restaurants, and buy nice things when you feel like it, more money ceases to be crucial. Don't misunderstand me: I'd rather have $50 million than $10 million. Five hundred million is too big a number for me to seriously contemplate, but I wouldn't say no. More is better. My point is that added increments of money do provide increased satisfaction, but they do so at a diminishing rate.

Why, then, do people who have a great deal of money—"enough" by all reasonable estimations—continue to chase after it? Adam Smith was intrigued by this question, and he offered a simple answer: there are strange and slightly pitiable people who don't know the meaning of "enough." So they keep chasing one opportunity after another, they serve those whom they hate, they are obsequious to those whom they despise, and yet they keep at it, hoping to become top dog, awaiting a tranquillity that never arrives. In other words, the sad, relentless engine of human discontent continues to drive the hugely successful to become even more successful.

To test Smith's theory, I asked Jim Barksdale, former CEO of Netscape and now head of the Barksdale Group, what kept him going long past the point where money could make any difference in his life. "I am very conscious of coming from the South," Barksdale said. "I know that people laugh at the southern accent. I know of many successful people with hardscrabble backgrounds. Many of us are driven to overcome what we came from." In a similar vein, Ted Turner has attributed his relentless ambition to a "latent inferiority complex" based on his childhood inability to satisfy a demanding father. Several years ago, in the middle of a speech, Turner held up a copy of a business magazine with his face on the cover and called out, "Is this enough for you, dad?"[34]

In Michael Lewis's biographical sketch of Jim Clark, who has founded three billion-dollar companies, the author explores the question of how much money Clark needs to be happy. At first, he discovered, Clark wanted to have $10 million. When he reached that goal, he raised it to $100 million. Soon he has set his sights even higher: "I just want to have a billion dollars." Lewis pushed him: "What happens after you have more money than Larry Ellison? Would you like to have more money than, say, Bill Gates?" Clark dismissed this as a ridiculous idea, but a few minutes later he confessed, "You know, just for one moment, I would kind of like to have the most." Lewis poignantly observes, "He was the least happy optimist there ever was."[35]

The contest to better everyone else, to accumulate the largest pile of money, remains the primitive drive behind the inexhaustible energies of our entrepreneurial elite. In other words, although the gratification of spending is subject to diminishing marginal returns, the gratification of accumulation is not. And Adam Smith concludes, "It is well that nature imposes on us in this manner. It is this deception which rouses and keeps in continual motion the industry of mankind."[36] Translation: Let these pathetic bastards keep at it! Who knows if they're really adding to their happiness? What we do know is that they are producing things that make society better off. Far from them exploiting us, we are, admittedly with their full consent, exploiting them.

Short-term inequality remains a problem, but is it a problem we can live with? I believe it is if two basic conditions are satisfied. First, we should make sure that the gains of the successful are not accompanied by losses on the part of the less successful: "I win, you lose." When the rich are getting richer and the poor are getting poorer, society has a serious problem. We should strive for an economy where the rich are getting richer and the poor are also getting richer: "I win, you win." In such a case it doesn't matter very much if inequality rises over the short term.

This condition, in which all the social classes gain, even if not at the same rate, has not always been satisfied in the West, but it is being generally satisfied in today's American economy.

The second condition is that economic equality be attended by as much social equality as is feasible in a given society. Fortunately, America does very well in this regard. This is a country where there are no clear distinctions of dress and demeanor that set economic classes apart. How you speak English in Britain immediately classifies you; the English spoken in the United States is equally abominable across all sectors of society. Perhaps most surprising, in America even menial jobs, such as janitors and maids, don't involve the fawning and toadying that one sees in other countries. The United States is one of the few nations in the world where people call waiters "sir," as if they were knights.

Even where there is no equality, American culture provides adequate illusions of it. My favorite example: sports teams. What possible kinship can there be between the millionaire athletes who play professional sports and the vast majority of fans in their cheering section? None. In truth, they don't even come from the same city. But sports terms such as "Dallas Cowboys" and "Los Angeles Lakers" are a magnificent mechanism for building civic solidarity because they enable the losers in society to identify with the winners. By jumping and screaming "We're number one! We're number one!" people whose number is pretty far down the list can vicariously share in their team's triumphal quest for enduring greatness.[37]

Inequality is not a virtue in and of itself, but it is an inevitable by-product of a free society that seeks to reward citizens in proportion to their productive worth. Still, even short-term inequalities of a certain magnitude continue to disturb the social conscience, and they should. The Party of Nah cannot win the debate on this issue, but it is right to keep raising it. And it does have one consolation: over time, more and more ordinary citizens are going to move from the lower ranks to relative affluence. They too will find themselves in a position where they can do what they want with the rest of their lives. Thus they will have crossed the point where money produces diminishing marginal gains. At that juncture the issue of inequality might cease to matter.

CHAPTER FIVE

EYE OF THE NEEDLE

The Moral Critique of Prosperity

It is fortunate for men to be in a situation in which, though their passions may prompt them to be wicked, they have nevertheless an interest in not being so.

—Montesquieu, *The Spirit of the Laws*

Wealth and success may buy you freedom and make your life easier, but in the process of acquiring them must you sell out your principles and lose your soul? Rich societies have extended longevity and comfort for their citizens, but haven't they also complicated—and corrupted— life so that people in poorer, simpler societies may actually live more wholesome and happier lives?

The "right-wing" critique of technological capitalism is deeper and more profound than its left-wing counterpart. I use the term "right-wing" advisedly; as I said earlier, many conservatives have been supporters of capitalism and are only now questioning its social and moral implications. Talk to many conservatives today, and you will get a less favorable view of capitalism than you would have a decade or two ago. Oddly enough, these former devotees of capitalism have now formulated a critique of it that goes beyond anything that the traditional enemies of capitalism ever conceived.

The "left-wing" egalitarians, after all, accept that technology and markets generate wealth and that wealth is good. Their only complaint is that wealth is not being properly distributed. The emerging right-wing argument is based on the premise that it doesn't matter how the prizes are distributed, because the game itself is evil. So what if the system is successful in reaching its goals when they are immoral ones? This critique questions the ethical legitimacy of the market system itself. It holds that the very engine that motivates technological capitalism is greed and selfishness.

This rapacity is said to have reached new heights in the new economy, where many people want instant riches and will sacrifice virtually anything to get them. Moreover, all the previous restraints on the impulse of greed have come off. At least in the 1980s greed was identified and deplored; now we don't use the word but celebrate the thing itself. The social consequences, in this view, are materialism, the proliferation of vice, the vulgarization of culture, broken families, uprooted communities, environmental ruin—in other words, a breakdown of both nature and society. Does it really matter that our portfolios are flourishing if, at the same time, we are wrecking the natural and social ecosystem and relinquishing our moral principles?

Several leading tech entrepreneurs have voiced their concern about the pervasive influence of greed in today's society. Craig McCaw, the telecommunications mogul, argues that greed has become a kind of cancer, corroding the fabric of the new economy. "When greed becomes this prevalent," he says, "something bad always happens."[1] In a recent article in *Fast Company,* Jim Collins wagged a deploring finger at all the young entrepreneurs who are rushing to take their companies public and strike it rich. The best-selling author of the book *Built to Last,* Collins indignantly asked, What happened to the early new-economy ideal of making better products and lasting companies so that the world would be a better place? Collins implied that the younger generation had simply lost its sense of higher purpose. All you greedy capitalists care about, he complained, is making a bunch of money![2] These concerns were echoed in *The Wall Street Journal* by Kim Polese, founder of Marimba. "I worry about the greed factor," she said. "The entrepreneurial common wisdom is that the most important thing you do when you're starting a company is deciding on your exit strategy."[3]

Others in the Party of Yeah are outraged by charges of greed because they see themselves as pioneers who are helping to shape a better world. Yet faced with concrete moral challenges, these champions of the new economy are often flummoxed. When critics made Nike a poster company for corporate ruthlessness and greed—accusing it of using "slave labor" in the Third World—Nike responded by hiring "storytellers" to disarm critics with touching stories about Nike's "corporate heritage" of trying to help people.[4] This is a good example of the "well-meaning but stupid" defense.

There is an alternative strategy of meeting criticism that can be labeled "no defense at all." When Ted Turner announced that he was donating a billion dollars to the United Nations, John Stossel of ABC News asked him, Why are you throwing your money down such a rat hole? Why don't you invest that money in your own company, create more jobs, and make people better off? Turner walked off the set.[5] Apparently, he could not bear the thought that his business practices themselves had socially beneficial effects.

Turner has been accused of guilt-trip capitalism—some people suspect that Jane Fonda got to him—but his premises seem to be shared by some of the market's strongest defenders. In his book *Compassionate Capitalism*, Richard DeVos, the founder of Amway, insists that entrepreneurship is a thoroughly moral pursuit. At the same time he reveals that he donates 10 percent of his pretax income to his church and charities. Again, the question arises: Why? DeVos says it's because God asks him to, because of the tithing provision in the Bible.[6] No doubt DeVos is familiar with the New Testament pronouncement that it is easier for a camel to go through the eye of a needle than for a rich man to enter the kingdom of heaven.[7]

My friend Tom Monaghan, the founder of Domino's Pizza, also feels the sting of the biblical injunctions against the wealthy. When I stopped by to see him recently, Monaghan told me he had taken a "millionaire's vow of poverty." He had sold his antique car collection. He stopped flying first-class. "I don't deprive myself of comforts," Monaghan said, "but I won't indulge in luxuries because I don't want to commit the sin of pride. I don't want material things to be the center of my life." So what's he going to do with the $1 billion he recently got for the sale of Domino's? "I'm going to give it all away to Catholic causes," Monaghan said. As to a reward for his labors, "I expect to receive that in Heaven."

DeVos is an evangelical Christian, Monaghan a Catholic. But one does not have to have religious motives to act as they do. Innumerable CEOs who live secular lives speak of the need to "give back" to the community. But if you feel you need to give back to the community, that implies the admission that you have been *taking from* the community. Across the political and religious spectrum, philanthropy seems to have become the modern equivalent of indulgences purchased by the rich to atone for their participation in the sin of moneymaking.

"If capitalism had to rely for its defense on capitalists," Irving Kristol once remarked, "the system would long ago have passed into extinction." Kristol's comment contains the implication that even if entrepreneurs are inept defenders of the system that makes their wealth possible, there is a moral defense of capitalism to be made. But Kristol's own attempt, *Two Cheers for Capitalism,* is at best a halfhearted apologia that concedes most of the right-wing case. Can capitalism survive the accusation of enriching our portfolios while impoverishing our souls? To answer this question we must address, point by point, the right-wing critique of wealth acquisition and affluence.

The first and most familiar charge against capitalism is that it is a system based on selfishness and greed. Left-wing critics such as Karl Marx and more traditional sources such as the New Testament seem to agree on the depraved inclinations of rich and successful people. Adam Smith, the high priest of capitalism whose *Wealth of Nations* first articulated the case for free markets in 1776, resoundingly affirms this indictment: "It is not from the benevolence of the butcher, the brewer, or the baker, that we expect our dinner, but from their own interest. We address ourselves, not to their humanity, but to their self-love, and never talk to them of our own necessities but of their advantages."[8]

More recent apologists for capitalism, such as management sage Peter Drucker and technology guru George Gilder, recognize the insufficiency of a defense of capitalism that proclaims its efficiencies while conceding its low and dishonorable foundations. How can an economic system based on the premises of "me first" and "greed is good" be upheld by decent people? For years Drucker has maintained that "creating a customer" is the real goal of successful business enterprise and profits are merely the scorecard of how successfully this is being done. In a similar vein, today's high-tech entrepreneurs chant in unison, "We're not doing this for the money." They want us to believe that they aren't selfishly chasing big bucks, that their motives are the expression of creativity and passion. The magazine *Red Herring*—seeking to prove worthy of its name—would have us believe that profits are the unsolicited by-product of a labor of love: "Money comes to those who do it for love."[9]

Before we are lulled into sentimentality by the sound of violins, let us ask: Aren't profits the *raison d'être* of commercial enterprises? Drucker would seem to have it backward: companies seek to win customers so that they can profit from them. Profits aren't merely a barometer of customer service, they are the ultimate rationale of the whole enterprise. True, many Internet companies forgo profits in order to expand their customer base. But they do this only because they expect to harvest vastly greater profits from those consumers in the future. Moneymaking, not customer service, remains the bottom-line objective. Without denying that many tech entrepreneurs love what they do, it hardly follows that they are doing it "for love." If that were truly the case, many of them should be willing to work for free. But when I posed this option to Ron Carney, CEO of Florida-based Tantivy Communications, he became indignant. "You don't work for free, so why should I?" His wife vigorously nodded her head, as Carney let me have it: "What are you—some kind of Communist?"

A more audacious defense of technological capitalism, one that does not rely on putting the cart before the horse, comes from George Gilder. "The moral core of capitalism," Gilder writes, "is the essential altruism of enterprise." Excuse me? What? Capitalism is based on charity? Gilder is completely serious. "Capitalism begins with giving," he says, and "giving . . . is the moral center of the system."

The capitalists of ancient society, Gilder explains, were tribal leaders who held great feasts. In addition to sharing large portions of food with others, these feasts typically involved lavish gift giving, a virtual "contest of altruism." Gilder points out that while the gifts represented an outflowing of generosity, they were not entirely "free," since the giver did expect to get a gift in return. But gifts would be appreciated and reciprocated, he argues, precisely in proportion to their benefit to the recipient. Consequently, effective gift-giving required an "understanding of the needs of others."

Excursions into the habits of the Kwakiutl Indians and other ancient tribes make for interesting reading, but what do they have to do with modern technological capitalism? Everything, according to

Gilder. For him, capitalist investments are like gifts "in that the returns are not preordained and depend for success entirely on understanding the needs of others." In the most rewarding instances, according to Gilder, "the giver fulfills an unknown, unexpressed, or even unconscious need in a surprising way. The recipient, startled and gratified by the inspired and unexpected sympathy of the giver, is thus eager to repay him."[10]

I would like to believe Gilder's account of how capitalism works. The only problem is that it doesn't describe how I got my new computer, leased my Chevy Blazer, or made any of my other recent purchases. Gateway didn't give me the computer as a present, and no, I didn't open the gift-wrapping paper, shriek with delight, and then, filled with gratitude, write out a check to Gateway for what I felt like giving those wonderful people in return. As for my Chevy Blazer, my best memory is one of haggling with the salesman, calling in the manager, walking out of the dealership, being cajoled back, and finally arriving at a price that represented the most I would pay and the least they would take. Of course it would be lovely if they had just given me the car as a gift. Unfortunately, it didn't happen that way.

Although Gilder is guilty of overstatement here, he still has a point. His point is that the greedy, selfish guy thinks only of himself, while the successful capitalist makes a profit to the extent that he anticipates and satisfies the wants, even the unexpressed wants, of others. This allows Gilder to claim, correctly, that under capitalism "the good fortune of others is also finally one's own."[11] It is a point often overlooked by the critics of free markets. But it does not solve the problem of the intention of the capitalist, which has always been, is, and always will be to benefit himself and make a profit.

The indispensability of self-interest as a driving force behind business has led other defenders of capitalism, such as philosopher Ayn Rand, to proclaim selfishness itself as a virtue. Rand's book *The Virtue of Selfishness* is a candid celebration of self-interest and greed. Posing to herself the question why she would use a word like "selfishness" in her title, Rand replies, "For the reason that you are afraid of it." Rand's advice is: Be not afraid. For Rand it is altruism that is shameful and unethical, clear evidence of "the arrested moral development of mankind."

The reason for Rand's hostility to altruism is that it frequently militates against man's survival, his pleasure, and his happiness. In Rand's hedonistic philosophy it is rational and moral for us human beings to be concerned with our own interests, and we should be concerned with the welfare of others only to the degree that it gives us pleasure. Even love and friendship, Rand argues, are nothing more than "the spiritual payment given in exchange for the personal, selfish pleasure" that we derive from other people. Consequently Rand finds herself positively enthusiastic about selfishness as the ground of human happiness. "The attack on selfishness," Rand writes, "is an attack on man's self-esteem."[12]

This is a weird and unpleasant doctrine, and indeed Rand was a weird and unpleasant woman. Her intelligence, however, is not in doubt, and the failure of both Gilder's and Rand's attempts to vindicate capitalism morally show that the free-market system has a real problem in answering the charge of avarice. Ultimately, I don't think we can do better than Adam Smith's own analysis, albeit a fuller analysis than is contained in the single quotation given above. For what Smith affirms, with an attentive eye to both sides of the issue, is the moral paradox at the center of entrepreneurial activity.

Smith does not regard self-interest as a virtue. On the contrary, in his book *A Theory of Moral Sentiments*, Smith makes a surprising assertion: "To feel much for others, and little for ourselves, to restrain our selfish, and to indulge our benevolent, affections, constitutes the perfection of human nature."[13] Smith asserts that our deepest moral impulses express themselves in natural feelings of sympathy for others, especially those who are suffering. Morality, Smith argues, consists of putting ourselves in the place of an imaginary "impartial spectator" and then acting in a given situation as this voice of conscience dictates. The importance of this argument is that it shows Smith's recognition that morality is not based on self-interest; indeed, it involves transcending and even repudiating self-interest.

How, then, did this advocate of sympathy and conscience justify an economic system founded on self-interest? Smith argues that while we have a moral disposition to help others, human nature is characterized by a much more fundamental drive to help ourselves. This "uniform, constant and uninterrupted effort of every man to better his own condition," Smith writes, "comes with us from the womb and never leaves us till we go to the grave."[14] Even our sympathies move in a series of concentric circles with ourselves at the center: we care more for ourselves than for our family, more for our family than for our friends and relatives, and more for those whom we know than for those whom we don't. Indeed, we can hardly know firsthand the afflictions of strangers, and so we are unlikely to go out of our way to help them. Smith's conclusion is that self-interest, broadly understood, is the necessary foundation of a successful economy. Given the strongest drives of human nature, no other approach is likely to work.

Smith's case for the morality of capitalism is based largely on its social consequences; it has nothing to do with the virtuous motives of entrepreneurs. Instead Smith describes most businessmen as greedy and rapacious, adding that they seldom meet except to conspire against the public and raise prices. Smith's confidence lies not in the character of businessmen but in the force of competition and its effect on the behavior of people in business. Smith argues that competition is the "invisible hand" that compels the businessman to devote his energies to supplying the best possible product at the lowest possible price. So greed leads to empathy. Ironically, the businessman is driven by his motive of self-love to seek to meet the needs and wants of others. Even more remarkable, by pursuing his own interest the businessman advances the welfare of society more effectively than when he tries to do so directly.

Smith's argument that capitalism orients the energies of entrepreneurs toward serving others is vindicated by many examples from the contemporary business world. At Wal-Mart, for instance, Sam Walton worked tirelessly to develop an efficient inventory control system so that he could monitor consumer preferences and satisfy them as promptly and cheaply as possible. Customers flocked to Wal-Mart, and Walton profited handsomely. At Dell Computer employees are trained to fulfill the expectations, and address the individual problems, of customers. "We used to focus on how many calls we could take per hour," says Manish Mehta, senior manager of Dell services on-line. "Now we focus on first-time resolves—solving the problem once and for all—even if that means talking longer with a customer."[15] Jeffrey Arnold, founder of WebMD, outlines his modus operandi: "I always put myself in the other guy's shoes and think, what are they getting out of this? Name a company, and within 10 seconds I could tell you what the opportunity is at WebMD for them."[16]

The most successful entrepreneurs go beyond empathy as it is normally understood! As we saw in the previous chapter, those who develop new products not only identify and gratify people's wants, but they anticipate desires even before people have them. Think of Jay Walker of Priceline.com, who figured out that consumers would enjoy purchasing airline tickets and other merchandise by skipping the official price tag and bidding an amount that they considered fair and reasonable. This is an instance of "extreme empathy" because it involves feeling for the wants of consumers and getting there before they do.

Adam Smith emphasizes the benefit of competition in compelling businessmen to keep prices down. But he overlooks the way in which the incentive structure of capitalism regulates and even improves the actions of the self-interested businessman. This point is illustrated by an incident described by Gary Winnick, the founder of Global Crossing. While raising money for his new telecommunications company, Winnick encountered a powerful financier who said to him, "Your idea is crap and you are a jerk. I am going to bankrupt you." Winnick's reaction was rage. "If I was ten years younger I would have decked him," he says. "But being more mature, and a bit more frail, I decided to make him my best customer. And today he is."

Winnick is the type of guy who enjoys chronicling his own achievements. He is very impressed with his ability to drive a hard bargain. There is little about him that suggests that he is an altruist or a lover of humanity. He is a lover of money and success. In dealing with the antagonistic financier, however, his avarice for gain forced him to suppress his natural instinct and "turn the other cheek." So insult was transformed into cordiality, and hostility metamorphosed into a productive alliance. Winnick's ability to do this, to convert a potential adversary into a business partner, is undoubtedly one of the reasons he is a billionaire today. And Adam Smith's point is that we should celebrate this result, because through the alchemy of the market, Winnick's self-interest has caused him to act decently and to promote the public good.

"Interesting analysis," one evangelical pastor said, responding to my comments about Adam Smith. "But from a moral point of view, a complete nonstarter." Greed and self-interest aren't virtues, he argues, any more than hatred and gluttony and lust are virtues. He reminds me of the biblical warning, "love of money is the root of all evil."[17] Should we admire the seducer who comes across as a nice guy in order to get his way with the girl? Sure, he's acting decently, but that's purely tactical, and it doesn't change the moral quality of his objective at all. In this pastor's view, it is even more ridiculous to say that the practice of vice— or as many Christians call it, sin—somehow leads to virtue.

In a recent book, the Reverend Jim Wallis argues that the theme of wealth and poverty is one of the most prominent in the Bible, surpassed only by the theme of worshiping God and repudiating idols. Yet, he argues, many so-called Christians and even some Christian churches downplay or ignore what the Bible has to say about the rich. But if you take a scissors and cut out from Scripture all the passages pertaining to poverty and riches, Wallis says, the gospels are "ripped to shreds," the epistles "turn to tattered rags," and the Bible becomes "full of holes."[18]

Wallis is the editor of *Sojourners,* a progressive evangelical magazine. Interestingly, his concerns are echoed by evangelical pastor Randy Alcorn, a longtime prolife activist and champion of profamily causes. Alcorn is far more representative of "born-again" Christians than Wallis is. Politically, Wallis and Alcorn are on opposite ends of the spectrum. Yet what is striking is that in their interpretation of what the Bible says about wealth, Alcorn and Wallis speak with a single voice. In his book *Money, Possessions and Eternity,* Alcorn provides a detailed analysis of biblical passages dealing with the rich and the poor.[19]

One example cited by Christ involves the rich donors who made generous contributions to the church and the beggar woman who gave only two copper coins, worth a fraction of a penny. But Christ dismisses the value of the gifts of the rich, which meant nothing to them. Instead he commends the charity of the beggar woman, who gave very little, but it was all she had.[20] The Christian lesson seems to be that our motives count for more than the social benefits produced by our actions.

Another teaching refers to a rich man who had a plentiful harvest. "What shall I do?" he asks. "For I have nowhere to store my crops." So he decides, "I will pull down my barns and build larger ones, and there I will store all my grain and my goods." He resolves to eat, drink, and enjoy himself because he has ample goods set aside for many years. But God says to him, "Fool! This very night your soul is required of you, and the things you have prepared, whose will they be?" Thus, the Bible tells us, is the fate of those who are attached to earthly things instead of being spiritually rich.[21]

These examples are from the New Testament. The Old Testament has a somewhat different tone; there wealth is often presented as a gift from God and a sign of his blessing. There are exceptions, of course, leading Job and Jeremiah, two righteous men who met with adversity, to ask God why he allows good people to suffer while the wicked prosper. Notwithstanding this dilemma, the God of the Old Testament generally rewards worthy men such as Abraham, Isaac, Jacob, Joseph, and Solomon with abundant lands, crops, and cattle. Consequently, in the Jewish tradition, based on the Old Testament, wealth is generally regarded as a good thing, especially when it is deployed in a manner that benefits both the rich man and society. But the New Testament— rejected by Jews but embraced by Christians—offers a much less benign view of wealth, which is presented as a snare and a dangerous form of temptation.

Alcorn cites the story from the Gospel of Luke of the rich man who lived in luxury, while the beggar Lazarus, covered in sores, crawled around and "longed to eat the scraps that fell from the rich man's table." The gospel tells us that when they died their situations were reversed: Lazarus was in Heaven, and the rich man was in Hell. When the rich man calls out to Abraham, urging him to send Lazarus to relieve his suffering, Abraham replies, "In your lifetime you received your reward, while Lazarus suffered, so now he is comforted here while you are in agony."[22]

Biblical scholars call this the "doctrine of reversal," and there are many examples in the New Testament. Here is a snippet from Christ's Sermon on the Mount: "But alas for you who are rich: you are having your consolation now. Alas for you who have your fill in this world; you shall go hungry. Alas for you who laugh now; you shall mourn and weep."[23] It goes on like this: Blessed are the poor in spirit, for they will have treasure in heaven. Blessed are the hungry, for they shall be filled. Blessed are the meek, for they shall inherit the earth. Blessed are those who are persecuted, for a heavenly reward awaits them. Those who are exalted in this life will be humbled in the next one. The first will be last and the last will be first. You cannot serve both God and mammon. None of these teachings seems to bode well for rich and successful people generally.

Alcorn mentions another case, that of a wealthy man who came to Christ and asked what he must do to enter the Kingdom of Heaven. Christ replied that he should keep God's commandments, and the man said, "I have kept them." Then Christ said, "Sell all you have, give it to the poor, and follow me, for then you shall have treasures in Heaven." According to the Bible, the man went away very sad, because he had a great deal and could not bring himself to part with his possessions.[24] The lesson seems to be that an attachment to wealth, and an unwillingness to part with it, is a sufficiently grievous sin that it can imperil one's soul even if one lives a good life in other respects.

Many Christian clergy do not merely condemn the malign intentions that drive technological capitalism; they also deplore the result. "Don't tell me about all the social benefits produced by these selfish producers," one preacher says. "The consequence of their actions is to feed an equally selfish materialism that reduces everything in society to money and focuses our energies on getting more, more, and even more. Our wants multiply entirely out of proportion to our needs, and the greed of the consumer complements and fulfills the greed of the capitalist. What a wonderfully perverse system, isn't it? My only objection is to pretending that it is consistent with Christ's message."

One clergyman who believes that Christ would have no problem with moneymaking under capitalism is Father Robert Sirico, a Catholic priest who runs a free-market advocacy group called the Acton Institute in Grand Rapids, Michigan. "All these tirades against the rich are self-defeating and unchristian," Sirico told me. "So many productive and decent people are being alienated from the church because they are treated as morally inferior." Sirico points out that the Bible is not hostile to ownership or trade; in fact, two of the ten commandments— thou shall not steal, and thou shall not covet thy neighbor's goods— presume the legitimacy of private property.

These two commandments, Sirico says, point to an evil that is often unmentioned by those who denounce greed: the sin of envy. If greed is the natural vice of those who have more, envy is the natural vice of those who have less. Moreover, "Greed is out in the open," Sirico says. "Greed cannot hide. But envy marches under the banner of equality. It is a vice masquerading as a virtue." One of the good things about a mobile, free-market economy, Sirico argues, is that it reduces the power of envy. People see their lives improve and they see an opportunity to move even further ahead, so they are less likely to wish ill upon their neighbors or to seek to claim what belongs to others.

"But what about the question of greed?" I persisted. "Isn't it unequivocally condemned?" Sirico said that the Bible had been written in an era of scarcity, when it was presumed that the wealth of the rich had been obtained at the expense of the poor. In a sense, Sirico's argument is that biblical strictures apply only to precapitalist society. Biblical principles, Sirico says, should be adapted to today's situation. "It's not enough to have noble-sounding sentiments about the poor," he told me. "If we care about the poor, if we want to implement Christ's teaching, then we have to celebrate the creation of wealth that relieves people of the pain of poverty." Sirico prefers to regard entrepreneurs by the consequences of their actions, in keeping with the biblical principle "By their works ye shall know them."

Even on the question of intentions, Sirico defends businessmen. The Bible isn't against self-love or self-interest, he says. "Jesus tells us to love our neighbors as ourselves. He assumes that we love ourselves and that this is a good thing. He asks us to try and have a regard for others which corresponds to the natural regard we have for ourselves." In practice, Sirico contends, entrepreneurs and businessmen don't work just for themselves but to provide for their families. Sirico asks rhetorically: Is providing for one's family an immoral activity?

Sirico points out that it isn't money but *love of money* that is held to be the root of all evil. The sin, from Sirico's perspective, isn't capitalism but idolatry, manifested in excessive attachment to wealth at the expense of devotion to God. This is precisely the moral of the story of the rich man who couldn't bear to get rid of his possessions. "God didn't have a problem with his wealth," Sirico explains. "The problem was that the man had made of his possessions a god." In a similar vein, Sirico argues that the rich man in the Lazarus story found himself condemned not because he was rich but because he was uncharitable.

Not surprisingly, one of Sirico's favorite Scripture passages involves the Parable of the Talents. Christ tells the story of a master who, preparing for a long journey, entrusted five talents to one servant, two to another, and one to a third, asking each to manage his investments to the best of his ability. Upon his return the man discovered that the first servant had converted his five talents into ten and the second had also doubled his investment to four talents, while the third had buried his talent in the ground and done nothing with it. And the master congratulated the first two servants but chided the third, even taking away his talent and giving it to the man who had ten. "To every one who possesses not," the master said, "even that which he has shall be taken away. Cast that useless slave into outer darkness."[25]

This is music to the capitalist ear. Sirico interprets the term "talent" in two ways: as a monetary unit of the time and also as the various abilities that God has given us for our use. The moral of the story is that our talents and resources are ours not to hoard but to invest, so that their fruits can be multiplied. Sirico argues that God wants us to be stewards of creation, and by multiplying God's abundance we worship Him. "Turning a profit," Sirico concludes, "is not greed, it is the proper use of the gift." Sirico defines greed as an "excessive or insatiable desire for material gain."[26]

I asked Sirico if he knew any entrepreneurs in whom the desire for gain was moderate and satiable. Not many, he conceded. "Capitalism is an economic system created for sinners, not saints," he said. "Of course, human beings are selfish, but not more so under capitalism than under any other economic system." Sirico says that the churches, both Catholic and Protestant, have to come to terms with the laws of economics just as they have to come to terms with scientific laws: "We can't repeal the law of supply and demand, any more than we can repeal the law of gravity." At the same time, Sirico says, "the truths of economics, like the truths of science, are not the whole truth."

Sirico concludes on a somber note, distinctly uncharacteristic of the Party of Yeah: "Wealth is a temptation because it lures us into believing that we should orient our lives toward the goods of this world. But the truth is that all the wealth in the world finally comes to nothing, because we are dust. The poor are aware of this, but the rich are disposed to forget it. So the poor are vulnerable today, but the rich will also experience vulnerability at their death. Our solace is that the rich can save the poor, and the poor can save the rich by reminding them that they too are poor."

*   *   *

"I don't mean to disagree with anyone's religion," says T. J. Rodgers, the CEO of Cypress Semiconductor, with a grin, "but my own view is that money is the root of all good."

We are driving in Rodgers's shiny BMW, and I notice that he doesn't slow down for speed bumps. "I'm tired of all these stupid restrictions," he says. He is still wearing his tracksuit (he showed up at the office straight after the gym), and now he is taking me to the airport. The car leaps over a bump, landing with a slight crash. A little perturbed at this reckless behavior, I ask, "What about the car?" Rodgers isn't fazed: "To hell with the car." That, I tell myself, is the voice of affluence. You know you are rich when you can afford to say, *To hell with the car.*

I'm delighted to be discussing with Rodgers the morality of capitalism and affluence because it's a subject on which he's positively loquacious: "I keep hearing feed the poor, clothe the hungry, give shelter to those who don't have it. The bozos that say this don't recognize that capitalism and technology have done more to feed and clothe and shelter and heal people than all the charity and church programs in history. So they preach about it, and we are the ones doing it. They want to rob Peter to pay Paul, but they always forget that Peter is the one that is creating the wealth in the first place.

"I don't mean to single out the clergy here," Rodgers continues, "but haven't you noticed how many people freeload off the rich and then condemn them for lacking the virtues that the freeloaders supposedly possess?"

Rodgers doesn't wait for an answer: "It's simply astonishing how many people who produce absolutely nothing can go around calling the entrepreneur a bad guy. Like Sister Gormley. A very ignorant and arrogant woman. So I figured I'd zap her."

Sister Doris Gormley is a Catholic nun who wrote to several Silicon Valley executives, including Rodgers, demanding that they consider more women and minorities for positions on their boards of trustees. Rodgers responded with a lengthy, single-spaced letter in which he asked Sister Gormley to "get off her moral high horse" and recognize that the consequences of her ideology would be disastrous.

"If I started loading up my board with politically correct placeholders," Rodgers explains, "we're going to lose our edge, and our thousands of employees and shareholders are going to be at risk. This is a competitive industry. Her methods of running a business produce terrible results, reducing wealth and hurting the standard of living of lots of people, including old nuns who want to eat and be housed reasonably well in their retirement, thanks to investment earnings shared with them by productive business enterprises."

A few years ago Rodgers was approached about running for Congress. "I said, no way. No way could I do that. We have a midsized company. We're worth $1.2 billion. We've created a few dozen millionaires. We create astounding technology. We make chips with over ten million transistors on them. And we pay $100 million a year to our people, which supports a whole lot of families, houses, cars, college educations, what have you. That's more good than any congressman does, ever. So for me to go from wealth creator to wealth distributor, I would become depressed, probably suicidal."

Rodgers emphasizes that he's not defending businessmen across the board. He contrasts wealth-creating entrepreneurs with people he calls "statist businessmen." Statist businessmen, he says, "are not capitalists at all. They got their positions the way politicians do—by building the right constituencies and kissing the right people's butt. These guys are into corporate jets and all the perks of success. They are happy to lobby for protectionist measures that put their competitors out of business. These are the thieves who take their shareholders' money and give it to political causes, and then act as if they are doing something virtuous. The business magazines profile them as the captains of capitalism, but in fact they are the enemies of capitalism."

Rodgers is a great admirer of Ayn Rand; he even hired a professor who specializes in Rand's work to conduct a course for his employees at Cypress. Rodgers explains how Rand's doctrine of the "virtue of selfishess" plays out in his own life: "Money is not my prime motivator. But that's only because I have as much money as I'll ever need. So what drives me now is winning a difficult competition, reaching my goals for success, and learning. This doesn't mean I'm indifferent to rewards, although my relatively low salary may give you that false impression. My salary last year was something like three hundred thousand bucks, putting me, I believe, ass-last among CEOs of companies my size in Silicon Valley. Why do I choose to limit my salary? Because I'm a good capitalist.

"Let's say I decided to pay myself two million dollars a year. I have several vice presidents today who make $150,000 a year. They're going to tell me how grossly underpaid they are, relative to me, and how perhaps a five-to-one differential between my salary and theirs is appropriate, but not fifteen-to-one. Over time I'm going to be forced to pay them a lot more, because otherwise many of them would be unhappy and some of them would resign. So I made a decision a long time ago, not because I'm a good guy who thinks CEO pay is bad, that my own self-interest would be best served by taking a modest salary and relying on my ownership of a fraction of the company for my long-term compensation. That's an entrepreneurial view. That's why Bill Gates is a billionaire."[27]

Rodgers makes several points that strike me as important. The first is that capitalism makes people behave better than they otherwise would. Implicit in Rodgers's comments is the insight that capitalism civilizes greed, just as marriage civilizes lust. Greed and lust are human emotions. As such, they cannot be eradicated. And to the degree that greed leads to effort and lust to pleasure, who would want to eradicate them? At the same time, it is widely recognized that these inclinations can have corrupting and destructive effects. So they have to be regulated or channeled in such a way that they serve us, and society, best. The institution of marriage allows the fulfillment of lust, but within a context that promotes mutual love and attachment and the raising of children. Lust is refined, purified, and in a sense ennobled by marriage.

Similarly, capitalism channels greed in such a way that it is placed at the service of the wants of others. Destructive forms of greed, in which we seek to seize and appropriate other people's possessions, are outlawed in a capitalist society. We can acquire what others possess only by convincing them to give it to us, and the best way to do this is to give them something in exchange. The point isn't just that capitalism makes society better off; it is that capitalism makes us better people by limiting the scope of our vices. T. J. Rodgers likes to sound like a bad boy, but for all his Randian revelry in greed and selfishness, his everyday actions are the actions of a decent, productive person who is also a valuable member of American society. In the way he runs his business, T. J. Rodgers *does* stop for speed bumps.

A second point, which Rodgers makes more explicitly, is that whatever their motives, entrepreneurs are doing more than anyone else to fulfill the Bible's practical mandate to improve the living standards, and the dignity, of the disadvantaged. To pose the issue in its most provocative way, who has done more to eradicate poverty and suffering in the Third World, Bill Gates or Mother Teresa? To the extent that he has placed the power of information technology at the disposal of millions of people, the obvious answer is Gates. It doesn't follow that Gates deserves a higher heavenly perch than Mother Teresa. Still, if the moral value of actions were to be judged solely by their consequences, Gates and other tech entrepreneurs have done an awful lot of good, far more good than their detractors in the Party of Nah.

Rodgers's third point is more controversial. The rich businessman is accused of selfishness and depravity, he says, but compared to whom? This is an issue that has always puzzled me about the Bible. Both the Old Testament and New Testament extol the virtues of poverty and deplore the avarice and exploitation of the rich. One assumption seems to be that the poor are less materialistic than the rich. But is this really so? Aren't there just as many ordinary people who are obsessed with the material things they don't have as there are successful people obsessed with the material things they do have?

In my experience the very poor, such as those who grow up in the slums in India, learn to accept the little they have because they cannot envision changing their lot in life. In America, however, where wealth seems more accessible, it seems that the poor are *more* obsessed with money and possessions than the rich. Why? For the same reason that dwarves spend more time than the rest of us thinking about height! The absence of money and possessions makes the poor feel inadequate and becomes an obsession. By contrast, rich people may want even more, but they are less likely to be consumed by such thoughts.

These speculations raise the broader issue: Are the poor in a society such as the United States a more virtuous group than the affluent? Libertarian thinkers, members in good standing of the Party of Yeah, tend to venerate the rich and assure us of their enduring contributions to society. But most people probably share the Party of Nah's view that while the rich may be smarter, more talented, and more hardworking, the poor are better people because they have not been corrupted by the trappings of wealth and success. Who is right? Not surprisingly, the rich people I know are quick to testify to the moral benefits of affluence. A friend, who together with his wife runs a successful business, told me, "Jane and I have been poor, and now we are rich. We are much better people today than when we were broke." I must have given him a strange look because he laughed and said, "I know, I know. But you should have *seen* us when we were poor."

George Orwell, a strong partisan of the political aspirations of the poor, casts doubt on the poor as a moral example for society. In his book *Down and Out in Paris and London*, a firsthand account of low life in two of the world's richest cities, Orwell gives numerous examples of the laziness, meanness, and dishonesty of poor people. To his horror, he even notices these qualities emerging in himself. The temptation to cheat other people seems irresistible. Sloth and self-pity seem to come with the territory. For one reason or another, "all day you are telling lies." Orwell's implication is that by raising the poor out of poverty we can help make them better people.

I was reminded of Orwell recently when, on a visit to San Francisco, I stopped at the intersection of Market Street and Powell Street to play chess against the bums. The bums are dirty and disheveled, but they are good chess players. They play against the tourists for small bets, typically between $2 and $5 per game. I am no Gary Kasparov, but I am a decent enough player that I can usually give the bums a fair game. This time I took on one particularly sorry-looking fellow for a $2 bet. I blundered in the opening moves, promptly resigned, and paid him my $2. Emboldened, he suggested we play the next game for $5. This time I settled down, found my stride, and fifteen minutes into the game I was measurably ahead. "I'll be right back," my opponent excused himself. "I have to take a crap." He made his way to the rest room of a nearby hotel visible from the street.

I waited for him, studying the position and contemplating my forthcoming triumph. After several minutes of waiting, a bystander alerted me to the obvious. "There's no point waiting. He isn't coming back." Uh-oh. I should have expected something like this. I guess I was naïve, because taking off to avoid paying my bet isn't something I would have considered doing. Admittedly, my virtue was largely made possible by my means. To me, how could you be such a jerk for a mere $5? To him, $5 was probably a significant amount of money. Necessity became, in a sense, an accomplice to his deception.

Being captives to necessity, poor people are far more likely than rich people to perpetrate certain social atrocities. For example, the poor are much more likely to resort to violent behavior than the rich. Just look at the data: poor people are ten times more likely than rich people to commit crimes such as burglary, mugging, rape, and homicide. The Sentencing Project reports that only 10 percent of U.S. prisoners had incomes exceeding $25,000 in the year prior to their arrest. Nearly 90 percent of inmates today come from low-income households and have a high school education or less.[28]

If you want to check, you will probably find that the poor indulge far more than the rich in other social pathologies. They are disproportionately found in the ranks of drug and alcohol abusers. They are far more likely than rich people to beat their wives and children. The poor have higher divorce rates than the rich. Illegitimacy is far more widespread among the poor. Contrary to what some people think, the poor have abortions at a higher rate than the affluent. Poor men are much more likely to be deadbeat dads than their rich counterparts.

None of this is intended to overlook the moral offenses of the rich, who are disproportionately represented among the perpetrators of white-collar crimes. It is not easy for a poor person to compete with the depravity of a rich tycoon who steals from his employees' pension plan or who puts five-year-old children to work in Cambodia. Undoubtedly, there are plenty of rich people who live carelessly and leave a wake of broken things and injured lives, like Tom and Daisy Buchanan in *The Great Gatsby*. We see the evidence in our tabloids, which for years have been treating us to the outrageous behavior of superrich athletes, Hollywood celebrities, and business tycoons. Flamboyant divorces, weird sexual habits, and an occasional bout of violence are a necessary code among celebrities, if only to entertain the masses. "Wealth, sex, and murder" appear to be the three ingredients for a good *Vanity Fair* story, and there are plenty of rich people to oblige. Moreover, quite apart from celebrities, there are countless examples that will never make the papers of well-off men unloading their spouses in order to secure "trophy wives" or "upgrades."

Yet if the crimes of the poor are partly the product of necessity, it must similarly be acknowledged that the offenses of the overclass are partly the product of opportunity. Donald Trump's dumping of Marla Maples, a beautiful woman with whom he had a beautiful daughter, shortly before the minimum-payment provision of their prenuptial contract expired, is an act so shamelessly cynical that few would seek to defend it. Yet after giving Maples the heave-ho, Trump, a chubby middle-aged man, was able to take up with a succession of beautiful models because his money and his celebrity made them available to him. A supervisor in one of Trump's hotels could not possibly attract the attention of a Miss South Carolina or a Miss Virginia; his hopes are more likely to descend on one of the non-English-speaking maids whom he oversees. So Trump's celebrity becomes a catalyst for his promiscuity, while the hotel supervisor's more virtuous conduct may be due to the fact that he has fewer options.

If one pays any attention to their boasting, it seems obvious that the superrich are vastly more arrogant than the poor. I can't say that Trump is representative of rich people, but it's interesting that everywhere he goes he tells people how good-looking he is.[29] He seems confident that his ability to score with top models derives from his incredible physical attributes. Other tycoons such as George Soros seem equally starstruck by themselves. In his autobiography Soros confessed to "godlike and messianic impulses" and terms his accomplishments "quite awesome."[30] Even some of the young moguls are rising in their own esteem. As Henry Nicholas of Broadcom recently told *Fortune,* "It's hard being me."[31]

Some will find this pomposity amusing, but self-importance is a natural weakness of people with well-endowed bank accounts. Consider: if you lived in a world where everyone laughs at your jokes, you too would conclude that you were extremely witty. The general principle here is that the greater means available to the rich make them more vulnerable to temptation, just as the Bible warns. At the same time, those rich people who are able to resist temptation deserve the highest credit because they have a chance to engage in vice but don't. The Bible itself notes, "Blessed is the man that endures temptation," because he has been tried and found worthy.[32]

The greater resources of the rich make temptation more affordable and insulate the rich from the consequences of their actions. These same resources, however, give the rich a chance to pursue philanthropic and spiritual aims to a degree that the poor cannot hope to match. Poor people are no less generous than rich people; in fact, they contribute a slightly higher proportion of their income to charity. Yet the income of the poor are so measly that most poor people are simply incapable of doing much social good. If a poor man contributes 5 percent of his income, he can provide someone worse off with a meal, but if a rich individual contributes 5 percent of his income he could cover an

AIDS patient's medical expenses or pay for a poor child's college education.

The problem is that many rich people are too cheap to contribute even that much. Consider the success stories profiled in *The Millionaire Next Door*. The authors have unreserved admiration for how their subjects became rich. One of their biggest secrets turns out to be stinginess and lack of charity. Those qualities are, I suppose, the downside of the virtue of frugality. In preparing for their interviews, the authors told their affluent subjects that they would contribute $300 to the subjects' favorite charity in exchange for an hour of their time. The typical response they got from people who are worth, on average, $3 million apiece: "But I am my favorite charity." Wow. Regrettably, the authors contend that these sorry specimens are representative of wealthy people in the United States.

So virtue does not seem in overabundant supply in any socioeconomic camp. At the same time, the widespread notion that the poor are somehow more virtuous than the rich does not stand up to scrutiny. Indeed, it seems that as a consequence of their condition poor people are pressured to do harmful and degrading things that they would be much less likely to do if they were well off. Thus my conclusion is that the movement from poverty to affluence represents a kind of moral progress. It is a beneficial thing for individuals and societies because it expands the opportunity to act virtuously and help others.

Finally, I want to consider here what these moral evaluations of selfishness and materialism mean in terms of human happiness. Ever since Immanuel Kant, morality in the West has suffered from a reputation of being indifferent to happiness. That's because Kant defines morality as something that we must do in obedience to our rational will, even if it makes us miserable. In today's society most people think of morality in terms of restrictions and prohibitions: "Don't do this" and "Don't do that." But as philosopher Charles Taylor points out, there is an older, classical tradition that considers morality less in terms of what not to do and more in terms of how to be and what to love. In this tradition morality is central to the good life and the happy life.

To see the truth of the proposition that morality is central to happiness, consider this: our sense of well-being depends in large part on how others see us and on how we see ourselves. We don't just want others to admire us for our wealth, we also want them to respect and cherish us for who we are. This means that most of us care about how others evaluate us morally. Bill Gates doesn't want people to think he's a rich jerk; he wants them to think he is a really nice guy. Moreover, it probably wouldn't be sufficient for Gates to fool people into thinking this about him. He wants to see *himself* this way. This example illustrates the point that our self-image and our happiness depend upon our ability to convince others, and ourselves, that we are decent human beings.

But to raise an old question that has new relevance in an age of affluence, do money and material possessions give us the good life that we seek? In the previous chapter we saw that money buys all kinds of wonderful things—security, comfort, luxury, beauty, and so on—so it stands to reason that people who have this stuff would be a lot happier than people who don't, right? Wrong, say members of the Party of Nah. And they have studies to prove it.[33]

One set of studies looks at how miserable lottery winners are several years after they collect their winnings. These winners at picking numbers or beating the slot machines typically turn out to be losers in life: they divorce their spouses, quit their jobs, invest in South African gold coins, alienate their friends, get sued by their relatives; sometimes they end up just as poor as they were before they won the lottery. These studies seem designed to produce *Schadenfreude*—a German word that means delight in other people's misery. I'm not sure they prove very much. What they do show, alas, is that some people are imbeciles who have very little idea of what to do with money.

A more sophisticated set of studies overcomes these limitations. These studies ask rich and poor people, or sample populations from rich and poor countries, to say how satisfied they are with their lives. Amazingly, they reveal that, for both individuals and nations, there is a very low correlation between increased material wealth and human happiness. This is not to say that there is no connection whatsoever. If we can trust their self-descriptions, people in rich countries are happier than people in poor countries. But not very much. Similarly, poor individuals in a given society report lower levels of satisfaction than their more affluent counterparts. But this applies only to those at the very bottom of society; after a certain level of comfort, the linkage between increased wealth and increased happiness disappears.[34]

How is this possible? How can greater wealth fail to provide greater happiness? Economist Richard Easterlin says it is because as individuals and nations become richer they are able to satisfy more of their wants, but since their wants multiply as fast as their resources, the distance between their desires and their ability to satiate them remains as great as ever. "As incomes rise," Easterlin writes, "the aspiration level does too, and the effect of this increase in aspirations is to vitiate the expected growth in happiness due to higher income." The reason for the increase in aspirations is that as we get richer, we compare ourselves to a new group of peers who have roughly as much as or more than we do. Since there are always people in this world who are richer, we always have someone to make us miserable, we can never be truly content. So we don't feel happier even when we are measurably better off. Easterlin's conclusion, a real bummer, is that "there has been no improvement in average happiness in the United States over almost half a century—a period in which real GDP per capita more than doubled."[35]

Speaking in relative terms, Easterlin is probably right. Most of us today live a lot better than our parents, yet we don't compare our position in life with that of earlier generations; we compare it with that of our peers. Based on this comparison, we probably don't feel any more content with our lot than our parents did with theirs. This relative compass of perception does not, however, take into account absolute gains that improve our lives even if we don't fully recognize them. For example, if I park my forty-five-foot yacht in a slip in the back of my ocean-view home, I might still be irked that the guy in the next slip has a sixty-foot yacht. But I'd rather be in this position than find myself driving my rust-ridden Jeep to my trailer home, only to be mighty pissed off to see that the guy in the next trailer has a brand-new pickup! Let's just say that the former type of unhappiness is superior to the latter. And the near-universal aspiration of poor people and poor countries to improve their material circumstances testifies that the weight of human experience is on my side on this point.

How, then, to account for the studies that deny any significant relationship between material well-being and happiness? An important clue is provided by sociologist Richard Sennett. While researching a book on the American class structure twenty-five years ago, Sennett encountered a janitor named Enrico and his young son, Rico. Recently, by chance, Sennett found himself sitting next to Rico on a long plane journey. Enrico had been a poor man all his life; Rico was clearly doing well for himself. Enrico had been humble, even fatalistic; Rico was arrogant and had high hopes for his career in the future. Even so, in the course of his conversation, Sennett found a hollowness to Rico's life that Enrico had not experienced. Enrico's life had been linear, coherent, it had had a purpose. Rico's was more abundant but less purposeful. And somehow Rico knew it. His outward bravado concealed a frustration and bewilderment about life that his simple father had never experienced. Sennett never puts it this way, but the clear conclusion is that Rico is better off, but not really happier, than his father, Enrico.[36]

I think Sennett is onto something very important here. Let me put it another way: my parents, and probably yours, derived a powerful sense of meaning and fulfillment in life in the struggle against necessity. They worked hard to put a roof over our heads, to make sure there was food on the table and that we were dressed in clean clothes for school every day. There was a monotony to this life, to be sure, but the battle for dignity and against degradation also provided a seriousness to life, a sense of victory over the elements, an unquestionable moral depth. But today many of us are in a situation where that struggle for existence is effectively over. Obviously my daughter will have plenty to eat and a place to live; there is money in a mutual fund for her college education; and if she needs braces or wants to take ballet, money is not an issue. I love the feeling of security, even power, that money provides. My parents never really had that. At the same time I realize that feeding and clothing my family cannot give me the same depth and fulfillment that my parents derived from taking care of us. I have to find it elsewhere.

My conclusion is that the happy life is not simply the life filled with good things; happiness also requires a life that is meaningful. I think it is quite possible that people in earlier generations who had a lot less than we do were nevertheless just as happy as we are because they had a moral purpose to life that is not as easily found today. I know what members of the Party of Yeah will say: okay, brother, let's go find meaning. But where do we start looking? And what if affluence itself is partly responsible for eradicating the moral horizons that give significance to life? If this is so, we have to find alternative horizons of significance— a daunting prospect. Before we embark on that quest, however, let us explore the sources of moral coherence that apparently once existed in America and the West but now have been largely obliterated.

CHAPTER SIX

THE WORLD WE HAVE LOST

Goodbye Nature, Family, and Community?

Will you tell me how to prevent riches from becoming the effects of
temperance and industry? Will you tell me how to prevent riches
from producing luxury? Will you tell me how to prevent luxury from
producing effeminacy, intoxication, extravagance, vice and folly?

—John Adams, letter to Thomas Jefferson

"What I'm going to do here," the poet and farmer Wendell Berry says, surveying a patch of land in the Kentucky River Valley, "is grow an old-growth forest. It will take about two hundred years, and I won't live to see it, but there will be some nice trees here if somebody doesn't cut them down." Berry is accompanied by the journalist Jordan Fisher-Smith, who observes that there are already hundreds of trees on Berry's land and Berry is able to identify each one: wild cherry, black walnut, ironwood, beech, sugar maple, honey locust, and sycamore. He knows their names, Fisher-Smith reports, "not as a botanist, but the way a country boy who grew up to be a farmer knows trees."

If you want to interview Berry, the telephone won't do you much good. Berry doesn't like using such contraptions. He prefers you to stay with him for a while and join him in chores like milking, cutting wood, and cleaning the animals. (This is why I passed on the opportunity to interview Berry.) Fortunately, Jordan Fisher-Smith, a rancher himself, agreed to Berry's terms. After their chores they sat around the dining table, sipping coffee, while Berry's two sheepdogs loitered around the back door. Berry's wife, Tanya, leaned into the room from the kitchen; she reported from the day's newspaper that funding for NASA's space program was being cut. Berry casually remarked that this was excellent news.

Later Berry led Fisher-Smith to a nearby graveyard, where several Civil War soldiers are buried, but also a number of Berry's relatives and friends: "The women tell stories about the sad things that happened, people who died young, women who died in childbirth." Berry reflects, "The old have an obligation to be exemplary, if they can, and they also have an obligation to be intelligent about their failings. The young have an obligation to remember these people and live up to them—be worthy of them." Berry says he wants to live in a world where there are no institutionalized "child care centers" or "homes for the aged." Young and old should live together and learn from and care for each other.

But that's not how it is in today's world, Berry knows. He talks about developing "a relationship with land and with place" that is very rare today. He's referring to "a settled, thriving, locally adapted community, which we don't have anywhere." Why not? Because mobility—what Berry calls "being moved around"—has become America's dominant social institution. Young people "find themselves living far from where their ancestors are buried, in unfamiliar land that they didn't grow up with and don't know much about." Having no enduring attachment to specific place and specific community, they are unable to develop a consistent moral narrative for their own lives.

Rich in material possessions, these young people, in Berry's view, are nevertheless poor in their relationships—to land, family, community, even work. "The specialist system fails from a personal point of view," Berry wrote several years ago, "because a person who can do only one thing can do virtually nothing for himself. In living in the world by his own will and skill, the stupidest peasant or tribesman is more competent than the most intelligent worker or technician or intellectual in a society of specialists."

Specialization seems indispensable to efficient production, yet Berry argues that the effect of an economy based on maximizing output is "the squandering of our natural and cultural inheritance." We are victims of what Berry calls the "most dangerous superstition" of our age, that "you can make people better by means of technological progress."

Berry says he isn't a Luddite who opposes technology per se. What he opposes is the recklessness of those who uncritically welcome technology even when it has socially harmful effects. He appeals to the wisdom of the Amish. The Amish farmers, he says, ask a single question of all new technology: What will this do to our relationships with land, family, and community? If it will enhance those relationships, they welcome the technology. If not, they eschew it.

Berry is completely serious, to the point that he refuses to use a computer, even though as a writer he knows it would increase his literary output. In an essay provocatively entitled "Why I Am Not Going to Buy a Computer," Berry outlines his daily writing routine. He prefers to write with pencil or pen; then his wife types his work on a Royal standard typewriter "bought new in 1956 and as good now as it was then." Berry says a computer would cost "more money than I can afford, and more than I wish to pay to people whom I do not admire."

But for him the expense is more than monetary. He doesn't want to get rid of the "old model—the old model in this case being not just our old Royal standard, but my wife, my critic, closest reader, fellow worker." Some may say that Berry has turned his wife into a lowly stenographer—a human tool—but the Berrys view it differently. They say they have developed a working relationship, a productive intimacy, that would be eroded if Wendell Berry switched to the latest model from IBM or Compaq.

Berry understands that he cannot re-create the world that has been lost. What he's trying to do is re-create it in miniature; he wants to live the life of a local farmer who preserves the natural and moral ecology, and he wants to encourage others to inhabit self-reliant communities and develop long-term relationships to place and people. Berry knows this is not a cost-free move. It means doing local work, such as being the manager of a hometown credit union, instead of seeking opportunity in a global market. It means eating the local food, whether it's corn, crabs, or catfish. It also means combating the narrow-mindedness and xenophobia that are inevitable features of parochial environments.

Despite these limitations, Berry is convinced that his philosophy—rooted in principles of local economy, neighborliness, family commitment, and stewardship of land—promises to restore our moral horizons and thus enhance human happiness. Berry's advice to people on the move is simple: "Stop somewhere! Because you can't recover what's lost.

You just have to start again. What people have to experience is the knowledge and understanding and even happiness that come with long association with people and places and kinds of work."[1]

Berry's arguments, and his lifestyle, offer what I consider to be the most serious alternative to the global technological economy routinely celebrated by the Party of Yeah. I must confess at the outset that I cannot see myself living like Berry. But perhaps this only means that I, like so many others, have been so warped and corrupted by the cosmopolitan urban lifestyle that we have closed ourselves off to a more difficult, but ultimately more rewarding, mode of living. I am especially intrigued by the way in which Berry combines the left-wing and right-wing critiques of technological capitalism—he is both a "natural ecologist" and a "moral ecologist"—and offers up an "alternative lifestyle" that is egalitarian and environmentalist but also family-oriented and civic-minded.

According to Berry, we are at a crossroads: we must choose either to pursue the prosperity that is promised by the global technological capitalism that is sweeping the world or to inhabit a local economy that allows us to live more harmoniously with nature, to form lasting relationships, and to live more meaningful lives. The obvious response from the Party of Yeah is, Why *do* we have to choose? Why can't we cash in on the opportunities available in the new economy and at the same time preserve nature, enjoy a wholesome family life, make friends, and discover a purpose to life? Advocates of this viewpoint acknowledge that their participation in a global technological economy involves a mobile, cosmopolitan lifestyle. This means that obviously they will have to relate to nature, friends, family, and community in a new way. But they find Berry's alternative—that people should stay in the same place, like trees—so impractical and unattractive as to be virtually unthinkable. After all, we admire the moral cohesion of the Amish, but who of us would be willing to go in for their haircuts?

In order to see whether we can have it both ways, as the Party of Yeah would like, we have to confront a serious argument, advocated by members of the Party of Nah, that traces the despoliation of nature, the dissolution of the family, and the erosion of civic and communal ties, to forces unleashed by technological capitalism itself. One version of this argument was made in the early twentieth century by the economist

Joseph Schumpeter. Schumpeter warned that technological capitalism, based as it is on novelty and change, looses a "gale of creative destruction" that uproots traditional social institutions and transforms human attachments and mores.[2] Consider how radically the steam engine or the automobile transformed rural and small-town life in the nineteenth and early twentieth centuries. Can you think of anyone or anything that has done more to destroy the mores of the heartland than the car? I can't.

While Schumpeter located the destabilizing social impact of capitalism in the productive process itself, sociologist Daniel Bell argued in *The Cultural Contradictions of Capitalism* that the problem lay mainly on the consumer side. In Bell's view, capitalism and technology conspire to produce riches, and riches foster a consumer culture. The guiding principle of this culture, Bell suggested, is hedonism, "the idolatry of the self." Bell concluded that the consumer vices produced by affluence could be expected, over time, to erode the habits of industry, thrift, and deferred gratification on which the productive success of capitalism depended.[3] In a sense, Bell's was a formula of capitalist self-destruction.

In a recent book Francis Fukuyama draws on the arguments of Schumpeter and Bell to show how technological capitalism has undermined the traditional family. The crucial event, Fukuyama argues, was the exodus of women, including mothers of young children, from the home and into the workplace. Feminists present this move as one of ideological emancipation from centuries of male oppression—a nice morality tale. But think about how difficult it would have been for most women in the past to have careers. In the nineteenth century, for example, women had no effective way of controlling their reproduction because contraceptive devices were unavailable or unreliable. Only with the invention and mass-market availability of the birth control pill during the 1950s and 1960s, Fukuyama suggests, could women contemplate a life relatively liberated from the serendipity of future pregnancies. Modern technologies such as the washing machine, vacuum cleaner, dishwasher, and microwave oven have made housework, once a full-time job, into a part-time occupation. Moreover, jobs outside the home became increasingly mechanized, so that women could now enter fields that had once been considered too physically demanding for them. Finally, the explosion of consumer products convinced more and more Americans that the domestic sacrifices imposed by mothers' working would be more than compensated for by an improved standard of living for the family. As a result, Fukuyama concludes, a great moral shift took place, and the traditional family with a single provider has become a minority lifestyle.[4]

In a recent essay called "The Spirit of Capitalism, 2000," published in *The Public Interest,* David Bosworth takes the Schumpeter-Bell-Fukuyama thesis to a new level. Bosworth argues that the acquisitiveness of capitalist production and the hedonism of capitalist consumption were traditionally restrained by strong traditions of local self-government and Protestant Christianity. These restraints have now been stripped away, Bosworth writes, so that we find ourselves in a commercial culture in which everything has been reduced to its market price, in which all other values have been trivialized, commercialized, and cannibalized. As for the higher human values of heroism, sacrifice, and respect for the transcendent, Bosworth laments that they no longer seem to have a place in a society that is now unambiguously dedicated to greedy acquisition and self-indulgent consumerism.

If these arguments seem abstract, Bosworth outlines their real-world consequences. He cites the recent case of a white, middle-class midwestern couple who left for a nine-day winter vacation while leaving their two daughters, ages four and nine, at home unattended. One of the girls accidentally set off a smoke alarm, and a neighbor called the police. The parents were taken into custody when they got home from their Acapulco getaway.

Bosworth knows that most of us will be quick to deplore the extreme selfishness and irresponsibility of this professional couple. But who are we to throw stones? Although they transgressed the permissible bounds of behavior, Bosworth says, "their ways of thinking are not that far removed from the newly emerging cultural norms" in today's America. After all, he points out, countless young children are left on their own every day by parents who are off pursuing various forms of self-gratification. How far, Bosworth asks, are our own values from theirs? Don't we too define marriage and childbearing in terms of the instrumental fulfillment they give us? Aren't we willing to jettison marriage partners who "don't work out"? Don't we frequently neglect or get rid of offspring who are "unwanted"? Bosworth suggests that all our talk about moral horizons and cultural renewal is the purest hypocrisy because it is radically contradicted by our behavior. Bosworth's unsettling conclusion is that the selfish and disgusting conduct of the professional couple is no aberration, nor is it the conduct of an aberrant segment of society; rather, it is an apt illustration of *the way we live now.*[5]

Are these dire prophets of social apocalypse right? I decided to test some of their arguments by calling Daniel Bell. I began by challenging his thesis that there is a "contradiction" built into the workings of technological capitalism. Even though Americans are avid consumers, I asked him, what evidence is there that the entrepreneurial ethic or the work ethic has declined? Bell startled me by saying that there was none. His answer, and his irritable tone, baffled me. I moved to my next question. As we talked, I realized to my amazement that Bell no longer seems willing to defend his original argument. From all indications this learned curmudgeon has defected to the Party of Yeah.

"The world is a much better place today than at any time during the twentieth century," Bell told me, adding that the so-called virtues of the past had been exaggerated by people who saw them through the lens of nostalgia. "Morality has never been in very good shape," Bell said. "Look at what went on in the port cities like San Francisco. Crime, gambling, and prostitution were widespread. The only difference then was that these things weren't publicized. We think of the old Hollywood as a decent place, but it wasn't. Things got so bad that there had to be a moral code established."

What about the values of the ethnic neighborhood that Pat Buchanan and Gertrude Himmelfarb extol? "Have you lived in those neighborhoods?" Bell exploded. "I grew up in the tenements. They were crowded, abusive, and sometimes violent. Try living decently in the middle of all that filth and noise. Morality doesn't thrive very well when people have to survive in conditions of such forced intimacy. This notion of close-knit community is a big myth. Where I grew up, there was lots of screaming and hating. Of course, the divorce rate was low, but that's only because fathers who didn't want to take care of their families simply deserted them."

Bell's new claim—that capitalism cannot be held responsible for a decline in social morality because moral communities have never really existed—surprised me coming from him, but it is hardly a novel or surprising position. Indeed, this view is widely held by many business executives who find any discussion of cultural breakdown very irritating. When I talk to tech entrepreneurs about the relationship between capitalism and social decay, they typically respond with the same visible annoyance that Bell conveyed: "Don't talk to me about that"; "It's all bullshit."

As I probe a little further, three names keep popping up: Bill Bennett, Gary Bauer, and Pat Robertson. Apparently in the tech universe, and probably in the business world more generally, discussions of social morality are viewed with disdain because they are seen as a kind of painful prelude to a sermon by a member of this trio. Businesspeople simply detest public moralizers whom they see as trying to lecture them, as well as others, on how to conduct their sex lives. Indeed, it is the influence of people such as Bennett, Bauer, and Robertson that seems to be the main factor keeping the tech community from embracing the Republican Party. It doesn't matter if this group has a correct understanding of what Bennett and his pals are attempting; those guys are seen as the sex police, and many people want nothing to do with them.

Philosopher Michael Novak is one of the few people to address social issues in a manner appealing to both parties in this debate. A round-faced man with an affable disposition, Novak is considered the most eloquent living defender of democratic capitalism. In his books, such as *The Spirit of Democratic Capitalism,* Novak argues that free markets have produced enormous moral gains. In Novak's view the free flow of goods and information has enabled millions of people to have a better life by liberating them from grinding poverty, political tyranny, and op-
·pression of conscience. Still, sitting in his office surrounded by mountains of books, Novak acknowledges in his soft, serene tone that the cultural maladies identified by critics such as Bosworth and amplified from the political podium and religious pulpit by others are quite real.

A descendant of immigrants of Slavic background, Novak, like Bell, grew up in an old ethnic neighborhood. The Catholic neighborhoods of Johnstown, Pennsylvania, Novak says, were tough and in some ways unsavory places. "I'm not saying that people lived decently then and we do not. But we grew up in a world where there was an acknowledged difference between right and wrong, so that when people fell short of that it was clear what they should do to reform their lives. Today our public culture does not acknowledge those distinctions. We pretend that they don't exist." Historian Gertrude Himmelfarb makes a similar point about the Victorian era. It's not that the Victorians were particularly virtuous, she says, but they were acutely conscious of their vices, and they struggled to raise themselves and their society to a higher standard. Such efforts are sometimes seen as evidence of religious fanaticism, but Himmelfarb notes that the Victorians sustained them in the face of *declining* religious faith; indeed, some saw them as a necessary substitute for such faith.[6] Many people today, by contrast, try to make virtues of their vices or deny that there is any basis for telling the difference between the two.

The problem, in other words, is moral relativism. "You can't hold capitalism responsible for this," Novak says. "We've had a capitalist society in America for two hundred years. Moral relativism has only become widespread in our society recently." Novak argues that capitalism is not a comprehensive social system like socialism. The economic framework supplied by capitalism is only one part of a three-part social structure. Novak argues for a tripartite system of a free-market economy, a democratic polity, and a Judeo-Christian social ethic that will help to direct democratic decisions and market choices toward morally desirable ends.

Novak argues that technology and capitalism expand our freedom by giving us choices, but it is the responsibility of parents, schools, churches, and political leaders to teach us—especially the young—to make wise choices. As a result of the failure of our cultural and moral institutions to uphold traditional standards, Novak says, many in today's society are choosing the consumerist lifestyle, valuing things more than relationships, neglecting or abandoning their children, succumbing to the temptations of promiscuity and drugs. "Initially," Novak concedes, these experiments in living outside the traditional moral framework can seem "satisfying and liberating." But over time, he says, they are "a dead end." The novelty wears off, disillusionment sets in, and what once seemed like thrilling liberation ends up producing a hollow, fractured, and unfulfilled life.

"I am an optimist because I believe that people learn from their mistakes," Novak says. He points to the recent declines in crime and illegitimacy rates as evidence of a cultural turnaround. He also argues that technology and affluence give us the means to improve our natural environment, strengthen family values, and enrich our civic lives. Finally, he makes a remarkable prophecy: "We are going to see a spiritual revival in this country, and it is going to be led by rich people. I realize that sounds odd, but it really isn't. The Bible tells us that man cannot live by bread alone. But you have to have bread to realize that. Rich people are finding that wealth by itself does not bring meaning and fulfillment, and they are starting to search for answers. In the past people came to God because they were suffering, because they were broken. But increasingly, in the West, it is going to be affluence that leads people to God."

Carl Pope is, by his own confession, a tree hugger. "As a kid, I loved to climb trees," he says. "I would wrap my arms around them and propel myself upward with my legs. I'm not young enough to do that now, but every now and then I'm tempted to try." Pope is executive director of the Sierra Club. "I feel the same way about nature today as when I was six years old," he notes. "When I'm out in the wilderness, I feel an excitement and awe that is almost childlike."

Pope became an environmentalist, he says, because "I had the experience of losing the places I grew up with. One day there was wilderness, and another day it was gone." While maintaining his determination to undo that damage and prevent further loss, Pope acknowledges that in recent years the environmental movement has been compelled to rethink its strategy. For one, Pope acknowledges that the evidence of the past few decades has been that "centralized bureaucracies do not do things well." But at the same time he insists, "Apostles of the free market have to realize that are many things that we value as human beings that markets do not do well."

Here in America, Pope says, "we're blessed to have some of the most beautiful landscapes in the world." He mentions the Arctic National Wildlife Refuge, a 19-million-acre wilderness that is home to the full spectrum of arctic life, including musk oxen, grizzly bears, wolves, red foxes, and more than a hundred bird species. The problem, Pope says, is that the oil industry wants to drill in the coastal plain, which harbors "an incredible diversity of wildlife." Pope envisions miles of roads and pipelines, massive production facilities, oil spills; in short, a natural disaster caused by human beings. The Sierra Club is fighting hard to protect public lands from what it perceives as private greed.

Or consider the northern Rockies. Pope recalls that Lewis and

Clark ventured across this spectacular landscape, encompassing parts of Montana, Wyoming, Idaho, Oregon, and Washington State. "The gray wolf is just starting to make a comeback," Pope says. There are also bison, mountain lions, and elk, and the rivers are thick with salmon and trout. "Many of the species here require undisturbed habitat to live," he notes. The problem? Agricultural development. Highways. Loggers. Miners. "We need to maintain the grizzly bear's status as an endangered species," Pope says. "We need a permanent ban on new road building in our National Forests."

Pope told me that in the years ahead the environmental movement will face a new challenge that will require an appeal not just to people's self-interest but to morality. In years past, Pope says, we have worked to convince Americans that it is worth a considerable expense of taxpayer money to preserve our natural habitats and to keep the air we breathe clean. This argument was based on asking people what they value and are willing to pay for, and it has been largely successful. But now, Pope argues, we have to convince people that their actions have consequences that are distant both in time and in place: "My choice of automobile can influence the incidence of cyclones in Sri Lanka." Will people in America and the West impose restraints on their behavior and incur costs in order to secure environmental benefits that are not readily apparent to them? Pope isn't sure, but this, he is convinced, is the next battle he must prepare to fight.

Pope has an unlikely ally in biologist E. O. Wilson, a political conservative who can hardly be accused of tree hugging or any sort of sentimentality. Wilson points out that the tropical rain forests cover only 6 percent of the earth's land surface but are home to more than half of the species of plants and animals in the world. By various estimates, Wilson says, we are destroying around 25,000 species a year. "Global warming is not the issue," Wilson told me. "Neither is the depletion of the ozone layer or pollution. Our environmental crisis is much more serious. We are in one of the great extinction spasms of history. There have been six so far, and we are in the middle of the seventh. We are the greatest destroyer of life since the ten-kilometer-wide meteorite struck the earth off the coast of Yucatán, ending the age of the dinosaurs."

Wilson argues that because we evolved in a given habitat, "that's where we are going to find mental peace, as prescribed by our genes. I don't think we will ever be able to find, or create, another setting as beautiful as this planet before we began to change it." Quite apart from its aesthetic benefits, Wilson argues that we depend on functioning ecosystems to cleanse our water, enrich our soil, and create oxygen for us to breathe. To say that we cannot create or sustain an artificial ecosystem to replace the natural one "is a massive understatement," according to Wilson. "Even bugs, weeds, and fungi have a role," Wilson says, "and it's one that we don't always appreciate or understand."

The biodiversity of the planet, Wilson argues, has proven an invaluable source of natural pharmaceuticals, including antibiotics, painkillers, and blood thinners. "We are wiping out species of plants and animals that we don't even have names for, that could be an invaluable source of scientific knowledge." If we continue to live the way we do now, Wilson forecasts, a majority of plant and animal species will be gone by the end of the twenty-first century. The consequence? "Humanity will have to wait for millions of years of natural selection to replace what we have destroyed in a single century. Our descendants are not likely to forgive us for this."

So what can we do? The moderate answer is "Live well but conserve." This is the preferred solution of most environmental organizations, as well as of Christian groups that invoke the Bible to call for "responsible stewardship" of the earth. The most influential recent work from this school is *Natural Capitalism,* written by three well-known ecologists, Paul Hawken, Amory Lovins, and Hunter Lovins. The authors want people to keep eating natural foods and recycling their trash, but they also want a basic redesign of society in order to make the world more efficient in terms of resource conservation.

Finding almost every aspect of our society wasteful—roads are too wide, cars use too much fuel, home insulation is inadequate, offices are poorly designed—the authors of *Natural Capitalism* propose ingenious solutions, such as "green cars" that get a hundred miles per gallon of gas, superrefrigerators that use 80 percent less electricity, and eco-designed office buildings powered by solar energy. Retrofitting the farms, factories, homes, offices, cars, and appliances of the world may seem like an expensive proposition, but the authors insist that it is a transitional cost that promises fantastic economic savings in the future. Written to win the allegiance of the business community, *Natural Cap-*

italism offers entrepreneurs and executives the attractive vision of a future that is not only earth-friendly but also immensely profitable.[7]

But radical environmentalists, including so-called deep ecologists, are unconvinced. If all the ambitious proposals for social redesign outlined in *Natural Capitalism* truly portend big cost savings, they ask, why haven't they already been embraced by corporate America? Hawken, Lovins, and Lovins invoke a familiar bugaboo—the opposition of "powerful vested interests"—but a more likely answer is that their solutions involve huge investments and questionable payoffs. Moreover, deep ecologists worry that even if the entire ecoefficiency agenda is implemented, it still won't be enough to prevent the degradation of the planet. Consequently, they offer a more radical solution: leave nature alone; repeal the techno-capitalist drive to conquer and manipulate the environment. Deep ecologists argue that in terms of both population and standard of living, humanity must learn to stop growing and start living like Wendell Berry. "Growth," in the words of biologist Paul Ehrlich, "is the creed of the cancer cell."

Deep ecologists argue that the entire earth—including the land, plants, animals, and human inhabitants—constitutes a single community. This means that members of the community should treat one another with respect and consideration. Deep ecologists reject the notion that land is a commodity, that animals are mere property, and that human beings have a proprietary right to lord it over the rest of nature. They are appalled by the notion of reducing nature to its property value or even its scenic value. Insects and microbes, they insist, are full members of the community, just as humans are. This view holds that in a sense, "lower creatures" have a higher position on the moral scale because they instinctively fulfill their role in maintaining ecological balance; human beings, by contrast, occupy the bottom rung of the totem pole because we are uniquely capable of destroying the ecosystem. The Unabomber, a remarkably intelligent advocate of this viewpoint, used it to justify sending mail bombs to maim and kill people whose work in high technology allegedly contributed to environmental devastation.

I cannot do full justice to this argument here, although let me note that contrary to the rhetoric of some anti-environmental groups, the deplorable violence of the Unabomber does not constitute a sufficient refutation of deep ecology. In a sense radical environmentalists such as the Unabomber are challenging the basic premises of modern science, technology, property rights, indeed of modern Western civilization. These premises will be examined further in the next chapter. At this point all I want to say is that any environmental program that subordinates the interest of human beings to other living creatures is unlikely to be implemented by human beings. What this means is that we cannot count on animals to enforce animal rights or on plants to stand up for their prerogatives. It is equally ridiculous to expect people to stop swatting mosquitoes or stamping on ants that come into our homes. Consequently, deep ecologists who wish to influence human action must argue for a course of action that appeals to our moral framework and our welfare.

But this reality gives rise to a paradox that is not lost on members of the Party of Yeah. The paradox, pointed out by Peter Huber in a recent book, is that "the rich, not the poor, are the ones actively committed to conserving wildlife, forest, seashore, and ocean." Huber's point is that the hardest guy to persuade that trees are valuable is the logger whose livelihood depends on cutting them down. Similarly, mine workers are unlikely to be sympathetic to the conservation needs of rare plants, butterflies, and animals; they would much rather feed their families and allow the earth to go on minus an endangered species or two. Environmentalists, who have already tried, know how hard it is to convince Brazilian and Ecuadorian farmers and woodcutters to leave the rain forests alone so that ecological balance can be preserved and the prospects for scientific knowledge enhanced.

Who, then, are the people most likely to respond to environmental pleas on behalf of animals, birds, and greenery? The answer, of course, is the overclass. They are the ones who value green pastures; we know this because they are willing to pay $3 million for a tiny apartment overlooking Central Park. They are the ones who can afford to eat organically produced eggs and lettuce even though such items may cost more. They probably are also the ones who make up most of the contributors to environmental groups such as the Sierra Club. Huber writes that only when well-off, well-fed people from the West show up in fuel-guzzling planes does the protection of the African and Indian elephants begin and "not a moment earlier."[8]

Not only are the rich more likely to be socially conscious than the poor, they also have the resources to put their money behind their ideals. Recently the David and Lucile Packard Foundation, set up by the founder of the Hewlett-Packard Company, pledged $175 million to preserve thousands of acres of farmland in California's Central Valley and along the California coast. What does the foundation intend to do with this property? Nothing. It wants to keep it out of the hands of developers; it wants to conserve it as it is.[9] Other foundations and wealthy individuals are following the Packard Foundation's lead and purchasing land for conservation in Colorado, Utah, and Washington State.

Huber contends that whatever the role of affluence and technology in ruining the environment, affluence and technology are today the best hope of improving it. He dismisses as unrealistic the proposal to limit growth, to leave nature alone. "Our atavistic appetites," he writes, ensure that "however much our plenty, we will hunt and gather more." Huber writes that artifice is now the best way of conserving nature. He argues that by using technology to get more food and timber out of an acre of land, we leave more room for wildlife. In his view, hybrid seeds, chemical fertilizers, irrigation pumps, pesticides, and growth hormones all increase the efficiency of land and livestock; otherwise farmers would have to graze and plow down millions of acres of wilderness to maintain the current levels of food production.[10]

Party of Yeah enthusiasts also point out that birthrates around the world are plummeting, due mainly to affluence and urbanization. Rich people in cities typically don't have enough kids to replace themselves. The yeahsayers predict that this demographic reality will reduce consumption pressures on the environment over time. The Internet, they expect, will enable more of us to work at home and read and shop online, saving enormous amounts of energy and natural resources. Finally, they promise that biotechnology and cloning will allow us in the not-too-distant future to solve the problem of endangered species; we could manufacture in the laboratory as many spotted owls, snail darters, and Bengal tigers as we want.

In practical terms, I have to agree with these yeahsayers. Their solutions promise to produce far better results than can be achieved by people turning down the heat in winter or sorting out items to recycle from their trash. I am not competent to evaluate the cost-saving proposals outlined in *Natural Capitalism,* but it seems to me that any radical redesign of our society to promote environmental objectives is unlikely. The deliberate halting of growth rates, either in the West or in the Third World, is incomprehensible. Thus our most feasible option is to employ wealth and technology to preserve nature with human tools. Even if we win this battle, however, we will have still lost something very valuable. Techno-affluence may be able to restore nature, but it cannot restore our *connection* with nature. No amount of chemical fertilizers, growth hormones, and cloning can restore our sense of living as part of nature, in harmony with it. In some sense, they diminish it. No longer are we inhabitants of the planet; rather, we have become its overlords, deciding what shall be preserved, what shall be consumed, and what shall be cast away. Even that which is protected or produced does not have the same significance as that which is discovered in nature itself. A tiger in a zoo or in a game preserve is not the same as a tiger in the wild. A landscape produced and maintained by the apparatus of modern technology is scarcely more "natural" than a naturalist oil painting. A cloned daffodil or bald eagle inspires awe, but is the awe directed at nature or at our own scientific ingenuity? William Wordsworth would have understood the problem. The deep ecologists have a point: our natural landscape may be retained, but our moral landscape has been tragically narrowed.

We have spoken about natural ecology; what about human ecology, which is to say, family and community? For decades critics of free markets have charged that technological capitalism contributes to urbanization, specialization, and mobility, all of which have had the effect of isolating the individual and to some degree alienating him from his family, his work, and his neighbors. We associate one version of this critique with Karl Marx, but it may surprise some to discover that similar concerns were articulated by the founding father of capitalism, Adam Smith.

Here is what Smith wrote about the effect on the worker of division of labor: "The man whose whole life is spent in performing a few simple operations . . . has no occasion to exert his understanding, or to exercise his invention. . . . He naturally loses, therefore, the habit of such exertion, and generally becomes as stupid and ignorant as it is possible for a human creature to become. The torpor of his mind renders him, not only incapable of relishing or bearing a part in any rational conversation, but of conceiving any generous, noble or tender sentiment, and consequently of forming any just judgment concerning even the ordinary duties of private life."[11]

Members of the Party of Yeah concede these shortcomings, but insist that those were problems of the Old Capitalism, the product of the Industrial Revolution. They are confident that the New Capitalism, driven by the Internet, will help to solve them. By contrast to the mindless tasks performed under the old economy, the magazine *Fast Company* promises a cornucopia of new-economy jobs that will not only pay well but also provide a sense of personal fulfillment. Christopher Locke, one of the authors of *The Cluetrain Manifesto,* a collection of theses pertaining to the Internet economy, remarks that "people finally have permission to be human in the context of their work."[12]

New-economy enthusiasts admit that job responsibilities, especially when they involve dual-earner families, can place a heavy stress on family life. But they argue that technology and wealth are offering ways of ameliorating these strains. George Vradenburg, a vice president at America Online, told me that "a lot of American families today live in diasporas. The Internet cannot bring these families together in physical space, but it can bring them closer in cyberspace." Vradenburg argues that technology is also making it possible for more and more people to work at home. That's good not only for women, who can sometimes combine motherhood and work in a single venue; it is also returning many fathers to the home, where they used to work prior to the separation of home and factory wrought by the Industrial Revolution. The argument, in sum, is that while the Industrial Revolution may have harmed the family, the Information Revolution will undo some of that harm.

Advocates of the new economy say it will not only benefit workers and families but also help to restore a sense of community. Jeff Skoll, the vice president of eBay, says that in the craft economy that preceded the Industrial Revolution, chairs and other goods were customized for customers, with whom the craftsman typically enjoyed a personal, not just a commercial, relationship. The Industrial Revolution introduced mass production, which was a mixed blessing. Prices came down, Skoll writes, so "now everyone could own a chair," but it was "the same chair, with no variation in design," and moreover, "the customer and craftsperson no longer had the ability to form a relationship." The Internet economy, according to Skoll, enables mom-and-pop operations to sell merchandise alongside multinational companies, and once again customers can form relationships over the Internet and order customized products. Potential customers can even exchange gossip in chat rooms and via e-mail: "What do you think? Have you tried this out? Is that any good? Can I send it back?" The consequence, Skoll argues, will be a "great global on-line town square," not so different from the markets of old.[13]

New-economy advocates hope that the Web will go beyond market relationships to facilitate genuine ties of friendship and solidarity among people. In his book *The Virtual Community* Howard Rheingold expresses the hope that "perhaps cyberspace is one of the informal places where people can rebuild the aspects of community that were lost when the malt shop became a mall."[14] Jeff Bezos defines a community as "neighbors helping neighbors" and argues that companies like Amazon.com are helping the Internet put people in touch with one another so that they can form authentic communities. Similarly Steve Case, the CEO of America Online, argues that companies like AOL aren't just money-making enterprises; they are catalysts for a restoration of community.[15]

Obviously, Bezos and Case aren't talking about the rebuilding of communities of the old sort; I can't see people borrowing sugar from their on-line "neighbors." But so what? Columnist Virginia Postrel says that while the old communities were involuntary, the good news is that the new ones established over the Internet are communities of choice. Today, she writes, people who "collect strange memorabilia or read esoteric books, hold unusual religious beliefs or wear odd-sized shoes, suffer rare diseases or enjoy obscure movies" can all find each other on the Net. The great benefit of the Internet, according to Postrel, is that "you don't have to be alone—no matter how unusual you seem to be."[16]

Physicist Freeman Dyson writes that in addition to facilitating virtual community, the Internet is making close-knit physical communities viable again. He points out that jobs in the Internet economy are increasingly portable, and this freedom to work where you live means that more people are going to leave the overcrowded cities and suburbs and return to the villages. Villages have always been sources of peace, security, and beauty, Dyson says. Now they are becoming sources of wealth. "The typical English village today," Dyson remarks, "is not primarily engaged in farming. Wealthy homeowners pay large sums of money for the privilege of living under a thatched roof. The thatching of roofs is one of the few ancient village crafts that still survives." The new residents rebuild the dilapidated churches, Dyson notes, and the church bells ring again. Of course, not everything is the same: "The old population of peasant farmers, who used to live in villages of poverty and squalor, disappeared long ago. Discreetly hidden in many of the villages are offices . . . engaged in high-tech industry."[17] Dyson's comments imply not only a craft revival but also the possibility of the restoration of community in a setting that is close to nature.

It's a hopeful vision, but is it plausible? Not surprisingly, the Party of Nah has its doubts. Sociologist Richard Sennett isn't impressed by the "flexibility" of the new economy; to him, that's a euphemism for the absence of job stability. For the past several decades, Sennett argues, most Americans had careers. From janitor to company president, they worked steady jobs, and they worked their way up in life. The word "career" in its English origins meant a road for carriages. Sennett points out that until recently people viewed their careers as "a lifelong channel" for productive activity. Of course, some of this work was laborious and routine, Sennett concedes. But ordinary labor has its dignity, he says, and "routines beget narratives" that give meaning to life. In Sennett's view, character is the product of "mutual loyalties" sustained amid "the pursuit of long-term goals."

In the new economy, Sennett writes, workers are offered "free agency" and "flexibility" but no coherent life path, no chance to build sustained loyalties: "Time's arrow is broken." The new economy offers grand promises of personal fulfillment, but many people experience instead a life like "a collage, an assemblage of the accidental, the found, and the improvised." The self is perpetually in formation; it never finds coherence or completion. For all the uplifting rhetoric about "networks" and "teams," the new-economy self makes only the most fragile and ephemeral connections with others. It is free, but free to float in a void: "To imagine a life of momentary impulses, of short-term action, devoid of sustainable routines, a life without habits, is to imagine indeed a mindless existence."[18]

I agree with Sennett that efforts to find an enduring life purpose in the fast-changing new economy are likely to fail. The error here is the assumption that work is the venue for discovering one's purpose in life.

Most people, now as in the past, would be quite happy to find jobs that pay well and give them a sense of doing something productive. I don't see why today's workplace cannot fulfill this aspiration better than its predecessor. So Sennett holds the new economy to an unfair standard, while showing himself to be overly sentimental about the old one.

Sure, most people were loyal to their bosses in the past, not because they felt a sense of devotion or attachment but because they had no other choice. Stock options were extremely rare; workers had pension plans that shackled them to the company. No doubt many lost interest in their jobs but kept showing up for work, waiting for the clock to strike five, waiting for the weekend, waiting for retirement. Today, by contrast, companies must compete to hire and retain good workers. Many workers are offered options so that they can act like owners of the company. To prevent others from being lured away, they must be given good wages, good benefits, and a pleasant work environment. Companies do not achieve loyalty through long-term acquiescence; they must earn loyalty. How can this be regarded as a bad thing?

Clearly, the new economy places some difficult strains on family life. In particular, the grueling hours invested in their jobs by tech entrepreneurs and others cannot be regarded as good for their relationships with their spouses and children. Many start-ups are headed by young men who are single, so family is not an issue. But successful business executives who are married and have kids usually subordinate their home life to the requirements of staying on top. "I'll never know my kids as well as most people," confesses Scott McNealy of Sun Microsystems.[19] Mukesh Chatter, the former CEO of Nexabit who now works for Lucent Technologies, spends so much time on the road that he can rarely find time to relate to his two young children. "There has been night after night of reading bedtime stories on the phone," he complains.[20] One is tempted to ask why a man who doesn't need the money chooses to travel so much. But let's remember that in previous eras successful businessmen also played a minimal role in the raising of their children; indeed in many upper-class families this task was mainly performed by servants. At least today's fathers are making the effort to participate in their children's development.

One reason it's important for parents to be closely involved with their children's upbringing is that it is harder to raise them well in an atmosphere of comfort than in an atmosphere of deprivation. Among affluent families the child-rearing dilemma has become a major topic of discussion and concern. "When I was a kid I had to wait two years before getting a train set," one successful executive told me. "My son has more trains than he knows what to do with, and he doesn't give a damn about any of them." Not long ago our family was watching our big-screen TV when the screen suddenly went blank. My wife punched away at the remote control, while my daughter, taking in the situation, coolly remarked, "Hey, it looks like we need a new TV." A couple that lives down our street was recently outraged when their little girl came home from school and said, "Mommy, why do we have only one house? Brittany has two houses."

What to do in these depressing situations? Many very rich people have hit upon a late-term solution—they have decided to limit their children's inheritance to compel them to learn self-reliance. Other affluent parents wring their hands. One of my wife's friends recently said, "I wonder if I should simply lie to my children and tell them that we cannot afford to buy them all those new toys." David McCourt, CEO of the telecommunications company RCN, says, "I think it would be very good for my kids if they lived in a modest, three-bedroom house." The problem, McCourt added, "is that if *they* live in a three-bedroom house, then *I* have to live in a three-bedroom house." McCourt has worked hard to get where he is; who can blame him for being reluctant to make this sacrifice?

While all good parents know they must frequently say "no" to their children, there is no way that the affluent will, or should, impose on their children the same scarcity that they grew up with. The parents have struggled to give their children more than they ever had, and the children are quite aware that their parents can afford to buy them stuff, so there is no point in lying. The best strategy for parents is to develop close relationships with their children, so that the good sense and responsibility previously inculcated in the young by scarcity can be developed in them through parental teaching and example. What this approach requires, however, is time to spend with the children, and time today seems more scarce than ever.

In this connection, probably the greatest benefit of affluence is that it means that both spouses don't need to work. Indeed, in the nation's most affluent neighborhoods, such as Grosse Point, Michigan, and Medina, Washington, and Rancho Santa Fe, California, few of the mothers work outside the home. These are the wives of cardiologists and attorneys and investment bankers and software developers. Their reasoning is impeccable: "Fred is pulling in four hundred thousand a year. Why should I bust my butt for another forty?" In our neighborhood I know of only one mother who works, and she sells ads part-time for an alternative newspaper. Most of the women choose to devote themselves to their families and to take up various self-improvement and social causes. Observing these mothers' relentless dedication to their children, it seems obvious that affluence has made the traditional family viable again.

Even the extended family is doing better. Cheap telephone rates make it easier for me to talk with my family in Bombay every few days. Thanks to the Internet, I can load photographs of our five-year-old daughter and e-mail them to her grandparents and relatives all over the world. Of course, I cannot eliminate the physical distance between me and my family, but my countryman Anil Godhwani did. When Godhwani sold his software company, he was able to buy four adjacent 3,000-square-foot homes in a gated community near Fremont, California, so his whole family could live in one place. Godhwani said, "It's always been my dream to bring my family together."[21]

As George Vradenburg says, technology is making it possible for a larger group of people than ever before to work out of their homes. A recent article in the magazine *Citizen*, published by the group Focus on the Family, illustrates this point. The author, Ann Morse, points out that in the colonial era families worked together in the field or making shoes or baking bread. It was a hard and rugged life, "yet one conducive to strong family bonds." The Industrial Revolution, however, introduced specialization and factories, and men started to work outside the home. Industrialization introduced a radical separation between making a living and raising a family. Indeed what we consider the "traditional" family, made up of a male provider and a female homemaker, is an artifact of the Industrial Revolution. Now, one response to this, advocated by many feminists, is that women should join their husbands in the workplace. But another, made possible by the Internet and other communications technologies, is that both husband and wife can work at home. Morse welcomes the future because it makes possible a family life that resembles the one her forebears enjoyed in the past.[22]

*   *   *

If the new economy is helping families, is it doing anything to promote community? Political scientist Robert Putnam and others have warned of a steep decline in community attachments among Americans. Putnam's famous example is that Americans don't participate in bowling leagues anymore. Some people may ascribe this to the advance of civilization, but in a recent study Putnam insists that on a wide measure of indices, community affiliations in the United States have become fewer and less robust.[23] Other scholars, such as sociologist Seymour Martin Lipset, have disputed Putnam's thesis. Lipset argues that while some forms of association have declined, others are thriving. Americans may bowl less, but pool and golf are more popular than ever. Smoke-filled card parties are out, but smoke-filled cigar clubs are in. Parents are less likely to join the Parent-Teacher Association, but they are heavily involved in various other school activities.[24]

If the strength of a community is measured simply by involvement in group activities, Lipset has a point. But according to the sociologist Robert Nisbet, simply doing things with other people does not really create community. Nisbet defines "community" as a set of relationships characterized by a personal intimacy, emotional depth, moral commitment, social cohesion, and continuity in time. In Nisbet's view, communities absorb the whole person, not just a particular role or interest. To some degree, they subordinate the individual will to the collective sentiment and moral authority that the community represents. By this standard of deep connection and irrevocable attachment, Putnam's thesis holds: unquestionably the tight-woven fabric of community has unraveled in America over the past several decades.

The real issue, however, is whether technology and the new economy will help or exacerbate the problem. Stephen Doheny-Farina argues that the much-vaunted community of the Internet is a mirage. He writes, "The society of the net isolates individuals. Once we begin to divorce ourselves from geographic place and start investing ourselves in virtual geographies, we further the dissolution of our physical communities."[25] Doheny-Farina's premise is that authentic community requires a sense of place, of belonging. How can you call a thousand guys sitting alone in their computer rooms typing away a "community"? Far from healing the breakdown of traditional communities, Doheny-Farina warns us, the Net will further isolate us from one another.

Is this true? I've been visiting various Web sites that promise "relationships" and "community," and I must confess that these concepts take on a strange new meaning on the Web. First, I visited Multi-User Dungeons and game sites such as Ultima Online, where players take on virtual identities, live in virtual homes, hold virtual jobs, and even marry and have virtual families, all while performing feats such as killing dragons and each other. Some of these environments are quite realistic: you can stop in the tavern and play a game of checkers or listen to hoof-beats as a troop of armed knights thunders toward your castle. Many people find these sites addictive. That's the only explanation for why otherwise reputable people—engineers, computer scientists, and so on—can spend hours a day living out a virtual existence as a dragon slayer or a captain on an interplanetary voyage.

While on-line I briefly encountered a king, the monarch of Talossa. Don't look for it on the map; it exists only in cyberspace. Even so, Talossa issues its own passports, its own money, and its own edicts. Tired of being a nobody in Peoria? Then perhaps you should join the nobility of one these cyberkingdoms. The top spot is usually taken, but perhaps there are still openings for a cyberknight or cyberduke. As for the king of Talossa, he is thirty-four-year-old Robert Ben Madison, whose real-world headquarters are considerably more mundane. He lives with his father and sister in Madison, Wisconsin. The only furniture in his study is a swivel chair and a computer. But in cyberspace, he becomes King Robert. He is an absolute ruler, at least as far as his cyber-subjects are concerned. He pretends to give orders, and they pretend to follow them.

Somehow I don't think Nisbet would call this "community." Next I checked out some romantic sites, where the main challenge; faced by members of the male sex, involves finding and conversing with female partners. Part of the problem is that the number of men seeking to meet women on the Web greatly outnumbers the number of women seeking to meet men. Men are also reputed to make clumsy on-line overtures that scare away women. The best strategy for a man trying to strike up a conversation with a woman, I was told by a veteran of these sites, is to pretend to be a woman by assuming a female name such as "Stacy" or "Hotchick." The only problem with this strategy is that most of the women you meet turn out to be men in virtual disguise. Since you can't see or hear the person you're talking to, the Net permits this fluidity of sex roles. There are even sites where you can assume the virtual identity of furry beasts, cannibals, and so on; it seems safe to assume that the regular inhabitants of such "communities" are terminal weirdos whose online obsessions can be justified only on the ground that they might otherwise devote their time to dissecting animals or stalking people.

There are, of course, sites where a regular group of people assemble to chat and joke and argue with one another. The best description of a genuine on-line community I have read is Howard Rheingold's *The Virtual Community.* Unfortunately the community that Rheingold describes, "The Well," no longer exists. Set up by a group of San Francisco Bay Area activists, the Well attracted a thriving, mostly West Coast–based following for eight years. These were people into Michel Foucault, the Grateful Dead, and alternative lifestyles. They were a diverse, even outlandish, bunch, but they did have quite a bit in common, if only their outlandishness. Consequently, they became very attached to one another, and these online connections spilled over into face-to-face contacts. Rheingold attended real-life Well marriages, Well births, even a Well funeral. At one Well party, he writes, "I looked around at the room full of strangers. I had contended with these people, shot the invisible breeze around the electronic watercooler, shared alliances and formed bonds, fallen off my chair laughing with them, become livid with anger at some of them. But there wasn't a recognizable face in the room. I had never seen them before." As Rheingold recognizes, "The Well felt like an authentic community to me from the start because it was grounded in my everyday physical world."[26]

To the extent that it facilitates real-world interaction, the Web is clearly a catalyst for building community. We should not expect cybercommunities to do the work that real-world communities do; they cannot. To the degree that people immerse themselves in cyberspace, there is the danger that they will become disconnected from the people around them. But Doheny-Farina and others who issue this warning seem to have forgotten that the original cyberspace tool, the telephone, supplemented direct interaction; it did not replace it. Moreover, many of the communities made possible by the Web would not otherwise exist. The Web can connect people who study ancient Persian poetry, people who play chess, people in wheelchairs, people who like to listen to Jim Croce, in other words, people who have little in common with their neighbors but on-line can find soul mates who share their passions.

Admittedly, this argument for chosen affiliations cuts both ways. If chess aficionados and Melville scholars can share intelligence through the Web, so can racists and Nazis and child molesters. It's a mixed blessing to say, "The Web brings people together," especially when you contemplate pedophiles exchanging intelligence on where they can find young prey. Comedian Richard Jeni is not being entirely facetious when he says, "No matter what kind of a twisted sexual mutant you happen to be, you've got millions of pals out there. Type in, 'find people that have sex with goats,' and the computer will say, 'specify what type of goat.'"[27]

There is a second downside to the prospect of "voluntary lifestyles": they tend to restrict our associations to those who are most like us. C. S. Lewis once said that one of the great benefits of involuntary communities—and this includes the family—is that they enable us to discover the virtues of people whom we might never have chosen to hang out with. Lewis's point is repeatedly confirmed through experience: the annoying fellow who happens to be your neighbor or your brother turns out to be a very loyal person or a deep thinker or extremely empathetic in relating to old people. Over time you build a relationship that under other circumstances would never have developed. If our affiliations, both on-line and in the real world, are entirely voluntary, we risk shutting ourselves off from the broader range of human experience.

So where does this leave us? The old communities that many people long for were built on ethnic affiliation and scarcity: people banded together to face the challenges of the outside world. In an era of cosmopolitanism and affluence, there is no way of getting those neighborhoods back. Nor do I think that cyberspace will compensate for the loss; the relationships it fosters are too thin, too ephemeral. Nor is it always easy to translate cyberspace meetings into real-world relationships: the common experience seems to be that the sexy young thing with whom you've been flirting via e-mail turns out to be somewhat older and somewhat more obese than the picture on her home page led you to suspect. But there is one reason to be optimistic. If Freeman Dyson is correct—and only time will give us the answer—affluence and the Internet will liberate more and more people from a life chained to their jobs, and they will be free to migrate to villages or form communities where they can enjoy lasting associations.

CHAPTER SEVEN

A FUTURE THAT WORKS

Why Techno-Capitalism Prevailed

There are few ways in which a man is so innocently occupied than in getting money.

—Samuel Johnson

The last few chapters have, I hope, shown clearly the rift that has developed between the Parties of Yeah and Nah. On the surface, these are two contemporary groups who vehemently disagree over whether the new affluence and new technologies will enhance or diminish our lives and our society. When we probe a little further, however, we discover that this is an argument with much deeper roots. It is a fundamental clash over the principles that have shaped the modern West and that are at the core of America. While the current debate focuses on new wealth and the new technologies, the schism between the Parties of Yeah and Nah goes back to the two institutions—capitalism and science—that have generated this techno-affluence.

Recently *Wired* magazine featured a debate on the merits of our technological society between techno-utopian Kevin Kelly and self-proclaimed neo-Luddite Kirkpatrick Sale. Here is an excerpt from their exchange:

Kelly: You did smash a computer recently, right?

Sale: I did.

Kelly: I hope it made you feel better.

Sale: It was astonishing how good it made me feel. . . . This was a statement better than anything else I could possibly say.

Kelly: Other than arson and a lot of vandalism, what did the Luddites accomplish in the long run?

Sale: The Luddites established themselves as the symbol of those who resist the new technologies and demand a voice in how they are to be used.

Kelly: Where . . . do you think the hundreds of millions of jobs in America in the last 100 years have come from? They certainly didn't come from farming or handicrafts.

Sale: The idea that the whole end of life is jobs and job creation is pathological. The question is, what do those jobs achieve and at what expense? A job in itself is not a virtue.

Kelly: The Luddite cottagers thought it was inhuman to be put out of work by machines. But what's really inhuman is to have cloth made by human labor at all. Making cloth is not a good job for humans.

Sale: They didn't think so. Nor do I. Nothing is superior to handicrafts.

Kelly: The point of technology is to make higher-quality and more diverse products than we can make by hand. . . . We have technology to make things we could not make in other ways.

Sale: I regard that as trivial.

Kelly: What was the effect of printing technology? It increased literacy. It allowed more varieties of books to be written, and faster. It allowed better communication.

Sale: At the same time, it destroys oral traditions and oral abilities. So let's not simply say how wonderful literacy is, without saying what the price is. The truth is that we are reading little of merit.

Kelly: I would say that in oral traditions, there was very little of merit said. There is this tendency to think that the old things, the old times, the oral traditions, the tribal traditions, were somehow more lofty. . . . This is complete nonsense.

Sale: If we lose oral tradition and all that goes with it, we lose a due regard for nature and the preservation of nature. The successive empires that have driven civilizations for the last 6,000 years have had, almost uniformly, no regard for nature.

Kelly: Do you see civilization as a catastrophe?

Sale: Yes.

Kelly: All civilizations?

Sale: Yes.

Kelly: The downsides of tribal life are infanticide, tribal warfare, inter-tribal rape, slavery, sexism. Not to mention a very short life span, perpetual head lice, and diseases. Is that what you want?

Sale: What you are describing are tribal societies that have become pathological because of the invasion of some outside force. In the case of the American Indians and of Africa, it's the Europeans.

Kelly: I'm very glad not to be living in a tribal society.

Sale: Don't dismiss the virtues of that society. The sense of comrade-ship and inner peace and harmony that we know happens in these societies is not to be lightly dismissed.

Kelly: So what would be a measure of a successful human culture?

Sale: That it's able to exist in harmony with the rest of nature.

Kelly: I totally reject that. It's not enough.

Sale: Not enough?

Kelly: Naked existence is for animals. That's basically all that animals do: they exist in harmony with their surroundings.

Sale: And what's wrong with that?

Kelly: Plenty. We left that phase eons ago.

Sale: Your optimism is contrary to all history up to the present, which suggests that given the values and norms of our particular civilization, we will perfect technology to the task of exploitation and destruction of nature. . . . My optimism is based on the certainty that this civilization will collapse.[1]

This is an astonishing exchange. Sale's position is all the more intriguing—and hard to fathom—when you discover that he lives in New York City. Kelly's bewilderment in encountering such a peculiar person and such a peculiar point of view are palpable. Throughout the interview Kelly sputters things such as, "Do you really believe that?" "How can you be such a hypocrite?" I will not defend Sale against the charge that he is living in the Stone Age. But then, neither would he. He is an apologist for what may be termed the Stone Age lifestyle. Most striking of all, he is an intelligent apologist for it. Frequently, Sale seems to have the rhetorical advantage because he knows exactly where Kelly is coming from, whereas Kelly seems utterly mystified about Sale's position. Kelly keeps citing examples of "progress" that Sale does not regard as progress at all. To Sale, Kelly is a deluded techno-maniac; to Kelly, Sale is a deranged lunatic.

I cite from this exchange at some length because it dramatically illustrates the complete breakdown in communication between the champions and critics of techno-affluence. For Kelly, as for his fellow members of the Party of Yeah, the "good old days" were pretty awful. In their view, the past was a long and dreadful tale of people living in mud huts, eating dirt, taking slaves, slaughtering people, and then dropping dead themselves. The Party of Yeah lives for the future. Its optimism derives from the certainly that increased affluence and new technology will make the future better than the past in every way. By contrast, the Party of Nah locates its golden age in the past; since then, it sees precipitous and uninterrupted decline.

Of course, naysayers may disagree about which past they are talking about. For Robert Bork and Patrick Buchanan, it was probably the 1950s, when Ike was president, Mom stayed home, and you didn't have to lock your door at night. For Richard Sennett, it was the New Deal era, when politicians and unions worked together to ensure steady jobs. For the Southern Agrarians, it was the early twentieth century, when the South was still an agrarian society. For Gertrude Himmelfarb, it was the Victorian era, when prosperity was accompanied by social morality. For some Catholic philosophers, it's the thirteenth century A.D., when people lived for the afterlife and Thomas Aquinas strolled the hallways of the University of Paris. For those who admire the classical era, it was the fifth century B.C., the heyday of Greek thought. And for radical environmentalists such as Kirkpatrick Sale, the golden age was 10,000 B.C., before the earth was corrupted by the rise of civilization.

So the date varies, but the theme of the Party of Nah remains the same: Things used to be so great, but they've really gone downhill since the computer was invented, or since women started working, or since the South became like the North, or since the rise of cities, or since the Reformation, or since the invention of the wheel. Members of the Party of Yeah mercilessly ridicule these sentiments and seek to contrast the rhapsodic invocations of the past with unpleasant realities such as recurrent toothaches that are somehow forgotten in the rhetoric of nostalgia. The naysayers acknowledge the relief of suffering produced by modern medicine, but they counter that the gains produced by science and capitalism have been unaccompanied by moral progress; indeed, material advancements seem to have accelerated moral decay. The yeah-sayers insist that material and moral progress go hand in hand: they are fond of citing psychologist Abraham Maslow's dictum that only when a man has food in his stomach is he capable of attending to higher aspirations, such as pursuing spiritual meaning or inquiring into the purpose of his life.

Who is right? To answer this question, we must uncover the historical origins of the Parties of Yeah and Nah. These origins are best understood in the context of a puzzle observed by the sociologist Max Weber.

Weber was reading the works of Benjamin Franklin when he discovered something quite remarkable. Franklin, the archetypical American, is a new type of person created by a new type of society. He is charming, open-minded, honest, industrious, frugal, curious, inventive, and optimistic. At the same time, he comes across as cunning, ambitious, self-interested, avaricious, this-worldly, and pleasure-seeking. Franklin confesses that he used to visit prostitutes when he was younger; now he avoids them. But his abstinence is not based on religious or moral principle; rather, he worries about contracting diseases and about the considerable inconvenience and expense involved.[2] Franklin's modesty and humility, such as they are, seem largely aimed at ingratiating himself with others and securing his reputation. In short, for all his affability and ingenuity, here is one cunning self-promoter.

But what is most incredible is that Franklin views himself as a thoroughly upright fellow. His goal, he announces in his *Autobiography*, is nothing less than "moral perfection." He presents his character traits as virtues and himself as a model citizen. Weber asks: How could such capitalist traits as shrewdness, calculation, inventiveness, ambition, and self-interest, develop out of a civilization that for more than a thousand years condemned these traits as base and sinful? Another way of asking the question is: Why did capitalism develop in the West, and specifically in the Protestant West, and not elsewhere? Weber's inquiry can be deepened by extending the investigation to technology: Why have the vast majority of technological inventions in the past three centuries occurred in the West? How did America, a very new country on the world stage, move so quickly into the forefront of technology, and why does it continue to lead every other nation in discovery and innovation?

I will not discuss in detail Weber's answer to the question, which is inadequate. Basically, Weber argued that capitalism developed in the Protestant West because John Calvin's doctrine of predestination was misunderstood by ordinary Protestants who thought that if they were successful in this life it was a sign that they were favored by God for salvation in the next one. Consequently, in Weber's view, Protestants developed a strong work ethic and free markets, and these institutions retained their vitality long after their theological foundations were abandoned or lost their public force. Weber's thesis remains controversial among scholars, and rightly so. What evidence did Weber produce that millions of ordinary Protestants so totally misunderstood the basics of their faith that they confused their bank balances with their prospects for inclusion in the heavenly kingdom? In truth, he produced none.[3]

But Weber's question remains a good one. Many members of the Party of Yeah tend to assume that the premises of capitalism and technology—the quest to better our condition through trade and the desire to make better tools—are universal human aspirations and, as such, have provided the guiding impetus for all societies at all times. It comes as something of a shock for partisans of this view to discover that the great thinkers of the ancient world, not only in the West but also in other cultures, were virtually unanimous in spurning the technological innovator and regarding the trader as a lowlife and a scum.

To understand these sentiments, we must say good-bye to our surroundings and make an imaginative leap to understand a world that is radically different from our own. Let's begin with ancient Greece. As one scholar puts it, "We must imagine houses without drains, beds without sheets or springs, rooms as cold or as hot as the open air, meals that began and ended with pudding, and cities that could boast neither gentry nor millionaires. We must learn to tell time without watches, to cross rivers without bridges, and seas without a compass, to fasten our clothes with two pins instead of rows of buttons, to wear our shoes or sandals without stockings, to warm ourselves over a pot of ashes, to judge open-air plays or lawsuits, to study poetry without books, geography without maps, and politics without newspapers."[4]

Yet this poor, technologically backward society was able to produce, several centuries before Christ, the greatest range of philosophical wisdom the world has ever known. In addition to great thinkers such as Socrates, Plato, and Aristotle, Athens also produced great political leaders such as Pericles, great historians such as Herodotus and Thucydides, great mathematicians such as Pythagoras and Archimedes, great poets such Homer and Hesiod, and great playwrights such as Aeschylus, Sophocles, Euripides, and Aristophanes. These Greek figures by themselves refute the notion that ancient people were a bunch of primitive barbarians. Yet these men were part of a consensus of great minds in antiquity that regarded the trader and the craftsman as objects of contempt, and Hannah Arendt tells us that the finest Greek sculptors and architects were "by no means excepted from the verdict."[5]

Aristotle says that in a decent society craftsmen and traders would not be granted citizenship. Plato in his *Laws* calls for citizens who engage in commerce to be punished. Lycurgus, the legislator of Sparta, implemented these provisions by completely banning trade in a republic that was considered by many Greek thinkers to be a model for the ancient world. Dante assigns the qualities that motivate the Benjamin Franklin type—ambition, desire for power, and avarice—to the bottom rungs of Hell. Speaking from the non-Western cultures, Confucius offers a typical assessment: "The gentleman understands what is moral. The small man understands what is profitable."[6] In general the ancients held that the best way to acquire wealth was through inheritance and that even wealth obtained through conquest and plunder was more honorable than wealth obtained through production and trade.[7]

The ancients spent little time on, and in general took a dim view of, technological innovation. Archimedes was the greatest technologist in Greece. Plutarch writes of Archimedes that he held the "science of inventing and putting together engines, and all arts generally speaking which tended to any useful end in practice, to be vile, low and mercenary." As a result, "he spent his talents and his studious hours in writing only of those things whose beauty and subtlety had in them no admixture of necessity." Since the ancients didn't care about utility, many inventions that occurred serendipitously or promised military benefit were disregarded. Once again Plutarch is revealing: in his *Moralia* he narrates an incident in the fourth century B.c. involving the Spartan king Archidamus, who was preparing for battle when he was shown a new military invention, a catapult that could launch projectiles into the ranks of the enemy. Archidamus was impressed but said he would not be employing the new technology. Why not? Because if such contraptions began to be used, Archidamus swore, "manly virtue will perish from the earth."[8]

You may think Archidamus was a bit of a nut, but that's only a failure of imagination on your part. Archidamus understood that the new technology would destroy the basis of Spartan society. The whole regimen of Sparta was based on cultivating a spirit of martial courage and esprit de corps among its citizens. Children were separated from their families at birth and raised in the equivalent of military boot camps. Their education and training were directed toward a single purpose: fighting alongside their comrades in land-based combat in defense of the fatherland. Spartan society was oriented toward fostering heroism in defense of country, to the extent that when the Spartans lost a battle—and they rarely did—the mothers who wept on the battlefield were those whose sons were still alive. The mothers of the dead rejoiced because their sons had achieved eternal honor and glory in Sparta by refusing to retreat even in the face of certain defeat.

Many of the great figures of the ancient world, such as Plato, Xenophon, and Thucydides, admired Sparta because it sought the cultivation of the virtues of martial courage and selfless devotion to the public good more strenuously than any other society. The Spartan regime was exalted by the ancients for doing precisely the thing that many of us would find deplorable: it subordinated all personal and even family attachments to the greater good of the fatherland. To us, Spartan policy may seem a blatant violation of liberty, but the ancients didn't see it that way. Sparta was a republic. The society was governed by ephors elected by, and accountable to, the people. Indeed, the citizens in ancient republics like Athens and Sparta had a much more direct hand in deciding the policies of their society than citizens in modern democracies do. This ability to shape the public life of society is what the ancients meant by liberty, and it's a very different understanding of liberty than our modern notion of doing as we please.

The example of Sparta points to the unifying principle of the ancient world, which was virtue. The Greeks called it *arete*, which means something closer to "excellence," although it includes moral excellence. The ancient view was that the basic organizing purpose of a society should be to improve the character of the citizens. Plato sums up this ethos when he writes in the *Laws* that politics is "the art whose business it is to care for souls." Aristotle, who wrote much of his philosophy in refutation of Plato, nevertheless agreed with him completely on this point. So did Roman historians such as Livy and statesmen such as Cicero, as well as medieval Christian thinkers such as Augustine and Aquinas. Mohammed, Confucius, and the Hindu sages would all have readily assented to Plato's statement.

Not surprisingly, the ancient thinkers disagreed over which virtue was most important. For Homer it was the virtue of courage, embodied in a soldier such as Achilles. For Plato, it was the virtue of contemplation, exemplified by a philosopher such as Socrates. The Stoics saw as virtuous the man who had the inner strength to detach himself from bodily pleasures and pains. The virtues most admired in the Greco-Roman era were courage, magnanimity, temperance, and prudence. Medieval thinkers emphasized a different set of virtues, derived from Christianity: faith, hope, and charity. Other civilizations sought to cultivate the virtues outlined in the Koran, the Bhagavad Gita or the *Analects* of Confucius. Despite these disagreements about content, virtually every serious thinker in the ancient world agreed that virtue or moral excellence should form the basis of society.

One might wonder, as Tocqueville did, whether the people who lived in past times were better than people are today. Tocqueville noted that many ancient figures "talked continually about the beauties of virtue" while studying its utility "only in secret."[9] One might think that Tocqueville is accusing his ancestors of hypocrisy, but his point is that the sense of shame that kept the study of utility a secret is itself revealing. The ancients knew that virtue was difficult. They understood that the self-conscious embrace of the virtuous life would be limited to a few. If the masses acted virtuously, it would be largely out of habit, because they were taught to behave this way, or because they could not afford the consequences of vice. Consequently, in the view of the ancients, the strong supports of education, custom, and law were necessary to make people better than they otherwise would be.

The ancients emphasized the loveliness of virtue, and attempted to base their societies on virtue, because they believed that it represented the highest and noblest capacity in human beings. They held that just as man has a "lower nature" in common with the animals, he also has a "higher nature" that is unique to him, or in the image of God. Man has the capacity of speech. He can reason. He has a conscience, an inner conviction of right and wrong. He is the "beast with the red cheeks" who can feel shame. He wonders if he is part of some transcendent reality, something greater than himself. So, in the view of the ancients, the best human life, and the best society, is the one that is focused on nourishing these higher capacities and aspirations. Thus it was that ancient societies vastly poorer than our own built exquisitely ornate monuments, temples, and cathedrals where even their poorest citizens could seek to elevate their souls. Maslow's theory—that poor people are so imprisoned by necessity that they cannot pursue higher fulfillment—turns out to be historically false.

Given its lofty conception of virtue, the ancient world naturally assigned a low position to trade and technology. At worst, the trader was seen as an exploiter and a cheat, taking advantage of the necessity of others to make the biggest profit for himself. The church father Saint Jerome put it bluntly: "All riches proceed from sin. No one can gain without another man losing."[10] At best, the trader and the craftsman were seen as helping to provide the basic necessities of food, clothing, and shelter that made life possible. For Aristotle, eating, sleeping, and wearing clothes are part of the infrastructure, the scaffolding, of the good life; they are not the good life itself, which is oriented toward contemplation and participation in public life. Aristotle recognizes that for some people to have the leisure to think and govern, others have to do most of the work. This, he says, is why we need slaves. The ancients regarded the slave as a low creature who, like an animal, values survival more than anything else. Aristotle conceived a slave's function as similar to that of a vacuum cleaner or a Cuisinart. He does the necessary work, he provides the infrastructure for a society to develop and express its higher capacities.

Aristotle's view raises an interesting question: If a slave is like a Cuisinart, why not develop Cuisinarts so that you don't need slaves? This question can be more broadly stated as follows: Why did the ancients invent so little? Why didn't they develop technology? The Roman writer Seneca tells us that the most important inventions of his time were the work of slaves, because only slaves were interested in devices that made their work easier. Historian Joel Mokyr writes that during the Greco-Roman era, "many inventions that could have led to major economic changes were underdeveloped, forgotten or lost."[11]

Mokyr emphasizes that the technological backwardness did not prevail because the ancients were unable to figure out the workings of nature or make better tools. It's because they didn't attach much importance to such projects. Socrates leaves the question of the laws of nature to the gods so that he can focus on the question of human nature. Socrates' position reflects the consensus of the ancients that technological development was peripheral to the most important questions, which concerned not how well you ate or how comfortably your house was furnished or even how long you lived. Rather, the most important questions concerned the meaning of life and the meaning of death. Socrates devoted his life to asking the question that obsessed the ancient world: What is the good life, and how should we live it?

Jacques Ellul, in his book *The Technological Society,* offers a second reason the ancients ignored or spurned technology. He points out that ancient communities all over the world have seen themselves living in harmony with nature. This doesn't mean that they were "environmentalists." They didn't recycle, and they didn't talk about "saving the planet." But many of them approached nature with wonder, and some cultures saw natural objects such as stones and trees as possessing living spirits that needed to be worshiped and propitiated. Not all the ancients viewed nature as magical in this way, but in the rising of the sun, the coming of the seasons, and the cycle of birth and death, they perceived an order in nature, and they saw themselves as part of it.[12] The term "mother nature," which is used in virtually every ancient culture, is not intended entirely as metaphor.

It is virtually inconceivable that people who lived in this enchanted world, who saw nature in this way, would conceive of and launch a scientific and technological project to comprehend, control, and manipulate nature for human ends. According to the philosopher Leo Strauss, the "conquest of nature" was a possibility that had occurred to the Greeks. They repudiated it, Strauss says, not because of its impracticality but because of its inhumanity. They feared that a project to control nature would end up destroying human nature, which is to say, all that is distinctive and noble about human beings.[13]

Here, then, in the ancient world, are the origins of the Party of Nah. This group should not be seen in the purely negative context that its name suggests. The Party of Nah has plenty to affirm. Its basic premise is that the cultivation of virtue is central to the good life. Its main grievance today is that virtue has lost its loveliness, that what is highest and noblest about human beings is being sacrificed in a contemporary culture that is oriented wholly toward getting rich, collecting things, and gratifying our libido. In a moment, we will explore the historical validity of this charge. But for now let us recognize that the virtues of the ancient world were aristocratic, which is to say they were restricted to a few; they were obtained at the price of institutions such as slavery; and they were sustained in the face of scarcity and war. Despite all this, I have to confess a deep attraction to the aspiration for greatness that was the characteristic feature of ancient thought. That world is long gone, but its principles continue to beckon, and they form the unifying banner of the Party of Nah.

The Party of Yeah emerged, like a phoenix, out of the ashes of the ancient world. Its ascent between the sixteenth and the eighteenth century was accompanied by jeers from partisans of the old world, who feared that moral corruption had become widespread and institutionalized. Even then, they warned that the West was slouching toward Gomorrah. Meanwhile, supporters of the new techno-capitalist order proclaimed themselves the party of enlightenment and termed their critics apostles of the "dark ages." This rhetoric is with us still. From a historical perspective, both sides were wrong. Virtue did not succumb to degeneracy, nor was ignorance replaced by enlightenment. There are good reasons why the *ancien régime* was replaced by the techno-capitalist society in the Western world. What happened, in effect, was a moral revolution, a remaking of common sense, so that one set of values was replaced by another and what used to be considered the vilest heresy eventually came to seem acceptable, even good.

The reason the *ancien régime* became unacceptable in the West and nowhere else is because of a peculiar set of events that occurred in Europe between the fourteenth and seventeenth centuries. First, there was a series of plagues that swept across the continent, killing a third of the population. The Black Death has been called the greatest natural catastrophe of the second millennium. The suffering it caused was so intense and widespread that it virtually became comic. The comedy of desperation is captured in Giovanni Boccaccio's *Decameron*. A typical Boccaccio story involves a monk who assigned a man who came into his confessional an elaborate penance that required him to be away from his home at night while the monk carried on sexual escapades with his wife. In short, the desecration wrought by the plague seemed to bring, in its wake, a complete breakdown of morality and social order.

Then came the acrimonious splits between Catholicism and Protestantism, which inaugurated the age of the religious wars in Europe. According to the mythology of some evangelical Christians, the Catholics persecuted the Protestants in Europe, leading freedom-loving souls to run away to the new continent, where they could practice their religion in peace. The truth is that both Catholics and Protestants believed it was more important to save a man's soul than to respect his liberty to dissent. If the Catholics controlled power in one country, the Protestants there fled elsewhere, hoping to find a place where they could fine, imprison, and incinerate Catholics. The Puritans who came to America are a good example of a people who escaped persecution in order to establish their own theocracy, put witches to the stake, and persecute others. If either the Catholics or the Protestants had won an outright victory, the religious wars in Europe would have ended and the history of the world would have turned out differently. But the conflict went on, utterly exhausting the continent and convincing a number of leading thinkers that an entirely new way of organizing society was required.

The three crises faced by Europe between the fourteenth and eighteenth centuries were extreme scarcity of basic provisions and rampant disease, widespread murder and war in the name of religion, and political chaos. The European thinkers who faced these problems wanted to stop people from killing one another over such questions as transubstantiation. They wanted a peaceful society where people who thought differently about religion could live together. They decided to abandon the entire ancient enterprise of trying to base society on a quest for greatness or virtue. The ancient scheme is unworkable, they concluded; in trying to make people better than they are, you end up making them act like beasts. These thinkers decided to establish a new society based on meeting human needs and wants rather than elevating human aspirations to a higher level. Such an objective might not have been very noble, but it was attainable.

To achieve their goals, they needed to redirect people's energy from the powerful force of religion, what Hobbes called "fear of spirits invisible," to something equally powerful, and they came up with a remarkable substitute: *love of material gain*. Science, they said, would give human beings the tools to live longer and live better. Mankind would become, in René Descartes's words, "masters and possessors of nature."[14] Commerce and capitalism would distribute these benefits unequally but widely. As a consequence, a new kind of human being and a new kind of society would be created, oriented around technology and prosperity. The basic reasoning was that people who live to gratify their everyday appetites, people who live for the weekend, people who are saving up to remodel their kitchen, people who are planning a vacation—such people are not going to go around spearing one another in the name of religion. Samuel Johnson reflected this point of view when he uttered the line quoted at the beginning of this chapter: "There are few ways in which a man is so innocently occupied than in getting money."[15]

The commercial society, built on the basis of trade and technology, was designed by its founders to solve the main problems of Europe in a single stroke. It would dissolve religious conflict, eliminate material scarcity, ameliorate disease, and at the same time establish peaceful and orderly conduct between nations and among peoples. But how did the early moderns figure out that they could use the power of science and commerce to achieve these ends? How did they succeed in implementing their ideas and in convincing a population descended from Athens and Jerusalem to adopt them?

*　　*　　*

The intellectual and political assault against the principles of the ancient world developed slowly and took until the late eighteenth century to mature. Some of the thinkers who made the most original contributions to the modern techno-capitalist world view were iconoclasts— Niccolò Machiavelli, Thomas Hobbes, and Bernard Mandeville—and they stated their views in so shocking a manner that they were denounced by respectable opinion across the European continent. Consequently, the widespread acceptance of the new philosophy had to await its formulation at the hands of more cautious and prudent thinkers, such as Francis Bacon, John Locke, Montesquieu, and Adam Smith. Finally, the chatter of the intellectuals would have remained just that, had it not been for the founding of a new nation, currently the most important nation in the world, on precisely the basis of technology and commerce. ·

First, the iconoclasts. The biggest bomb thrower of them all was Machiavelli, whose *The Prince,* published in 1513, represents the first serious break with the principles of the *ancien régime.* Basically, Machiavelli says that while previous thinkers tried to conceive men as they ought to be, his philosophy is based on human beings as they are. Virtue, Machiavelli says, is a wonderful course of action for a ruler who wants to be deposed. The reality of life, he writes, is that bad men frequently triumph while "a man who wants to act virtuously in every way necessarily comes to grief." The important thing, he counsels all rulers, is to be willing to do what is necessary while gaining a reputation for doing what is just. Machiavelli praised the "inhuman cruelty" of Hannibal and the Borgia princes for sheer effectiveness. While the ancients had held that all rulers are subject to the vicissitudes of fortune, Machiavelli counseled that a ruler could through decisive action bring fortune largely under his control: "Fortune is a woman, and it is necessary, if one wants to hold her down, to beat and strike her."[16]

Machiavelli wrote nothing about capitalism or technology. His intellectual innovation was to abandon the ancient project of making the moral improvement of human beings the basis of society. He wanted nothing, he said, of "imaginary republics and principalities which have never in truth been known to exist."[17] His politics sought to steer human behavior onto low but firm ground by manipulating elemental human passions, such as greed and fear. Machiavelli's critics, mostly senior statesmen of the Party of Nah, denounced his teachings as evil, and they had a point. He was evil. But that's what made his personality and his writing so compelling. He had a huge influence on subsequent Western thought and an especially large one on an English philosopher who became a specialist in the elemental passions, Thomas Hobbes.

Hobbes diagnosed the problem of the religious wars that had split Europe and Christendom very simply: they had arisen from the widespread supposition that "the knowledge of good and evil belongs to each single man." And the consequence of this belief was that men had inflicted grievous pain upon others and justified civil war against their countrymen and rebellion against their rulers, all in the name of their assurance that they were in possession of the truth. Hobbes rejected the classical view that reason could be summoned to adjudicate these disputes; his premise was that reason is the slave of the passions.

Hobbes invented a now-famous concept: the individual in the "state of nature." This is the hypothetical original condition of each member of mankind before the formation of society and government. In this state, Hobbes said, the deepest passion guiding human behavior is the fear of violent death. Later, religion introduces a second terror: the fear of damnation. Fear of violent death, Hobbes warned, goads men into a "perpetual restless desire for power" that is insatiable and would destroy everything in its path. Religion, Hobbes pointed out, subjects men to the campaigns of superstition that have already left behind a trail of blood.

"In such condition," Hobbes famously wrote, "there is no place for industry, because the fruit thereof is uncertain: and consequently no culture of the earth, no navigation . . . no commodious building; no instruments of moving; no knowledge of the face of the earth; no account of time; no arts; no letters; no society. . . . And the life of man, solitary, poor, nasty, brutish, and short." Hobbes counseled people to forget about the afterlife. "There is no natural knowledge of man's state after death." As for earthly fears about threats to life and security, Hobbes argued that every individual should be willing to abandon the state of nature and entrust himself and his rights to a Leviathan state, ruled by an absolute monarch, who would establish peace, pursue prosperity, and decide all questions civil and religious, and whose verdict would permit no appeal.[18]

The relevance of Hobbes is not in his solution, which was intolerable. Rather, it is in his diagnosis of the base motives that guide human behavior and of the need to tame these turbulent passions. Hobbes's frontal assault against religious authority appalled the Anglican authorities in England and compelled subsequent thinkers to avoid such open blasphemies. Even so, he strengthened the conviction of these thinkers that something drastic needed to be done to curb the influence of religion as a source of civil strife and that the goal of the state was to promote peace and prosperity. It was left to the Dutch-English philosopher Bernard Mandeville to offer a playfully outrageous suggestion about how this could be done.

In 1714 Mandeville published a long poem called *The Fable of the Bees*. Its theme was that "private vices" produce "public benefits." Mandeville claimed that a society organized around the promotion of traditional evils such as greed, selfishness, gluttony, avarice, pride, envy, and lust would produce an incredible burst of prosperity that could be enjoyed by all. Without these so-called vices, Mandeville wrote, the engines of commerce and consumption would grind to a halt. As for virtues such as honesty and innocence, Mandeville found them the special province of "the poor silly country people." Mandeville took his view to its logical conclusion and argued that virtue is the ruin of society and that evil is "the grand principle that makes us sociable creatures." It provides "the solid basis, the life and support of all trades and employments without exception." If evil were to stop, "society must be spoiled if not totally dissolved."[19] Who can be surprised that such views produced an explosion of outrage and denunciation throughout Christian Europe?

It remained for sober men to take these arguments—startling in their originality, outrageous to traditional sensibilities—and make them palatable to a civilization anchored in the beliefs of Athens and Jerusalem. Adam Smith, for example, roundly denounced Mandeville's views as "wholly pernicious." Smith was no fan of sloth and extravagance, as Mandeville was. At the same time he agreed with Mandeville that the traditional vices of selfishness and greed were the indispensable foundations of a commercially prosperous society. So he replaced Mandeville's notion of "vice" with the more palatable term "interest." Then he argued, very much along the lines of Mandeville, that self-interested motives, operating through the framework of a free market, would produce socially beneficial consequences. In fact, Mandeville's concept that the pursuit of private gain leads to the public welfare is the central premise of *The Wealth of Nations,* and economist Gary Becker told me that he regards it as "the most important idea in the social sciences in two and a half centuries." Mandeville's name is largely forgotten, but his ideas are with us still. He is an unsung hero of the Party of Yeah.

But before Adam Smith, there was Francis Bacon. This early-seventeenth-century thinker deserves to be known as the patron saint of our technological civilization. Proclaiming himself "much beholden to Machiavelli and others, that write what men do, and not what they ought to do," Bacon criticized the entire corpus of ancient philosophy, from Plato to Aquinas, for failing to produce "a single experiment which tends to relieve and benefit the condition of man." The relief of man's estate: that is Bacon's goal. He doesn't care, as the ancients did, about exploring the nature of truth, about discovering what things are. Rather, Bacon is interested in how things work. His litmus test is utility. Therefore, Bacon proclaims, true knowledge is not that which enables us to rise above our wants, it is that which allows us to gratify our wants. It is that which feeds and clothes and heals people and supplies other human desires.

Drawing on such examples as the compass and the printing press, Bacon argues that the way to relieve man's estate is to figure out nature's laws and then manipulate them to human ends. He wants nature "under constraint and vexed, that is to say, when by art and the hand of man she is forced out of her natural state, and squeezed and molded." Right here we see the promise of human welfare derived from the conquest of nature and also, perhaps, a ground for concern that nature is to be reduced to raw material for the fulfillment of man's desires.

Bacon's hero is not the priest or the philosopher but the scientist, and in his *New Atlantis* he presents the scientists as a new elite, placing their practical wisdom at the service of society. Bacon assigns to science the grandiose task of restoring man to the Garden of Eden. The fall, Bacon says, introduced hardship and scarcity into the world, and we can overcome those evils through applied knowledge. Bacon contends that God wants us to decipher nature's laws so that we can carry out his plan for us. By establishing dominion over nature, Bacon argues, we show piety toward God's creation while harvesting God's bounty for the benefit of mankind.[20]

We are all heirs of Bacon in that we trust in science to perform everyday miracles. Indeed, libertarian writer Virginia Postrel argues that science has restored for us the enchanted world that disappeared when modern men and women stopped believing that rocks had souls. Postrel invokes "the wonder of the bread machine" as evidence that our world, no less than that of the ancients, is full of magic.[21] I don't know if I can get as excited as Postrel about my appliances. "Look," I said to my wife the other day, "I pop the bread into the toaster and it comes out crisp and hot. Isn't that incredible?" She looked at me as if I had lost my mind. Still, Postrel's amazement in the face of technology is very much in the spirit of Bacon, and I have to admit that I share it, just a little bit, every time I get off an airplane.

Bacon was an aristocrat who served in senior positions, including as lord chancellor, at the English court. He knew what science should do, but he had no idea how society should be economically structured to benefit from the inventions of science. Nor did he have any practical solution to the religious problem. The philosophers of the French and Scottish Enlightenment—Locke, Montesquieu, David Hume, Voltaire, and Adam Smith—did. "When it is a question of money," Voltaire wrote in one of his philosophical letters, "everybody is of the same religion." In the London stock exchange, Voltaire slyly added, "The Jew, the Mohammedan and the Christian deal together . . . and apply the name of infidel only to those who go bankrupt." Hume and Montesquieu held similar views. These men advocated the formation of a commercial society to create an outlet for the fulfillment of material desire, as well as a diversion from the call of religion.

The genius of John Locke was to work out in the late seventeenth century a doctrine of property rights that formed the basis of the commercial society. In the ancient and medieval worlds, people had owned property, but the notion that they had a *right* to property would have been regarded as absurd. Property was usually acquired by inheritance rather than purchase. Feudal lords owned land, but it rarely came up for sale. The barons and lords of the late Middle Ages would no more have thought of selling their estates than today's royal family in England would consider putting Buckingham Palace on the market. The ancient view of property was summed up in Cicero's analogy: Owning a piece of property is like occupying a seat in a public theater. It's your seat, but only temporarily. You don't own it, and even its possession and use come with certain moral and social obligations. Finally, the ancients assumed that the amount of land, like the number of seats, is generally fixed, so it's not really right to take up more space than you need.[22]

Locke challenges this view by advancing the premise that each human being owns himself. This seems obvious to us today, but at the time it was a kind of heresy: it contradicted the medieval supposition that God owns us because he created us. Since we own ourselves, Locke continues, we have a natural right to ownership of the fruits of our own labor. It follows, of course, that nobody has a right to own somebody else or to forcibly seize the fruits of another person's labor. So where do property rights come from? Locke argues that when we "mix" our labor with land, we come to own the land as well. Why? Because land is abundant, and moreover it is labor that adds value to land. So in Locke's view men are entitled to seize as much unused land as they can cultivate and use, as long as there is enough left over for others.

But what happens when the land runs out? Here is where technological improvements and money come in. As long as we can keep increasing the value of land and other natural resources and as long as we can buy and exchange these resources for money, Locke argues, there will never be a natural shortage. Land and resources will accrue to the person who can add the most value to them. After all, Locke writes, nature by itself is almost worthless. What good are acorns, leaves, skins, and moss? It is labor that provides virtually all the added value—Locke estimates first 90 percent, then 99 percent, then 99.9 percent—that converts nature's provision into bread, wine, and cloth. Thus, Locke says, our right to acquire property is practically unlimited.

Locke goes further: in the "state of nature," he says, borrowing this concept from Hobbes, we are naturally free, but we are at the mercy of thugs who can harm us and seize what we have. The only reason we enter into society and accept the authority of government is to protect our person and possessions from foreign and domestic thugs. In addition to the protection of life, he writes, "the great and chief end of men uniting into commonwealths and putting themselves under government is the preservation of their property." Locke does not envision that the society he recommends will make people rich, but he does foresee that it will enable them to triumph over necessity. He is confident that a system of property rights and trade will eliminate the scarcities that were prevalent in the ancient world. Thus, Locke tells us that an American Indian chief who is head of a large tribe nevertheless "feeds, lodges and is clad worse than a day laborer in England."[23]

In 1776, Adam Smith published *Inquiry into the Nature and Causes of the Wealth of Nations,* a comprehensive account of how free trade and free markets, what Smith termed a "system of natural liberty," would benefit all nations and produce widespread prosperity. The publication of Smith's book, which had a huge influence in Europe, was a monumental event. It was surpassed only by the decision, in that year, of a group of upstart colonists to issue a statement declaring their independence of their mother country, England. About a decade later, these same upstarts, having broken free of English control, established a constitution based largely on the principles of Francis Bacon, John Locke, and Adam Smith. The United States, I am suggesting, grew rich off the principles of Locke and Smith and became the technological powerhouse envisioned in Bacon's "new Atlantis." America is the only country based almost entirely on the principles of the Party of Yeah.

The founders, and their European supporters, recognized the novelty of their cause: America was nothing less than a new experiment in what it means to be human. Tom Paine announced that America represented "the birthday of a new world." The framers themselves called their work a *novus ordo seclorum,* a new order for the ages, that broke with all forms of government that then existed or had ever existed. Alexander Hamilton, James Madison, and John Jay announced in *The Federalist Papers* that the new constitution "accomplished a revolution which has no parallel in the annals of human society."[24] The American Revolution was more than a new set of documents or even a new system of government. More than a quarter century later, John Adams wrote that the "real American revolution" was a "radical change in the principles, opinions, sentiments and affections of the people."[25]

At first glance this may seem like typical Party of Yeah bombast. To see that it is not, one must examine what America looked like and sounded like before the Revolution. It was a society based on duties, not rights. Primogeniture and dowry were regular features of inheritance and marriage. The ring of the church bell, not the cash register or the stock exchange, defined public life. Many local communities seemed determined to set up their own theocracy, and each religious camp viewed the others with hostile intentions. None of this should be surprising. The early settlers had imported from Europe what they knew, and what they knew were the mores of the *ancien régime.*

A revealing indication of this can be seen in the Mayflower Compact, wrongly portrayed in many high school textbooks as the first of many chapters in the history of American liberty. In fact, the principles of the Mayflower Compact stand in marked contrast with those of the American Constitution. The Pilgrim Fathers who signed that document in 1620 made no mention of rights but spoke instead of a journey "undertaken for the Glory of God, and Advancement of the Christian Faith, and the Honour of our King." They were men of an entirely different stamp from George Washington, Thomas Jefferson, and Benjamin Franklin. They might have gotten along with Washington, but they would have hated Jefferson, and they would have wanted to burn Franklin.

For their part, the American founders wanted to establish a society in which the Puritans and other believers could practice their religion, but they would not be permitted to dedicate the public life of America to Christianity, nor could they use the power of the government to impose their beliefs on others. The framers of the Constitution were terrified of importing to America the religious divisions that had wrecked much of Europe. The founders, who were mostly deists, did not want to eliminate religious conviction altogether; indeed they viewed religion as the necessary foundation of personal and civic virtue. Their goal was subtler: to weaken religious fanaticism and limit the operating sphere of religion so that people of different beliefs could coexist in peace, and so that the public work of society could be conducted on a secular basis. They didn't want witch burning. They didn't want Inquisition. They wouldn't have minded church potluck suppers and cheery-faced Christians saying to everyone they meet, "Let me tell you what Jesus means to me."

So what the founders did was privatize religion, which means that they expelled it from the sphere of government and consigned it to the local or private arena. This is the meaning of "separation of church and state." It implies that each individual and each group can subscribe to its own doctrine of revealed truth: your religion is true for you, and my religion is true for me. This had the beneficial effect of promoting religious freedom because it permitted different religious sects to flourish in harmony. But at the same time its effect was to downgrade religion from a publicly acknowledged truth to a privately held opinion.

To see this, try to imagine the American founders privatizing, say, mathematics. The government is constitutionally prohibited from advancing mathematical knowledge in any way. No one who runs for public office shall be consulted as to his understanding of mathematics. We all enjoy "mathematical freedom," which means that we get to solve equations and come up with answers in our own way. Would such a doctrine—that mathematical truth is relative to each individual or group—be viewed as a triumph for mathematics? I doubt it. It would only prove that as far as the Constitution and the government are concerned, there is no such thing as mathematical truth and therefore people are free to believe whatever they want.

I regret having to bring bad news to religious people who have been raised to think of the founders as deeply pious men who sought to establish a Christian society. The founders were not deeply pious men, and they sought no such thing. Thomas Jefferson was probably more anticlerical than most, but the founders would have agreed with his view of the Declaration of Independence as "the signal of arousing men to burst the chains under which monkish ignorance and superstition had persuaded them to bind themselves." If a society is peaceful and prosperous, Jefferson said, who cares what people believe about the afterlife? "It does me no injury for my neighbor to say there are 20 gods or no god. It neither picks my pocket nor breaks my leg."[26]

We can debate whether the founders would have approved such Supreme Court rulings as the one that excluded prayer from public schools, but in general the experience of the United States over the past two centuries has vindicated the founders' intentions: religious belief is widespread, yet religion has little, if any, public force, and most people spend far more of their time thinking about living longer and more comfortably than about their salvation. Religious peace has been secured but, as the early modern philosophers would have recognized, at the price of removing from society a shared conviction of participating in a transcendent order.

*   *   *

The indifference and even hostility of the founders to established religion should not lead one to believe that they were atheists who didn't
care about morality. On the contrary, even the most skeptical of them,
like Jefferson and Franklin, regarded morality as the only firm foundation of a lasting social order. Morality, they knew, derived mostly from
religion. So the founders hoped that diverse religious affiliations would
come together in supporting a rational code of moral conduct. As for
their theology, the founders may not have been orthodox Christians
but most of them were deists. If they rejected the God of Scripture,
they embraced the God of Nature. Moreover, they held that the existence of a Creator was a necessary foundation of their radical new notion of individual rights.

"We hold these truths to be self-evident," the Declaration of Independence says, and then proceeds to list a number of things that were
by no means evident to the ancient world. Each person, the Declaration continues, has a God-given right to "life, liberty and the pursuit of
happiness." The core of the American idea is stated here. America is
based on the notion that we all share a human nature and that human
nature offers a basis for dignity, being a gift of nature or nature's Creator.

We may differ in many ways, but the differences among individuals
are not so great that they equal, for example, the difference between
human beings and dogs. It is acceptable to enslave animals, as pet owners do, and put them to death, as hunters do. The argument of the
American founders is that because we are not like other animals, these
practices are forbidden when it comes to human beings. Since we share
a common human nature, there is a natural equality among men, which
means that we cannot be justly governed without our consent. Implicit
in this single principle is the argument for democracy, as well as the argument against slavery.

The "low" foundations of the early modern philosophers should
not blind us to the authentic moral gains achieved when their doctrine
was adapted to the circumstances of the American founding. Slavery,
which was widely accepted in the ancient world and required few defenders because it had no critics, suddenly came into deep moral question
in the new American system. Admittedly, the founders compromised
in practice with the institution. How else could they have convinced
the southern states to join the union? Surely it was better to have a

union based on antislavery principles, even unrealized ones, than no union at all.

Abraham Lincoln, who understood the founders' dilemma better than anyone else, argued that the founders had been right to found the new nation on principles of equality and freedom even though they had been unable to secure them for everyone, not even all whites, at the time. Of the founders Lincoln said, "They meant simply to declare the *right*, so that the *enforcement* of it might follow as fast as circumstances should permit."[27] Some of the greatest events of American history—the Civil War, the civil rights movement—can be seen as successful attempts to fulfill the basic human rights to freedom and equality promised by the Declaration of Independence.

If men were not beasts, at the same time the founders understood that they were not angels. Madison writes that if men were angels no government would be necessary. The American political system, with its separation of powers, checks and balances, judicial review, and periodic elections, was designed for flawed human beings who cannot be trusted with absolute power. So also the free-market system enshrined in the Constitution accepts that people are motivated by self-interest and cannot be counted on to serve others through angelic benevolence. As the twelfth book of *The Federalist Papers* elaborates, the new government was set up to enable the efforts of "the assiduous merchant, the laborious husbandman, the active mechanic and the industrious manufacturer" to multiply their "means of gratification" and thus "vivify and invigorate all the channels of industry and to make them flow with greater activity and copiousness."[28] Adam Smith could not have put it better.

The founders believed in equality of rights, but they did not believe in equality of outcomes. Indeed, it is hardly an exaggeration to say that, in their view, equality of rights provides the moral justification for inequality of outcomes. "The first object of government," Madison writes in the tenth book of *The Federalist Papers*, is "the protection of different and unequal faculties of acquiring property."[29] Note that this is not one of the goals of the new regime; it is the primary one. Moreover, inequality of outcomes is not seen as a necessary evil that government should seek to remedy; rather, the government itself exists to guard citizens' right to accumulate unequal fortunes.

The word "right" appears in the original Constitution only once, in

Article 1, Section 8, where Congress is given the power "to promote the Progress of Science and useful Arts, by securing for limited Times to Authors and Inventors the exclusive Right to their respective Writings and Discoveries." Excluding the amendments that were added later, the only right specifically recognized in the text of the Constitution concerns patents and copyrights. Lincoln listed the founders' decision to promote science and technology as the last in the six great steps in the historical progression of human liberty. By adding "the fuel of interest to the fire of genius," the founders had, in Lincoln's view, aided "in the discovery and production of new and useful things."[30] Here one can see the legacy of Francis Bacon.

For more than two centuries, America has been carrying out the new experiment that the founders set into motion, based on the doctrines of Bacon, Locke, and Adam Smith. And the commercial society dedicated to "the pursuit of happiness" has proven massively successful. It has delivered to Americans unprecedented material prosperity within a framework of exhilarating freedom to chart the course of their lives. What could be more appealing? So America is now the model for the world, free markets and free institutions are embraced worldwide, and everybody wants the newest technology. The current popularity of the Party of Yeah is based on the simple fact that its formula has been tried and has proven successful.

The Party of Nah is on the defensive, because as yet it has no serious alternative to the commercial, technological society and is therefore reduced to whining. My sympathies for the principles of Athens and Jerusalem do not extend to sympathy for this whining. The reason is that the principles of the old world, however lofty, extracted over the course of Western history an unbearable human toll. By contrast, the principles of the new world have delivered on their promises. While I too admire Athens and Sparta and have a certain degree of fondness for the medieval village, I cannot imagine going back to a society where the classical or Christian virtues are sustained in an environment of tribalism, exclusivity, coercion, scarcity, and perennial conflict.

If the principles of commerce and technology, on which America is founded, are in some ways less noble than those of the ancient world, they are also more realistic and more practical. Moreover, they have produced not just material but also moral progress: the abolition of slavery, the elevation of countless people from poverty to comfort, the relief of suffering produced by disease, humanitarian campaigns against torture and famine all over the world, and a widely shared conception of human rights, human freedom, and human dignity. As a consequence, the United States can, in terms of material or moral excellence, hold its own against any contemporary society, even any ancient society. If it falls short, it is not by the standard of ancient practice, only by the standard of ancient principle. Thus I conclude that while the United States may not be the best conceivable society, it is probably the best society that now exists or has ever existed.

Yet if the Party of Nah comes across today as a bunch of whiners and losers, it may be this sorry bunch that has the last laugh. The American founders assumed that as people accumulated wealth through commerce and technology, they would prevail in the struggle against necessity, and they would be free, and have the means, to pursue happiness. The prosperity of the last two decades has brought millions of American families to the end of the Lockean road. They have triumphed against necessity; they are, by any historical standard, rich. So they are ready to pursue happiness, but this is where the problem begins: they don't know where to find it. If they turn to the early modern thinkers, and to the founders, for guidance, what they will find is nothing. On this crucial and relevant question, which concerns the content of the good life in a capitalist society, the founders and their intellectual mentors were silent.

CHAPTER EIGHT

THE CONQUEST OF HUMAN NATURE

Technology and the Remaking of Humanity

Aging and death do seem to be what nature has planned for us. But what if we have other plans?

—Biologist Bernard Strehler

In the years to come, many of the social and moral dilemmas surrounding wealth are likely to become dilemmas involving technology. There is a close connection between wealth and technology: they are both forms of control over the environment. Think about what it means to be rich. It means having sway over resources. It means being able to manipulate your environment to fulfill your desires. This is precisely the role of technology as well. We are familiar with technology as a *means* of the creation of wealth. It is capitalism's secret weapon, supplying producers and consumers with new tools for making nature do our bidding. Computing and communications technology are now driving growth, not just in new-economy companies but also in old-economy companies.

But technology can also be viewed as a *form* of wealth. This means that the common man who has a flush toilet, air-conditioning, a hip replacement, and a personal computer is in some respects richer than Louis XIV, who would probably have traded a wing of the palace of Versailles for these technological amenities. Today technology has displaced land, buildings, and even cash as the predominant form of wealth.

Thanks to wealth and technology, America and the West have become fantastically rich and powerful. We have realized the goals of the early modern philosophers and the American founders. We have largely completed the conquest of nature. We have overrun the skies with airplanes, we have plumbed the depths of the ocean, we have planted human footprints on every corner of the globe, we have bored down to the earth's core, and we have roamed the heavens. We have unmasked many of the mysterious laws of nature and found ways to turn them to our benefit, most recently by turning sand into silicon. We have prevailed over many diseases and pushed back the frontiers of death. In a manner that few could have anticipated, we reign sovereign over the natural world.

Consequently, it is hardly surprising that our attention is turning to new problems, including those raised by the enormous power of wealth and technology. How should we exercise these powers wisely? Should we impose any limits on their use? These questions are, in a sense, luxuries because they can arise only in a rich and powerful society. But in another sense they are indispensable because we are in the process of developing new technologies that are likely to raise human capacity, and human responsibility, to a new level. New technologies in biology and information science allow us to do more than transform our environment; they give us the power to transform ourselves—and our species.

What this means is that in a startling development, the project to conquer nature has turned its imperialist eye on human nature. In a reversal that Bacon did not foresee, we have become the objects of our own technology. The toolmaker has become the tool. This is a concept with such deep implications that it is likely to move to the center of international debate. It is impossible to avoid confronting this issue and the mighty dilemma it raises. Essentially, we are asking the question of whether we, or our children, should choose to be the last generation of ordinary human beings. How should we think about this possibility, which no previous generation has had to contemplate?

"I don't know why the concept of genetic engineering scares people," remarks Fred Gage as we walk through his laboratory at the Salk Institute for Biological Studies. With three Nobel laureates and nearly three hundred scientists, medical doctors, and researchers on staff, the San Diego–based Salk Institute is at the forefront of new research in the field of biotechnology. A slender man with hazel eyes and a mustache, Gage looked relaxed in jeans and a gray sweater when I stopped by to interview him in March 2000. As one of Salk's leading neuroscientists, Gage is studying ways in which the biological structure of the brain can be altered to reduce malfunction and improve brain capacity.

"People throughout history have engaged in genetic engineering," Gage says. "The American Indian chief who insisted that his son could only marry a certain type of girl—he's a genetic engineer. When couples get married today, they consider such factors as looks and personality—they are genetic engineers because they are selecting traits that will be passed to their children. The only difference is that in the past people have tried to engineer based on phenotype, in other words, based on the expression of the genes in a particular environment. What is new is that we are developing the capacity to alter and manipulate the genes themselves. We can introduce genes, and we can delete genes. We can directly shape the genetic constitution, and we can directly transform the human germ line."

Gage's laboratory staff is dressed in the white uniforms that one associates with a medical facility. They are surrounded by test tubes, bottles holding liquids of various colors, incubators, pipettes, funnels, laser microscopes, and refrigerators and freezers where the genetic material is stored. "This," one of Gage's assistants tells me, pointing to a machine that looks like a photocopier, "is a brain slicer. We can cut the brain into thin strips, like a block of Swiss cheese. Then we can see how each part of the brain works. When we understand that, we will be able to alter the brain in the same way that we alter the rest of our bodies."

Gage isn't interested in the clinical applications of his research. "I want to discover new things," he says. "All that the clinicians do is take what we've already discovered and try it out on humans." Of course Gage understands that his kind of work has social consequences. "What will be done with genetic research in Iraq or Bangladesh, I have no idea. But here people are going to want to enhance their brains, to improve their memory, to make their children smarter. Brain implants are going to be very risky, but that doesn't mean there won't be a demand for them. There are crazy people who will do anything to their bodies, so why should it be different with their minds?" Gage's serious face showed the slightest trace of a grin. "We might just see some people select themselves out of the gene pool."

Across the hall from Gage is Inder Verma, a portly, rumpled molecular biologist who is trying to apply the new techniques of gene therapy to repair or replace the defective genes of cancer patients. Unlike Gage, who usually speaks in a quiet, methodical voice, Verma is gregarious and animated. He seems especially pleased to be conversing with a fellow Indian. "Most people have no idea of the pace at which biological knowledge and technology are moving," he says. "I keep reading about the forthcoming completion of the genome project. What are they talking about? The genome project is done. Done. We know what the genes are. The next step is to ask what these genes do and what we can do with them. That will happen very rapidly."

Technology, Verma says, is accelerating the discovery and spread of biological knowledge. "The computer has changed our world," he remarks. "What used to take months of laboratory testing to do can now be done in a matter of hours, sometimes minutes. The information is coming at us much faster than our ability to process it. And in medicine we are approaching the final frontier, which is the brain, the mind, the soul."

A decade ago, Verma says, cloning was seen as a virtual impossibility. "Now we know as a medical certainty that we can clone people. Think about what that means. The clone is going to look at his father and know pretty clearly what he is going to look like when he gets old. In some sense, he knows his future before he gets there." Verma gives another example: "When you leave this room I can take your notebook, pick off a piece of your DNA, and know that you are disposed to get colon cancer. I mean, that's pretty incredible, isn't it?"

In the future, Verma says, people will use the new technologies to alter their genetic makeup or design one for their children. "I personally wouldn't do it," Verma says. "But I can't stop it. And I suppose I wouldn't try to stop it. If you want a child with a high IQ, a happy temperament, and a small nose, who am I to say your choices are bad? If people want designer children, then genetic technology will give them what they want. We scientists don't set the moral norms for society. It's not our job to think this through."

*   *   *

Among the Party of Yeah, there are plenty of techno-visionaries who are thinking it through. They have come up with a social vision so bold and breathtaking that in sheer force of imagination, it surpasses Plato's *Republic.* Like Plato, they intend to offer a utopia, not just a "city in speech" but a blueprint for where society should go and how we should get there. And as with the *Republic,* what to the utopians sounds like a triumph for humanity appears to their critics as a hellish nightmare. The critics warn of the desecration of everything that is sacred, the extinction of human freedom, plagues and pestilence, and nothing less than the final destruction of the human race and the world as we know it.

"Oh yeah?" comes the retort from the Party of Yeah. "Tell us something we don't know." The techno-utopians even welcome the worst-case scenarios raised by the critics. Among the smartest and most visionary members of the group, the destruction of humanity is a prospect to be *celebrated,* because the world as we know it is going to be replaced by something better. "I cannot believe that we are evolution's final product," remarks inventor and entrepreneur Danny Hillis, who builds supercomputers. "There's something coming after us, and I imagine it is something wonderful. But we may never be able to comprehend it, any more than a caterpillar can comprehend turning into a butterfly."[1] James Watson, who codiscovered the structure of DNA, asks, "Are we going to control life? I think so. We all know how imperfect we are. We'll make ourselves a little better."[2] Biologist Lee Silver asserts, "Today we can control our own evolution. We can decide what genes we give to our children. So we will take control over the evolutionary process by picking the genes we want our children to have. And then those children can pick the genes they want their children to have."[3] Technology writer Michael Malone has an equally ambitious idea: "Today we are all dreaming the ultimate dream—immortality."[4] And techno-futurist Stewart Brand, a founder of *Wired* magazine, frequently chortles, "We are as gods, and we might as well get good at it."

What on earth are these fellows talking about? Not about the Internet. The people in the vanguard of the tech world are convinced that the Internet will soon be passé, as in some sense the PC has already become passé. This doesn't mean the Web will disappear; rather, it will continue to be integrated into the fabric of social life through increased communication devices, smart appliances, and modes of recreation. But as a technology the Internet is already getting old and even a little boring. E-mail is no longer exciting, just useful, and who cares if you order your groceries on-line? To cutting-edge technologists, the greatest value of the Internet is as an *enabling device* for newer, more interesting, and ultimately more important technologies that will revolutionize our lives and transform the future of humanity.

The eminent physicist Freeman Dyson argues that biotechnology will shape the first half of the twenty-first century in much the same way that the computer shaped the last few decades of the twentieth century. "A new era will begin for architecture when buildings can be grown rather than built, using biotechnology applied to trees and corals," he writes. The same arts can be applied, Dyson argues, to restoring endangered habitats, cleaning polluted air and water, and replacing chemical industries with biological processes. Biotechnology also gives us the ability to make designer beasts. We can create "transgenic animals" that cross the normally inviolable dividing lines between species. That means that society will soon have the power to create an entire zoo of animals that have never previously existed. We can genetically modify cows and goats so that their milk contains medicinal properties. We can insert the genes of domestic dogs into wolves, thus turning them into docile pets. We may be able to produce a laughing cat or one that matches your furniture. We can insert firefly genes into fish, so that they glow in various colors. We can control pest populations by sterilizing them through genetic engineering. It may even be possible to bring back some extinct species. "It is not absurd," writes Dyson, to expect "reconstructed dodos and dinosaurs ornamenting our wild animal parks."[5]

Leading scientists contend that new research will give us unprecedented control over our bodies, including the power to extend life. "Over the next twenty to forty years, we will have the potential for eradicating the major diseases that plague the American population," remarks Leroy Hood, former chairman of the biology department at the California Institute of Technology.[6] "Aging is now a solved biological problem," declares biologist Michael Rose. "We know why aging occurs, and from that we know how to shape it, at least on the level of basic science."[7] Biologist Michael West says that there is no reason that humans in the foreseeable future should not be able to double their life spans and eventually approach immortality. "We are close to transferring the immortal characteristics of germ cells to our bodies and essentially eliminating aging," West says. "That sounds spectacular, but I believe those are the facts."[8]

Scientists say that these same biological techniques will empower us over time to escape the tyranny of our bodies. Society will finally be able to eliminate baldness and obesity, and "gender switching between the sexes will be commonplace," according to writer Jan Morris, who used to be writer James Morris before a sex-change operation.[9] Beyond this, biologists foresee that humans could reconstruct themselves to resemble a Cubist painting or favorite movie character, or even grow horns, wings, gills, and tails. Horns and tails may serve merely as fashion accoutrements. But wouldn't you like to have a biological sonar system, like a bat? Or be able to generate electricity, like an eel? Some biologists say that gills and tails could be part of a new apparatus that allows human beings—or rather human hybrids—to fly and to breathe under water.[10]

Molecular biologist Lee Silver, who teaches at Princeton University, is excited about cloning technology, which will give the human race a chance to completely separate sex from reproduction. In his book *Remaking Eden* Silver predicts that "sexless reproduction could become the norm." Silver perceives numerous practical applications for cloning and related technologies. If a couple loses a child in a terrible accident, for instance, Silver says that they will, in a sense, be able to bring the dead child back to life by taking some cells from the corpse and producing a clone. Silver writes that lesbian couples will soon be able to have their own biological children—two fertilized embryos, one from each partner, could be combined into a single "chimera"; or one partner could clone herself, and the embryo could be deposited in the womb of the other. Silver envisions that in the not-too-distant future, couples who want to have a child will review a long list of physical, intellectual, and emotional traits on a computer screen, put together combinations of "virtual children," and finally decide on the one they want, click on the appropriate traits, and, in effect, design their own offspring: "Parents are going to be able to give their children . . . genes that increase athletic ability, genes that increase musical talents . . . and ultimately genes that affect cognitive abilities."

But even this, Silver says, is a small step. By reengineering the human germ line, Silver concludes, people living today can "gain complete control over their genetic destiny." Many writers, including physicist

Stephen Hawking and social critic Francis Fukuyama, have suggested that genetic engineering could be used to reduce human aggression, thus solving the crime problem and making war less likely. Others have proposed raising the intelligence of the population, thus enabling our descendants to solve problems that we have not even formulated. Biologist Daniel Koshland argues that by raising the IQ of the common man, we may better prepare him to get jobs in an increasingly complex society.[11] Many years ago, biologist E. O. Wilson suggested that through genetic alteration of the species we could cultivate "new patterns of sociality" similar to that of gibbons or honeybees.[12] Steve Sailer of the Biodiversity Institute predicts that parents will seek better-looking offspring to maximize their chance of having grandchildren.[13] Feminists, no doubt, will lobby for the eradication of the genes that produce chauvinism or sexism. Others may call for a genetic "cure" for homosexuality. Some academics might argue that if human nature were sufficiently altered, socialism could finally work. Possibly all these eugenic objectives could be pursued simultaneously. Silver himself forecasts a general elevation of intellectual, athletic, temperamental, and artistic abilities so that we can over time create "a special group of mental beings" who will "trace their ancestry back to homo sapiens" but are "as different from humans as humans are from the primitive worms with tiny brains that first crawled along the earth's surface."[14]

Scientist and inventor Ray Kurzweil, a pioneer of voice recognition technology, contends that in a few years, computers will exceed the processing power of the human brain: "The emergence in the early twenty-first century of a new form of intelligence on earth that can compete with, and ultimately significantly exceed, human intelligence will be a development of greater import than any of the events that have shaped human history." In a couple of decades, he predicts, a typical home computer will have a capacity equal to a thousand human brains. The computer will read all the world's literature—including books, magazines, and scientific material—and exchange information with other computers. These machines will be both "intelligent" and "spiritual," Kurzweil writes, in the sense that they will sound like humans, act like humans, reproduce themselves like humans, invent things like humans, and even pray like humans and assert their dignity and rights. Ultimately, Kurzweil proclaims, computers will, through their superior processing power, start controlling events and telling humans what to do—unless human beings decide to merge with the machines. Kurzweil predicts that humans will opt to become cyborgs whose bodies are embedded with electronic and mechanical devices and whose minds have been transformed by neural implants "to enhance visual and auditory perception, memory and reasoning." In the most imaginative suggestion in his book *The Age of Spiritual Machines,* Kurzweil forecasts that some humans may even seek to use technologies now being developed to copy the entire neuronal structure of their brains, so that they could, in effect, "download" their brains into a computer and live eternally in the form of software. Indeed, this software could even be regularly updated and upgraded, allowing our electronic minds to become smarter over time. Thus even if our bodies perish, Kurzweil declares, we will be able to achieve digital immortality—our minds will live and grow forever.[15]

Kurzweil's vision may seem a bit fanciful, but computer scientist Kevin Warwick doesn't think so: he wants to become one with his computer. "I was born human," Warwick says, "but this was an accident of fate—a condition merely of time and place. I believe it's something we have the power to change." A professor of cybernetics at the University of Reading near London, Warwick has already begun implanting silicon chips in his body. He uses chips embedded in his arms to open doors and to be tracked by his secretary. Now he wants to make his computer communicate directly with his nervous system. He has also recruited his wife to participate in his experiments. Soon she will get silicon implants too. If these experiments succeed, Warwick is going to proceed with chip implants in his spinal cord, optic nerves, and perhaps even his brain. "I am most curious to find out whether implants could open up a whole new range of senses," Warwick writes. "We'd like to send movement and emotion signals from one person to the other, possibly via the Internet." For example, "if I move a hand or finger, then send those signals to Irena, will she make the same movement? If I sprained my ankle, could I send the signal to Irena to make her feel as though she has injured herself?" Warwick is willing to offer himself as a human guinea pig because he sees his work opening up new vistas of human possibility: "I can envision a future when we send signals so that we don't have to speak." He suggests that possibly students in the future won't have to learn any math because their thoughts will be able to activate entire databases of knowledge already implanted in their brains. Eventually, Warwick says he wants the computer to take over his mind and body. He concludes, "Linking people via chip implants directly to machines seems . . . a potential way of harnessing machine intelligence by essentially creating super-humans. Otherwise we're doomed to a future in which intelligent machines rule and humans become second-class citizens. My project . . . gives humans a chance to hang in there a bit longer." Warwick calls this "co-evolution with computers." Placing himself in an old scientific tradition of a seeker of knowledge, Warwick claims to be in the most acute suspense about what the future will bring, and he can't wait to find out. "The next implant," he concludes, "cannot come soon enough."[16]

What is one to make of all this? Among the Party of Nah, the reaction can be anticipated: a little bit of skepticism and a great deal of horror. Recall Burke's reaction to the French Revolution: "Everything seems out of nature in this strange chaos of levity and ferocity." For the Party of Nah, it's déjà vu all over again. Its skepticism arises partly out of disdain for the sheer confidence and chutzpah of the techno-futurists. Novelist Mark Helprin warns that they have been driven mad by "the electric flow of hubris."[17] Surely he's right—Warwick, in particular, strikes me as badly in need of a psychological evaluation—but, as in the case of Muhammad Ali, the hubris might be justified. Certainly science and technology have accumulated a pretty good knockout record over their opponents during the past few centuries. Imagine how people would have sneered at the beginning of the twentieth century if you had told them that their children would be able to fly across continents in a few hours and have heart transplants. We should expect similar scientific miracles in the years to come. Can anyone say with certainty that Bacon's new priests in their white robes are not going to be able to pull off any of this stuff? I wouldn't bet against them.

But let's not get too carried away either. There are valid historical grounds for caution: remember H. G. Wells's predictions about how our lives would be transformed by lumbering robots doing our laundry and serving us dinner? What happened to all the 1950s forecasts in *Popular Science* and *Popular Mechanics* promising that by now we would all commute to work in individual flying machines? Do you recall the hype in the 1960s and 1970s about how nuclear power would provide free and unlimited energy? Or the post–moon landing hoopla about how people would by now be living and working on the moon, if not on other planets? None of these things came to pass. Skeptics, who know this record, sniff a fair sprinkling of horse manure in some of the Party of Yeah's more outlandish predictions.

Personally, I am not interested in discussing science fiction or the wish list of every futurist with a biology or computer science degree. I don't care about items on the techno-futurist agenda that seem to exhibit insuperable obstacles. Thus I will not be exploring Kurzweil's intriguing notion of having the entire information grid of our brains electronically replicated and downloaded. Kurzweil says we should be able to do this in twenty to thirty years, but other scientists I've talked to are dubious. The brain has trillions of neuronal connections, and how they work together to produce a working mind remains largely a mystery to modern science. Kurzweil is a reputable scientist, so we'll have to wait and see if he's right. But for now I'm going to pass on exploring what seems at this point a remote possibility.

Kurzweil's claim that human beings will develop friendships and love affairs with computers strikes me as equally far out, unless he is referring to some iMac neurotics that I'd rather say nothing more about. Contrary to the fantasies of *Jurassic Park*, we are not likely to create a theme park with live dinosaurs unless we can find a way to recover their DNA. Nor will we be able to realize the plot line of several science fiction novels by incubating fetuses in artificial wombs, which scientists have no idea how to make. Futurist publications have speculated about controlling weather patterns; sorry, folks, but we can't make the climate of New Hampshire similar to that of Florida. Then there's the *Star Trek* fantasy that continues to haunt the imagination. "Clear the Line, I'm Sending Myself Right Now," reads a recent headline in *Wired* magazine. The article features quantum engineer Seth Lloyd's idea to vaporize people, copy the information content of their bodies, teleport this information to other planets, and then reassemble them photon by photon. It's a dazzling concept, except that Lloyd confesses, "We have no idea in practice how to carry out those operations."[18]

On the other hand, many of the things that the Party of Yeah wants to do are based on existing knowledge and techniques. They can be done now or require only more refined applications of discoveries already made, so they are almost sure to be done in the next decade or two. For instance, scientists have made enormous advances in their understanding of aging that are almost certain to result in techniques to increase human longevity over the next several years. Life expectancy has risen steadily over the past hundred years, and there is every reason to believe that this trend will continue. Part of the progress will come from ameliorating or curing the diseases that kill people; the rest will be the consequence of arresting the aging process itself. Over the next decade or two, many biologists say, hundred-year-olds will become an increasingly common sight.

Until recently, in animals as in human beings, aging unto death was considered inevitable. But researchers have found ingenious ways of increasing the life span of fruit flies, worms, mice, and cows. "My flies are super-flies," says biologist Michael Rose. "They are having sex when other flies are long since dead."[19] Aging works pretty much the same way in all animals. Human aging is now viewed as a failure of adaptation. Basically, our genes have been programmed by natural selection to stay fit through our peak reproductive years; after that, in a sense, our genes give up the struggle and we go into a phase of extended breakdown. But there is nothing intrinsic about our cells that makes them break down; the genes simply "turn off" once they have served their evolutionary purpose. By figuring out how this happens, scientists hope to be able to stop or reverse this process so that human beings can not only live longer but also preserve their youthful appearance and strength. How much the life expectancy of human beings will go up remains a matter of debate; that it will do so seems certain.

Similarly, the expansion of computer processing power is a technological given. Scientists can continue to load transistors onto silicon chips and to pursue improvements in chip design when Moore's Law approaches its technical limits. But even beyond that there is parallel computing, which is a way of linking computers together to increase aggregate processing power. There are also new forms of computers on the horizon, such as molecular computers, quantum computers, and DNA computers. Rapid progress is being made in these areas. Consequently, it seems reasonable to me that computing power will continue to grow rapidly, to the point where it will exceed the capacity of the human brain.

Does this mean that computers will be able to think? That's a more complicated question. Its relevance is established by the fact that already computers are prevailing in intellectual contests with humans. Chess is a game that requires a subtle combination of logical and strategic reasoning. There is no element of luck, but neither is success in the game a function of brute calculation. Computers have been playing chess for decades, but until recently many people believed that they would not be able to compete with the very best human players. Sure enough, in 1996 the world chess champion, Gary Kasparov, prevailed in a six-match contest against an IBM supercomputer named Deep Blue. But the next year brought a big surprise: a reprogrammed Deep Blue came back to defeat Kasparov narrowly in a rematch. This was widely seen as a humiliation for the human race, and it was. After the tournament Kasparov compounded the chagrin of the species by confessing that there were times during the games when he had "felt a consciousness, or something like it, within Deep Blue."[20]

In the 1950s, Alan Turing proposed what is now known as the "Turing Test" to determine if computers can think. Place a computer and a human being behind a screen, Turing said. Ask them questions to which they must provide text answers. If we cannot tell from the answers which is the computer and which is the human, then, Turing said, the computer is thinking. Even the best computers today cannot satisfy a Turing Test. Although computers can perform very sophisticated tasks within narrow domains, they cannot do what seem to us like quite simple things, such as describe the objects in a room, or distinguish between a dog and a cat, or give a summary of a book. With its complex reasoning requirements, chess is the best example of a computer's ability to meet the Turing criteria.

The philosopher John Searle argues that even if a computer can survive a whole battery of Turing Tests, it still isn't thinking. Searle offers an analogy that is instructive: Imagine that you, who can't speak Chinese, are placed in a room by yourself. Questions are put to you in Chinese. You have a manual for deciphering the answers with the appropriate Chinese symbols. If the manual is sufficiently extensive, Searle says, you will be able to give answers indistinguishable from those of native Chinese speakers. But the fact remains that *you do not know Chinese*. Searle concludes that similarly, a computer that plays chess or performs other mental tasks cannot be credited with thought because it is only manipulating symbols; it has no idea what these symbols mean. Indeed, the computer doesn't even know it's playing chess!

Searle notes that his pocket calculator can solve arithmetical problems faster and better than he can, but this does not mean that it is thinking. At best, the computer is a very sophisticated processing tool. In some contexts it can simulate human reasoning, but even a good imitation is not the real thing. The programmers who have given the computer its inputs—they are the ones who have done the thinking.[21]

Searle may be called an "intentionalist"; for him, thinking is a product of consciousness, the inner mental state that causes our minds to work in the ways that they do. As I mentioned earlier, scientists today barely understand how consciousness works, and they are not even close to building a computer that can reproduce it. But a group of thinkers known as "functionalists" have challenged this requirement. Why, they ask, should consciousness—the inner state—be necessary if the computer can produce the same results as a thinking human being? The philosopher Daniel Dennett argues that Deep Blue beat Kasparov by showing all the observable qualities, including planning and intention, that we associate with thinking. Dennett writes, "It was Deep Blue's cognitive capacity to recognize and exploit a subtle flaw in Kasparov's game. The purpose behind the attack was evident after it succeeded." Dennett insists that the programmers didn't beat Kasparov, the computer did. In Dennett's view we should no more congratulate Deep Blue's programmers than we should have congratulated Kasparov's parents, teachers, and practice coaches if Kasparov had won.[22]

Who is right: Searle or Dennett? I incline toward Searle's position, although I suspect a complete answer cannot be given for a while, until it becomes clear what exactly computers are able to do. If computers can precisely replicate the neurobiological workings of the brain, it will be hard for anyone to say that they are not thinking. Even short of this, if computers can perform a wide range of mental tasks that humans can, we must concede that, for all practical purposes, they are thinking. Of course, computers would still be incapable of feelings or morality. But in the capacity for thought and reasoning that many of the ancient philosophers regarded as the distinctive mark of humanity, computers would be able to produce results equal to, or better than, their human inventors'.

I feel strange in discussing these issues; not long ago they were safely consigned to the realm of science fiction. So were the concepts of cloning and genetic engineering. Then, in early 1997, using a technique called somatic cell nuclear transfer, Ian Wilmut and his medical team announced the successful cloning of a sheep named Dolly. Wilmut and his colleagues took the nucleus of an adult sheep cell, then inserted it into an egg cell whose nucleus had been removed. Once the cell began to divide, the Wilmut team took the newly formed embryo and implanted it into the uterus of another sheep, Dolly's surrogate mother. Since the nucleus contains virtually all the DNA in the cell, Dolly was produced as an exact copy of the adult sheep that had contributed the genetic material. Dolly's mother became the first "single parent" in sheep history.

A week after it published the article on Dolly, *Nature* editorialized on the significance of the new technology. "The growing power of molecular genetics," the magazine said, "confronts us with future prospects of being able to change the nature of our species."[23] Since Dolly's birth cloning has been performed on several types of animals: cows, mice, pigs, and monkeys. The genetic code of animals (especially monkeys) is very similar to that of human beings, so scientists say that there is no reason that cloning cannot be performed on humans as well. Of course, there are technological and safety issues that have to be resolved. But the cloning of humans, the biologists tell us, is now scientifically possible and is likely to be a practical option in the very near future.

Cloning, which reproduces a genetic formula, should not be confused with genetic engineering, which alters it. But cloning is the indispensable prerequisite for genetic engineering. Without cloning genetic engineering is virtually impossible; with it, genetic engineering is a virtual certainty. There are two types of genetic engineering. The first is somatic cell engineering, which involves changing the body's cells. Like plastic surgery, this is an alteration that does not affect the genetic destiny of future offspring. The second type of genetic engineering is germ-line engineering, which involves altering the sexual cells so that the new genetic configuration is passed down to the next generation. In animals germ-line engineering is easier to do than somatic engineering, and this may very well prove to be the case in humans as well. Somatic and germ-line interventions can be carried out for the purpose of *therapy,* that is, to cure disease, or for the purpose of *enhancement,* that is, to improve looks or height or intelligence.

Genetic engineering is currently widely practiced on animals, and scientists have been able to introduce both somatic and germ-line enhancements. In 1999, neurobiologist Joe Tsien boosted the intelligence of mice by inserting extra copies of a gene that enhances memory and learning; these mouse genes are virtually identical to those found in humans. Somatic gene therapy has been successfully carried out in humans, but as far as we know somatic enhancements and germ-line engineering have not yet been attempted. But the success of animal experiments and the new information provided by the Human Genome Project give a powerful impetus to proceed along this course. French Anderson, the first doctor to carry out somatic gene therapy successfully, says that "attempts to redesign human beings" will be scientifically feasible over the next decade or two.[24] But the fact that these things are possible does not mean they should be done.

Eugenics. That's the word that comes to Jeremy Rifkin's mind when he thinks about biotechnology. Rifkin knows all about the horrible history of eugenics: the doctrine of superiority; the contempt for people perceived as backward, inferior, and even inhuman; the campaigns of indoctrination; the forced sterilization; the rampages of extermination. Here in America such groups as the American Breeder's Association and the Eugenics Record Office, which had the support of the best scientific opinion and the elite segments of society, pursued the objective of breeding superior beings while seeking to eliminate the weak and the unfit. Then, as now, these doctrines marched behind the banner of progress.

Rifkin argues that the Nazi idea of the superman is very much alive, but now in a different form: the illusion of the "perfect child." In Rifkin's view the champions of cloning and genetic engineering deplore their eugenic forebears while, in a sense, pursuing their objectives. They don't talk about the "master race," of course; they speak of eliminating medical defects, giving our children the very best in life, and raising humanity to a higher level. But what crimes against humanity are they willing to commit to achieve these goals? Are they willing to trade human individuality, autonomy, and dignity for the Brave New World described in Aldous Huxley's 1932 novel?

Rifkin is a one-man juggernaut of antibiotech energy. His Washington, D.C., office may be termed the official headquarters of the Party of Nah. Rifkin doesn't confine his objections to books and articles. He leads marches outside laboratories. He testifies before Congress. He launches petition drives calling for moratoriums on research and bans on testing. He calls press conferences. He gets involved in discussions in churches and schools. He seeks to influence the way textbooks are prepared. What Jesse Jackson is to the race debate, Jeremy Rifkin is to the biotechnology debate: somehow, he always manages to show up.

Rifkin opens his recent book *The Biotech Century* with a shotgun blast. "Reprogramming the genetic codes of life," he writes, risks a "fatal interruption of millions of years of evolutionary development." Nature allows a certain amount of crossbreeding, but classical breeders could never have produced clones; or supermice that grow twice as large as normal mice; or transgenic animals such as a cross between a sheep and a goat; or man-animal hybrids called "chimeras." Ignoring evolution's time-tested design, namely the separation of the species, could cause biologists to unwittingly unleash deadly viruses that could produce innumerable deaths and immeasurable suffering. The "creation, mass production and wholesale release of thousands of genetically engineered life forms" into the environment might "cause irreversible damage to the biosphere, making genetic pollution an even greater threat to the planet than nuclear and petrochemical pollution." Indeed, we might even witness "the end of the natural world."

Rifkin charges that we are attempting to create new forms of life—a second Genesis—"to suit our own cultural and economic needs and desires." What, he asks, "are the consequences of reducing the world's gene pool to patented intellectual property controlled exclusively by a handful of multinational corporations?" He fears that we might become "aliens in a world populated by cloned, chimeric and transgenic creatures." We are heading for a nightmarish future "where babies are genetically designed and customized in the womb, and where people are identified, stereotyped and discriminated against on the basis of their genotype." A day may come when parents' failure to correct genetic defects or provide their children with available genetic enhancements will be seen as a form of negligence, perhaps even a crime. In this perverse situation, Rifkin mourns, living things "are no longer perceived as birds and bees, foxes and hens, but as bundles of genetic information. All living beings are drained of their substance and turned into abstract messages. Life becomes a code to be deciphered. How can any living thing be deemed sacred when it is just a pattern of information?"[25]

Within the biotech community, Rifkin is regarded as a reactionary, a man who opposes the scientific method itself and would shut down research labs and repeal three hundred years of scientific progress. There seems to be some truth to this perception. Rifkin has about him a touch of Robespierre, and he does seem to think there is something intrinsically exploitative about a scientific project aimed at the conquest of nature. Even so, the premises of modern science are not above criticism, and somewhere in his extravagant rhetoric—human sperm stored in animal testes, pig genes ending up in kosher food—Rifkin is raising some important concerns.

His main criticisms may be summarized in this way: The new technology is unprecedented, so we should be very cautious in developing it. It poses grave risks to human health and the biosphere, so it's not safe to develop right now. Historically, efforts to produce new and improved human beings have brought grotesque violations of rights, gulags, and concentration camps. Cloning and genetic engineering are unnatural; they tamper with the natural order and with millions of years of evolutionary development. Human beings have no right to do this to nature and to ourselves; we shouldn't play God. In the pursuit of a longer life and enhanced capacity for ourselves and for our children, we are extinguishing the sanctity of life.

These criticisms meet with guffaws and derision on the part of the leading spokesmen of the Party of Yeah. "Every time we have had a new technology we have had to put up with this crap," James Watson, the Nobel Prize–winning biologist who is head of Cold Spring Harbor Laboratory, recently said. "We've heard it all: 'The old ways are sacred, don't fool with nature, we shouldn't play God.' Yet every time we have gone ahead, and we have made things better. So now we're going through the same damn process. And in the end we *will* develop these technologies and make them available and no one will regret it. Twenty years from now people will look back and laugh their heads off that we made such a big deal out of this stuff. You'll see."

Speaking at a recent conference on genetic engineering sponsored by the University of California at Los Angeles, Watson offered a seemingly irresistible argument for proceeding full speed ahead with the new biotechnology: "We are talking about curing diseases and prolonging people's lives, and these morons are telling us that they have moral objections. I mean, what kind of ridiculous talk is that?" Watson's comment points to the treasure chest that is waiting for us if we are willing to follow the biotech trail. Most human diseases have a genetic origin. Some are monogenic, meaning they are the result of a single gene, such as cystic fibrosis, muscular dystrophy, and sickle-cell anemia. Other diseases are polygenic, which means they are the consequence of many genes interacting with one another. Still other ailments, such as diabetes, high blood pressure, and lung cancer, arise through genes' interacting with environmental influences such as foods, viruses, and toxic chemicals.

For centuries genetic diseases have been mostly incurable and untreatable. But new advances in biotechnology are making feasible the prospect of interventions to correct these diseases at the genetic level. Gene therapy was first successfully practiced in 1990 by French Anderson and his colleagues at the National Institutes for Health on a young girl suffering from ADA deficiency, or so-called bubble boy disease. "I'm really elated," the girl's father said afterward. "Our world has changed so much more for the better. A year and a half ago, Ashi could never have been playing out there with these other kids. You can't know what it means to our family to see her begin to lead a normal life."[26] Watson has a point—many ethical objections tend to sound silly in the face of testimony like that.

Watson asks us to imagine what it would be like to have genetic treatments for cancer, stroke, heart disease, epilepsy, Alzheimer's disease, Parkinson's disease, high blood pressure, and a host of other ailments that afflict millions of people every year. The Human Genome Project, he says, will soon result in a DNA chip that will enable doctors to take a sample of your blood, compare your genetic profile with that of all known diseases, and give you back the results in a few hours. Indeed, these new technologies will make possible "personalized medicine"—a health plan based on diagnosing your genetic predisposition to disease, treating your ailments even before they occur (imagine going in for medical treatments when you have no symptoms), and correcting those that do occur at the genetic level.

New frontiers are being crossed in areas such as stem cells, which may be used to grow skin and create bone marrow; artificial chromosomes, which when inserted into a human embryo could give that person lifelong immunity to certain diseases; synthetic viruses, which could be devised to destroy malignant cells; nanomedicine, which is microsurgery to repair individual DNA molecules and proteins; tissue engineering, which involves restoring or replacing damaged tissue; organ manufacture, the fabrication of artificial body parts; and xenotransplantation, which involves transplanting pig hearts and other animal organs into humans. Some of these medical techniques, which involve, for instance, experimentation on live embryos, are mired in controversy. Even so, Watson and other scientists say that biotechnology is making possible a revolution in modern medicine. How can it be ethical, they ask, to withhold these technologies from people who need and want them? Where is the point of moral qualms when life itself is at stake?

CHAPTER NINE

THE SEDUCTION

The Quest for the Posthuman

O, it is excellent

To have a giant's strength; but it is tyrannous

To use it like a giant.

—Shakespeare, *Measure for Measure*

The health benefits of biotechnology are undeniable and probably ir-resistible. But are the bioethicists from the Party of Nah right that there is a social and moral cost to be paid for these advances? To use the par-lance of the medical community, what are the "side effects"? The Party of Yeah can't think of any. Recently I was told by one of my techno-utopian friends that he intended to live to the age of 150. I asked him whether extending life expectancy that much—even presuming that we could do it—might have any negative social consequences. "Gee," he said. He could think of only one: "Our society might become too con-servative, because it would be dominated by old people."

The techno-utopians are greatly annoyed by critics like Jeremy Rifkin who keep raising the specter of apocalypse. They welcome the biotechnological future, and they are not scared by analogies from the past. Biologist Lee Silver doesn't believe the precedent of Hitler poses a problem. Nor does he think that the chilling prophecies of *Brave New World* and the crimes of early-twentieth-century practitioners of eu-genics are relevant here. Why not? Because, he writes, "it is individuals and couples, not governments, who will seize control of these new technologies."[1]

What he is saying is that the market, not the state, will be the channel for their development and distribution. The premise of the techno-utopians is that if the market produces a result, it is good. In this view, what is wrong with the old eugenics is not that it sought to eliminate defective types and produce a superior kind of being but that it sought to do so in a coercive and collectivist way. Apparently the old advocates of eugenics were operating on a twentieth-century mass standardization model rather than a twenty-first-century individual customization model. The new advocates of biotechnology speak approvingly of what they term "free-market eugenics." But is the practice of eugenics any less reprehensible because it is pursued through personal choice and unregulated commerce?

The term "eugenics" may ruffle some people, the techno-utopians concede, but soon the concerns will subside and the critics will be blown away. As U.S. Senator Tom Harkin put it when the issue of cloning was raised in Congress, how can anybody be against the advance of knowledge? The march of technology is inevitable! Progress is inevitable and should be welcomed! But this is too uncritical a celebration of social change, which has historically produced a lot of good things as well as a lot of bad ones. Was the invention of the hydrogen bomb "progress"? Were the discovery and manufacture of biological weapons that destroy the human nervous system "progress"? A bioethicist who does not share Harkin's enthusiasm for cloning remarked, "If termites could talk, I am sure they would call what they are doing 'progress.'"

But Harkin does have a point that there seems to be a kind of inevitability to technological change. Whether they do good or harm, new technologies appear to be unstoppable. Their use can be curtailed, as with nuclear and biological weapons, but can you think of a single technology that has not been developed because of moral or social qualms about its effects? Indeed, the techno-utopians gleefully point out that social change is expected to come especially fast in this case. What the Party of Yeah has on its side, after all, is the powerful desire on the part of people to have children of their own and to give their children the best possible future. What impulse could be more natural? What inclination could be stronger? Consequently, the techno-utopians argue, parents who don't have children are going to demand cloning, and parents who do are going to insist upon the availability of the best technological means to give their offspring the best genetic constitutions they possibly can. Wouldn't you like to give your children a few extra IQ points?

· Today's champions of biotechnology admit that cloning and genetic engineering should not be permitted in human beings until they are safe. A few people have already died from unsuccessful gene therapy experiments, sending a wave of trepidation through the general public. Ian Wilmut and several other biologists have supported a moratorium on cloning human beings on the grounds that it is not yet safe to do so. This caution is understandable: it is one thing to hazard deformity and death in animal experiments; it is entirely another to do so among humans. At the same time, scientists stress that "safe" does not mean "error-free." It means safe compared to existing forms of reproduction. But they are confident that the new forms of reproduction will soon be no less risky, perhaps even safer, than giving birth the natural way.

Tinkering with the human germ line introduces its own distinctive problems, however. What if you give your newborn a set of enhancements only to discover that they are obsolete by the time she is five years old? Biologists John Campbell and Gregory Stock want to make provision for future upgrades: "Our earliest genetic modifications should not become permanent parts of the human gene pool. . . . Children who received auxiliary chromosomes would one day want to give their own children the most up-to-date set of genetic modifications available, not the outdated ones they themselves had received a generation earlier."[2]

The techno-utopians are not very concerned that the availability of enhancement technologies will create two classes in society, the genetically advantaged and the genetically disadvantaged. They correctly point to the fact that two such classes exist now, even in the absence of new therapies. Physicist Freeman Dyson says that genetic enhancement might be initially costly, but it won't remain "permanently expensive." Dyson writes, "Most of our socially important technologies, such as telephones, automobiles, television and computers began as expensive toys for the rich and afterwards became cheap enough for ordinary people to afford them."[3]

Dyson is right that time will make genetic enhancements widely available, just as cars and TV sets are now widely available. But the poor family still drives a secondhand Honda Civic while the rich family can afford a new Porsche. This may not be highly significant when it comes to cars, because both groups can still get around fairly well. What about when it comes to genetic advantages conferred at birth? Democratic societies can live with inequalities conferred by the lottery of nature, but can they countenance the deliberate introduction of biological alterations that give some citizens a better chance to succeed than others?

As far as I am aware, the techno-utopians have not addressed this issue yet. The message from the Party of Yeah is one of reassurance. This group is eager to stress that while science is giving us the power to do many new things with ourselves, these powers have existed in nature and in other ways they have even been exercised by human beings. Clones, for example, are common among plants, bacteria, and other living things, so why not extend the practice to human beings? A clone, after all, is nothing more than a genetic copy. Identical twins are genetic replicas of each other. This doesn't make them the same person, because their environments are bound to differ. Consequently, despite their shared genotype, identical twins develop their own identity. There are plenty of identical twins living normal lives, and there is no reason to believe that clones could not do the same.

The reason many people are uncomfortable with cloning, the techno-utopians say, is that they have in their minds images of Hitler clones or Saddam Hussein clones. Advocates of cloning say that mass cloning is not likely, at least in the United States and Europe. Even if someone were to make a few dozen Hitler clones, it doesn't follow that we would see a revival of the Third Reich. As one advocate of cloning explained to me, Hitler was the product of a unique genotype interacting with a specific environment. If Hitler were to be cloned now, the clone would be raised in a totally different milieu and would turn out quite differently. The Hitler clone raised in New Orleans might well be seen traipsing the bayous looking for crawfish. Another Hitler clone raised in Dallas might find himself working on an oil rig and listening to Garth Brooks. "Hey," my techno-utopian acquaintance observed with a chuckle, "one of the Hitler clones might even end up marrying a Jew."

The techno-utopians contend that genetic engineering, like cloning, isn't new at all. "The selective breeding of animals directed to amplifying or eliminating certain traits has been a human activity since prehis-

toric times," remarks biologist Cornelius Van Dop. "The selective introduction of foreign genes into germ lines is thus a logical extension of
animal husbandry."[4] Similarly, the manipulation of human genes can be
seen as a logical extension of applying such practices to animals. In his
book *Who's Afraid of Human Cloning?* Gregory Pence argues that we
breed dogs to produce the traits that we want, and we are pleased with
the results; so what is so outrageous about breeding better children?
Pence writes that if a technology were developed to give his child an extra decade of life or 50 percent more memory, "then I personally would
feel *obligated* to give my future child such benefits."[5]

While genetic enhancement as a moral duty might strike many
people as a new concept, the techno-utopians emphasize that it is well
established in law, and widely recognized in society, that parents have
the right to determine what is best for their children. Moreover, this
group points out that parents have always taken steps to improve their
children's life prospects. As Fred Gage suggested in the beginning of
the previous chapter, when we seek attractive and intelligent mates, are
we not, in effect, seeking to shape the traits that will define our offspring? "There are already plenty of ways in which we design our children," remarks biologist Gregory Stock. "One of them is called piano
lessons. Another is called private school." Stock's point is that engineering your children's genes is simply one more way in which parents
can make their children better people. Pence is confident that any enhancements he can give his children will be much appreciated. "I believe that my child would be grateful to have been deliberately given
such a benefit."[6] One can envision young Pence proudly bringing home
his report card: "Thanks, Dad, those genetic enhancements really came
in handy."

The techno-utopians recognize that some people may have a funny
feeling about all this. There is something weird and unnatural about
fixing your child in the same way you fix your car. Yet this impulse, the
techno-utopians say, is reactionary. It is a function of habit. We're not
used to genetic engineering, so it seems "unnatural" to us. But think·
about how unnatural driving a car seemed for people who had previously gotten around in horse-and-carriages! Imagine how weird it appeared at first to take a person's heart out and put in an artificial one!
The techno-utopians gleefully point out that we engage in countless
"unnatural" practices today, such as wearing dentures, traveling in air-

planes, and using contraceptives. "The smallpox virus was part of the natural order," Lee Silver wryly observes, "until it was forced into extinction by human intervention."[7]

Diseases and death are natural; lifesaving surgery is artificial. Every time a doctor removes a tumor or performs a kidney transplant, he plays God. The techno-utopians are openly contemptuous of what they term the "if God had wanted us to fly, he would have given us wings" argument. They argue that it is equally absurd to speak of human action as contravening nature when we are part of nature; since we are part of nature, whatever we do is by definition "natural." At the same time, the techno-utopians emphasize that being part of nature does not make us genetic captives of evolution. The environments in which *Homo sapiens* evolved are long gone; they have nothing to do with the challenges and scarcities we face today. So we are free, the argument goes, to pick up where evolution left off and shape our genetic destiny as we see fit.

Technology booster Virginia Postrel argues that "revering nature means sacrificing the purposes of individuals to preserve the world as given." She outlines the consequence of this belief: "It requires that we force people to live with biological conditions that trouble them." People such as Rifkin, in her view, "oppose the extension of healthy, active human life beyond its current limits" that biotechnology promises. They want to force people to live with disease "or simply less beauty, intelligence, happiness or grace than could be achieved through artifice." Consequently they are aligning themselves against the hopes of sick and suffering people. Indeed they are, in Postrel's harsh term, "prodeath." Postrel's own view is that nature imposes no moral constraints on human behavior: "About the proper way to live, nature is silent. . . . What makes a human condition unhealthy is not that it is unnatural, but that it interferes with human purposes."[8]

Postrel makes a valid point about the futility of arguing that because something exists in nature, therefore it is good. But if nature is not a source of morality, as she and others insist, why should we care if people have a *natural* desire to have a child of their own? Why not treat their desire as no different from their desire for, say, a cable hookup to the Internet? Instead we give this desire a special moral status, and some people even speak of it as a "right." The concept of a "right," Tocqueville writes, is nothing but the concept of virtue introduced to the political world.[9] So there seems to be a problem with the attempt to establish a complete separation between nature and morality, between "what is" and "what should be." Here is a case where morality clearly appears to derive from nature: the "ought" arises out of the "is." Even so, the techno-utopians continue to resist the concept of nature because they see it as a constraint on human freedom.

The techno-utopians are not worried about diminishing the sanctity of human life because they say there is nothing intrinsically sacred about human life. This group is impatient with those who say that genetic interventions contravene a deep human conviction of the preciousness of life. "This is not an ethical argument but a religious one," Lee Silver retorts. "There is no logic to it."[10] Biologist David Baltimore, a Nobel laureate, argues that "statements about morally and ethically unacceptable practices" have no place in the biotechnology debate "because those are subjective grounds and therefore provide no basis for discussion."[11] Silver and Baltimore's shared assumption is that the moralists are talking about *values* while they, the hard scientists, are dealing in *facts*.

In this view, the subjective preferences of those who seek to mystify human life and raise it to some higher ethical plane do not square with the truths about human biology taught by science. The cells of human beings, Silver points out, are no different in their chemical makeup from the cells of horses, bacteria, and plants. Silver adds that living cells are, like stones and other objects, made up of molecules and atoms, so that life itself is only a particular way of assembling nonliving parts. Silver distinguishes between "life," which merely refers to cells made up of atoms, and "alive," which refers to the sentient creatures we see walking about.

If there is such a thing as human dignity, Silver argues, it derives exclusively from *consciousness,* from our ability to perceive and apprehend our environment. "The human mind," Silver writes, "is much more than the genes that brought it into existence." Somehow the electrochemical reactions in our brain produce consciousness, and it is this consciousness, Silver contends, that is the source of man's autonomy and power. While genes fully control the activity of all life forms, Silver writes that in human beings "master and slave have switched positions." So it is consciousness, after all, that enables man to complete his dominance over nature by prevailing over his human nature. Silver concludes that in a bold assertion of will, we can defeat the program of our genes, we can grasp the reins of evolution, we can choose the genetic code we want for our children, and we can collectively determine the future of our species.[12]

These triumphant notes are struck by many techno-utopians. Biotechnology, journalist Ronald Bailey writes, "will liberate future generations from today's limitations and offer them a much wider scope of freedom."[13] Physicist Gregory Benford is even more enthusiastic: "It is as though prodigious, bountiful Nature for billions of years has tossed off variations on its themes like a careless, prolific Picasso. Now Nature finds that one of its casual creations has come back with a piercing, searching vision, and its own pictures to paint."[14]

These are ringing statements, but do they make sense? Clearly, there are many problems with Silver's definition of human dignity as revolving around consciousness. Animals are conscious; do they deserve the same dignity as human beings? If so, should we view Silver as a kind of Doctor Mengele for experimenting on animals in his lab? Moreover, are human beings entitled to dignity only during the times they are conscious? Do we lose our right to be respected and become legitimate subjects for discarding or medical experiments when we cease to be conscious, as for instance when we are in a coma or when we fall asleep? Surely Silver would disavow these conclusions. They do, however, flow directly from his definition, which by the way is just as heavily freighted with values as that of his opponents.

I have stressed the issue of values because behind the proclamations of scientific neutrality there is clearly an ideology that needs to be spelled out. The unveiling is necessary because the ideology refuses to identify itself as such. Here, then, is the techno-Nietzschean doctrine that has arisen within the Party of Yeah. We are molecules, but molecules that know how to rebel! Our values do not derive from nature or nature's God; rather, they arise from the arbitrary force of our wills. And now our wills can make the most momentous choice ever exercised on behalf of our species: the choice to reject our human nature. For why should we remain subject to the constraints of our mortality and destiny? Wealth and technology have given us the keys to unlimited, indeed godlike, power. Why stop with the conquest of nature? Let us proceed with the conquest of our own limitations. Let us remake the life cycle. Let us remake ourselves. Immortality, here we come. From now on our children can be products of our design. Down with our evolutionary captors! Down with our human nature! Up, up, to something greater! Behold the dawn of the posthuman era!

The techno-Nietzschean is winning many converts in the high-tech world. The reason is that most tech guys don't consciously subscribe to an ideology. They are interested in technology, and their operating principle is that if something is possible, it should be done. At the same time, many people working on new technologies realize that their work has important social implications. So they are seizing upon the techno-Nietzschean ideology because it gives them a way to make sense of what is going on around them. Moreover, they are emotionally attracted to the techno-Nietzschean vision. Its rah-rah spirit is entirely congruent with the psychology of the Party of Yeah.

In evaluating techno-Nietzscheanism, I want to focus on two very different critiques. The first comes from Leon Kass, a prominent bioethicist identified with the Party of Nah. The other comes from biologist Richard Dawkins, a leading intellectual of the Party of Yeah. Kass faults the techno-Nietzscheans for going too far; Dawkins and his followers charge that they have not gone far enough. The Kass critique comes from outside the Party of Yeah; the Dawkins critique begins within the Party of Yeah but threatens to split it into two very different camps. Although the substance of their criticisms is very different, Kass and Dawkins seem to agree that the techno-Nietzscheans are shallow, overconfident people who have not thought through the implications and consequences of their ideology. Let us see what Kass and Dawkins have to say; then I will try to determine which position is right.

The problem with the techno-Nietzscheans, according to Kass, is that "they are people with scary ideas." The people themselves aren't scary, he emphasizes. "In fact, many of them are quite cheerful and nice. But they speak of terrible things like designing and manufacturing children, or changing the nature of humanity, with grins on their faces. They are intoxicated by power, but they show no evidence of responsibility. This is why they are so dangerous."

A medical doctor and philosopher, Kass teaches in the Committee of Social Thought at the University of Chicago. He is one of the most influential bioethicists in the United States; indeed, the typical bioethicist is to Kass what a Sunday school teacher is to a prophet. Kass speaks with the aura of a secular priest. "What alarms me," Kass says, "is this unlimited faith in technology and markets. Something is developed, so it has to be good. Whatever the market decides is always right. Never mind that companies are seeking patents on life itself. Never mind that we are trafficking in human eggs and embryos. We are being led down new paths by people who have no moral sense of what is at stake."

Part of the problem, Kass says, is the nature of modern science itself. "The ancients conceived of science as the understanding of nature, pursued for its own sake," he writes. "We moderns view science as power, as control over nature." One corollary of the scientific worldview, according to Kass, is that the only valid knowledge is that which can be known scientifically. The effect of this approach, he says, is to "shut our eyes to the most important human questions: what is good, what is bad, what is beautiful, what is happiness." In Kass's words, science and technology "supply knowledge of the means while professing ignorance of the ends."

Traditionally, Kass writes in his book *Toward a More Natural Science*, the purpose of medicine was to restore health, to make people well. Obviously, this goal requires some standard of health that is supplied by nature. Modern medicine has not abandoned its traditional goal, Kass writes, but it has gone beyond it to undertake projects that have a quite different end. A couple wants to abort a female fetus because they prefer to have a boy. A woman wants her breasts enlarged, to attract male attention, or reduced, because they interfere with her golf swing. A man seeks prescription drugs to alter his moods: Prozac when he is down; Ritalin when he is up. Bored with life, a person asks for a lethal injection so he can die a painless death. These cases occur routinely, Kass notes, but what is striking is that none of them involves producing better health; in fact, some of them conscript the doctor to help undermine, even destroy, health.

The stated justification for new advances in biotechnology, such as cloning and genetic engineering, is that they will advance the central goals of helping people to live longer, healthier lives and to give birth to children who can do the same. Kass concedes the legitimacy of this effort. In a recent article he writes, "Who would not welcome surgery to correct the genetic defects that lead to sickle-cell anemia, Huntington's disease, and breast cancer, or to protect against the immune deficiency caused by the AIDS virus?" I asked Kass: If his child needed gene therapy to recover from a deadly disease, would he pursue it? Unhesitatingly, he answered yes.

But it is precisely the benefits of these technologies, Kass hastened to add, that blinds us to their dangers. "It is easy to recognize evil pure and simple," he said. "It's much harder to recognize the evil in things that are partly good." Kass recently wrote that "the road to Brave New World is paved with love and charity." And, he says, we are all at different times of our lives vulnerable to the seduction. So what is the danger? The first one concerns the means used to achieve biotechnology's noble objectives. Kass recites a litany of modern laboratory techniques: experimentation on embryos and cadavers, sperm banks, organ transplantation, test-tube babies, surrogate wombs, sex-change operations, mind-altering drugs, and now cloning and genetic surgery. Many of these are standard practice, Kass says, and yet to thoughtful and decent human beings they violate some visceral sense of what is right and proper.

Kass gives an example. Over the years, he says, he has observed first-year medical students get ready to dissect their first cadaver. Invariably, he says, many of them show reluctance, qualms, and even disgust at the prospect of cutting up and experimenting on a human body. Eventually they get over this revulsion, of course, but Kass does not admire this emotional transition. He says they have simply become desensitized; their original moral reaction was the sound one. "The dead body is no longer the person who has died," Kass admits, "but neither is it simply the chemicals it is made of." The students' original reaction displays what Kass calls "the wisdom of repugnance."

Repugnance, Kass concedes, is not by itself an argument. Some people may be revolted at the idea of interracial marriage; it does not follow that this feeling is morally justified. While repugnance may sometimes reflect prejudice, Kass says that it usually reflects "a deep natural revulsion to violations we dare not condone." Morality, in his view, does not proceed by reason alone. Kass gives an example: the incest taboo. Incest is universally considered an abomination, but why? Can we give adequate logical reasons for this? Not really. Certainly incest may increase the chance of defective offspring, but if this were the sole problem we should approve of sexual relations between brothers and sisters, and also between parents and their grown children, as long as birth control is used. The horror of incest, Kass says, goes beyond a regard for the physical and mental health of offspring. It represents a profound natural wisdom that is no less wise because we cannot justify it scientifically. Why should we rationalize away our disgust?

But, I protest to Kass, practices such as dissecting cadavers, freezing embryos, transplanting organs, and making babies in test tubes are common. Isn't it absurd to believe that they can be resisted because of instinctive repugnance? I cite the example of in vitro fertilization. When the first test-tube baby, Louise Brown, was born in 1978, there was a big uproar. Many people were outraged at the notion of circumventing the natural process of reproduction by fertilizing the egg with sperm in a petri dish. But now thousands of babies are born each year by in vitro fertilization. More than 200,000 test-tube babies are alive today. What was once outrageous is no big deal.

Kass admits there is no way of going back. He is mainly concerned about the present. He wants people to trust the natural revulsion they have for new technologies such as cloning and genetic enhancement of children; he says that these instincts contain greater wisdom than we may be able to articulate. Kass's criticism of past technologies is aimed at preparing us to deal with future ones. His hope is that "a heightened awareness of what we have been doing" will prevent us from making more serious mistakes in the future. "If we recognize that we have gone too far," Kass says, "then we may realize that it makes no sense to go even farther."

Kass claims that the newest technologies pose a greater threat than anything we have encountered in the past: "Our greatest danger will be voluntary self-degradation or willing dehumanization." Even freely chosen uses of these biological powers, Kass says, "carry dangers of degradation, depersonalization, and enfeeblement of soul." We don't choose to be dehumanized, of course. We choose to "fight illness, and then to extend life, and then to pursue immortality, and then to design our children, and then to remake our species." Little by little, Kass says, "we are trading away our basic humanity." What the techno-Nietzscheans call progress, Kass calls "retail sanity and wholesale madness."

But what is wrong, I ask, with seeking to extend life, perhaps even indefinitely? "I don't have a problem with finding cures for diseases that kill people," Kass says. "But now we hear that aging and death are themselves diseases." In an essay subtitled "The Virtue of Finitude"

Kass argues that mortality and the natural life cycle are the foundations of our deepest and most meaningful experiences; indeed, they are the basis for taking life seriously, living it passionately, and finding fulfillment in it. "To number our days," Kass writes, "is the condition of making them count." Kass suggests that in a profound and inexplicable way, the beauty of flowers and sunsets is connected to their passing; the rose that never withered and the sun that hovered endlessly on the horizon would cease to command our astonishment and awe. Thus the project to extend life indefinitely carries with it the danger of "extending the body while diminishing the soul."

Kass is probably right that a sense of mortality adds richness and poignancy to human experience. The late Herbert Stein, a colleague of mine and a very wise economist, wrote in his last book that it is a bedrock economic principle that scarcity confers value: "The realization that one's days are few," Stein wrote, "increases one's appreciation" of their significance.[15] Still, Stein hung on to life as long as he could. Most people would probably welcome the opportunity to live a few more years, then a few more, then a few more. Beyond a certain point of frailty, this may no longer be the case. But what if antiaging drugs make it possible to retard the breakdown of the body? What if it's possible for a man of eighty to have the body and mind of a fifty-year-old of today? There is a wide consensus today that the extension of healthy life is a virtually unmitigated good, and to the degree that science makes it possible, why not postpone that appointment with the undertaker?

Kass understands this aspiration to stretch the limits of mortal life. The rhetoric of immortality bothers him, but it is not his real target. His real concern is aimed at the new technologies that are making possible cloning and genetic engineering. Kass recognizes the distinction between gene therapy, which is aimed at curing diseases, and gene enhancement, which is aimed at improving human beings. But Kass says that in practice there is no bright line separating the two. If it's okay to administer genes that increase height to midgets and dwarves, why isn't it okay for you to obtain them for your son who is three inches below average? It's going to be hard to say no to parents who believe that height confers confidence and other advantages in life and are willing to pay for their offspring to be taller than they otherwise would be. Kass points out that plastic surgery, which was developed to reconstruct the features of accident and burn victims, rapidly became a cosmetic industry. Today most plastic surgeons spend virtually all their time on "enhancement."

While Kass regards plastic surgery as a foolish indulgence, he takes a much firmer position against producing clones and genetically engineering our children. These practices are "inherently despotic," Kass says, because they reflect our desire to make other people after our own image or in accordance with our wills. In such situations, Kass says, children are no longer surprises to their parents and to the world; rather, they become "custom-ordered products" that are likely to be evaluated in accordance with their conformity to the traits that have been picked out for them. Cloning and genetic selection are exercises in narcissism and ego projection, Kass says. With them, he warns, we risk destroying the natural bonds of procreation and beginning the chilling process of turning children into "objects of manufacture." Kass says that the use of these technologies would amount to "a new form of child abuse."

Kass points out that several of the justifications of cloning make the clone an instrument of the fulfillment of someone else's desire. A sick child needs an organ transplant, so a clone is produced to provide one. A dying child is cloned to provide a "replacement." Clones are produced for the purpose of medical research or to resolve the nature-nurture debate or to send on space missions or on dangerous military expeditions. These may be seen as abuses of cloning, but Kass notes that they are suggestions that have been made by cloning advocates. Moreover, Kass says, even more benign goals, such as providing a cloned son and daughter for an infertile couple, reduce the clones to objects of other people's desires.

I ask Kass whether the same instrumental motives aren't present today. A couple may want a child because their relationship is faltering, and they think a child will bring them closer together. Or a tennis enthusiast may pressure his child to become a professional tennis player. These distressing cases exist, Kass admits, but at least nature frequently frustrates the instrumental desires of the parents. Cloning, he says, would make an existing social problem immeasurably worse.

Despite the efforts of cloning advocates to emphasize the continuity between cloning and existing reproductive practices, Kass points out that cloning is a form of asexual reproduction. Yes, cloning is common among plants and bacteria, but human beings are neither. Kass charges that cloning would represent a complete redefinition of the relationship between parents and their children. Kass worries about a "confounding of all normal understandings" of father, mother, sibling, and grandparent, and of all the moral relationships implied by those terms. In the case of cloning "the usually sad situation of the single parent is here deliberately planned." Women would be able to clone themselves and have children without any male involvement. A man too could rent a womb and reproduce himself without a female partner. Moreover, the clone would have a very strange biological relationship to her single parent. Since the clone would, biologically speaking, be an identical twin, she and her mother would be *twin sisters.* The clone's biological parents would be her grandparents! When the clone grows up and has children, her children would also be her mother's children! Cloning, Kass argues, represents a radical assault on the already fragile institution of the family.

When parents attempt to design their children, they are, in Kass's view, committing a similar abomination. Are we arrogant enough to believe we are wise enough to decide such questions? What makes us think that we know better than our descendants how their lives should turn out? Perhaps the well-meaning father who gives his daughter blue eyes will confront an angry teenager many years later who says, "Daddy, I can't believe you gave me blue eyes! I want brown eyes!" Against this perversity, Kass offers a very different understanding of the role of parents: "When a couple now chooses to procreate, the partners are saying yes to the emergence of a new life in its novelty, saying yes not only to having a child but also, tacitly, to having whatever child the child turns out to be. In accepting our finitude and opening ourselves to our replacement, we are tacitly confessing the limits of our control."

What this means, Kass writes, is that "our children are not *our* children: they are not our property, nor our possessions. Neither are they supposed to live our lives for us, or anyone's life but their own. To be sure, we seek to guide them on their way, imparting to them not just life but nurturing, love, and a way of life; to be sure, they bear our hopes that they will live fine and flourishing lives. . . . Still, in their genetic distinctiveness and independence are the natural foreshadowing of the deep truth that they have their own and never-before-enacted life to live. They are sprung from a past, but they take an uncharted course into the future." Kass concludes that the project of designing one's children is a grotesque violation of the profound meaning of parenthood.

Where does this leave us? Kass argues that in our endless quest for power over nature, we have lost sight of the ends that this power is meant to serve. So we strive desperately for control—control over nature, control over our lives, control over death, control over our children, control over our species. In Kass's view this pursuit is a response to "a deep human longing that is not fully satisfied with earthly life," and so we labor to extend it and change human nature in the hope that we will find true happiness, true wholeness. But we haven't found it yet, and Kass says we are not going to. Indeed, he says, the path we are on is the path to self-destruction, and true progress in such a situation can only mean turning back.[16]

I have cited Kass's views at length because they strike me as both thoughtful and humane. Yet although I admire Kass and agree with much of his outlook, I cannot always support his conclusions. Even though Kass is vastly more sophisticated than Rifkin, both strike me as too broad in their rejection of existing and emerging technologies. In the case of widely used techniques such as experimentation on cadavers, organ transplantation, and in vitro fertilization, I believe that the gains in terms of life extension and the provision of children to infertile couples outweigh the cost in terms of desecrating the body or moving the process of conception to the laboratory. Moreover, while I agree with Kass that earthly immortality would completely redefine the meaning of human life, and not necessarily for the better, I have no problem with antiaging drugs and therapies that may give me five, ten, perhaps even twenty years beyond my normal life span. That would mean more time with my family, more books to read, more books to write, an extended opportunity to confound and annoy my critics. Under certain conditions I will make a case for cloning and genetic engineering. At the same time, there is a very great evil in these new technologies that I intend to identify in the concluding chapter. Kass raises it but understates its moral and social harm.

But before we get there, I want to present a very different critique of the techno-Nietzscheans. It comes from biologist Richard Dawkins, who has emerged as perhaps the most serious thinker associated with the

Party of Yeah. The author of several highly acclaimed books on the implications of Darwinism, Dawkins is an Englishman who exudes a calm sense of his own superiority. His characteristic facial expression hovers between a smirk and a sneer. His attack is aimed just where the techno-Nietzscheans are proudest of themselves: in their triumphant assertion of the will to power.

Dawkins begins from a point that is in complete agreement with the techno-Nietzscheans. In 1997, Dawkins and several other leading scientists, such as E. O. Wilson and Francis Crick, issued a public statement defending cloning. They argued, "Some world religions teach that human beings are fundamentally different from other mammals. . . . Human nature is held to be unique and sacred. . . . As far as the scientific enterprise can determine, human capabilities appear to differ in degree, not in kind, from those found among the higher animals. Humanity's rich repertoire of thoughts, feelings, aspirations and hopes seems to arise from electrochemical brain processes, not from an immaterial soul that operates in ways no instrument can discover. . . . Views of human nature rooted in humanity's tribal past ought not to be our primary criterion for making moral decisions about cloning."[17]

Like Lee Silver, Dawkins is denying the sanctity of life on the grounds that our human bodies are made up of nothing more than molecules. For Dawkins, as for Silver, any claim that human beings have a soul appears to be a form of mysticism or irrationalism. Both of them are in agreement with Gilbert Ryle's assertion that our bodies are entirely made up of machinery: there is no "ghost inside the machine."

But recall that Silver goes on to justify human autonomy and dignity on the basis that "the human mind is much more than the genes that brought it into existence." This is the basis for Dawkins's attack. What to Silver must have seemed like a profound statement is to Dawkins a nonsensical one. The cells of the brain, no less than the cells in the rest of our body, are in Silver's own account made up of nothing but molecules. So what gives these cells any special right to be respected? Having disposed of the mysticism of the soul, Silver now seems to be promoting the mysticism of the mind. Having expelled the ghost from the machine, Silver appears to be trying to bring it back.

From Dawkins's point of view it makes no more sense to say, "The human mind is much more than the genes that brought it into existence" than to say, "The human pancreas is much more than the genes that brought it into existence." Or, for that matter, to say, "Water is much more than the hydrogen and oxygen molecules that brought it into existence." The point is that all chemical compounds do more than the molecules that brought them into existence. For Dawkins, the scientific reality and therefore the only reality is that our minds are simply the by-product of the electrochemical processes of our neurons. What principles of autonomy or dignity derive from such chemical reactions? None. Free will itself is exposed as an illusion, and the exaltation of will on the part of the techno-Nietzscheans is revealed as a form of self-deception.

Dawkins's philosophy is *materialism*, and it should be distinguished from that term as it is normally used. In everyday conversation we use "materialism" to refer to the mania for material things, as when we discuss whether our society is becoming too materialistic. This is not what I mean here. Materialism in this context is the view that material things are the only reality and that knowledge of material objects is the only valid claim to knowledge; all else is simply a matter of belief or opinion. Materialism is the ideology of many of the best minds in the Party of Yeah—including biologist E. O. Wilson, philosopher Daniel Dennett, and neuroscientist Steven Pinker. Dawkins is worth paying attention to because he is the group's leading theoretician.

Dawkins argues that there is a deep symbiosis between the biological revolution and the computer revolution; indeed, that there is a deep connection between human beings and computers. Departing from the familiar materialist concept that human beings are machines, Dawkins argues that it is more accurate to say that human beings are *software*. The reason is that our humanity is best defined by our genes, and in Dawkins's view our genes are "long strings of pure digital information." Indeed, life itself is "just bytes and bytes of digital information." When we reproduce, we are like a software program that makes copies of itself. Our genes are "replicators," and evolution is the mechanism of determining the survival, through natural selection, of those replicators that best adapt to their environment. All living things, Dawkins writes, "are survival machines programmed to propagate the digital database that did the programming."[18]

Since genes are entirely oriented toward the single goal of survival, Dawkins contends that the characteristic quality of the gene may be described as "selfishness." This does not mean that genes have motives, but their survival machines do: selfish genes make selfish people. Even altruism, Dawkins writes in his book *The Selfish Gene,* is rooted in genetic self-interest: the reason a mother gives her life to save her child is that this is the best way for her genes to perpetuate themselves.[19]

Yet genes cannot survive without bodies, just as software needs to operate through some form of hardware. Even bodies are not always enough, Dawkins writes; sometimes the pressures of survival require artifacts or tools. Birds build nests, beavers build dams, and those animals that do the best job in constructing these necessary artifacts are the ones that survive. Dawkins concludes that the nest is not some cultural add-on; it is part of the genetic expression of the bird. In his book *The Extended Phenotype* Dawkins argues that our artifacts and our technology arise out of the physical expression of our genes. They are the "extended phenotype" of our digital code. It follows from Dawkins's argument that there is no real distinction between natural and cultural evolution. Our technology is part of what determines our evolutionary fitness. In a sense, we coevolve with our tools.[20]

Dawkins's views have become hugely influential in the fields of biology and computer science. Indeed, his disciples have constructed entire fields of investigation on Dawkins's intellectual foundation. No doubt they have sometimes proceeded in ways that go beyond Dawkins, perhaps even in ways Dawkins might not approve of, but this should not be surprising. Christianity developed doctrines far more elaborate than anything Christ ever said, and Marxism went considerably beyond Marx. Dawkins's theories are equally radical, although whether they will have anything like the consequences of Christianity or Marxism remains to be seen. I have taken the liberty of drawing out the implications of Dawkins's theories to show how they provide the intellectual scaffolding for some of the farthest-reaching ideas advanced by the Party of Yeah.

Dawkins has convinced some leading figures in the tech world that computers should be designed entirely differently from the ones that are built today. Reflect for a moment on Dawkins's claim that software and genes are virtually identical systems of digital information. If this is so, if software and genes operate on the same principles, then software, like genes, should be able to perpetuate itself through the principle of natural selection. Computer scientists Danny Hillis, John Koza, and others are trying to make software that breeds other software. They are convinced that the best kinds of software will not be devised by a single creator but will be "grown" in a "digital ecosystem." These scientists want to create a new type of software that will perpetuate itself through the same evolutionary dynamics that for millennia have governed genetic selection in natural environments.[21]

An even more ambitious group of scientists is involved in a new field called "artificial life." If life is fundamentally made up of information, shouldn't it be possible to use information technology to create life? These researchers don't just want to make computers that can think. Thinking, after all, is just one of life's functions. Rather, they want to use silicon to replicate all the essential features of life, including thought, mobility, expression, and reproduction. Indeed, they are trying to create a parallel Darwinian universe that will differ from the human world in only one way: while we human beings are presumed to be carbon-based computers, the new universe will contain silicon-based computers.

Whether this project will succeed remains to be seen. But let's take the logic further. It seems obvious that silicon computers, which continue to evolve at a rapid rate, will surpass carbon computers, whose digital database evolved a very long time ago. Indeed, over time, silicon computers can be expected to be so much more advanced than carbon computers that the distance between the two will be as great as that between the processing power of a human being and that of a fly. At this point, the carbon-based computers, which initially created the silicon computers, will be subordinate to their control and will have to follow their instructions. To avoid this foreseeable defeat, which may be as degrading as the experience of being swatted is to the fly, the carbon-based computers may decide to merge with the silicon computers, thus ushering in the cyborg era.

While this merger may seem a defeat for humanity, it is completely consistent with Dawkins's notion that even though carbon-based evolution has, for all practical purposes, stopped, the evolutionary struggle goes on. The contest has merely shifted to new ground. In the past human beings struggled for survival with other carbon-based life-forms; in the future we will struggle against the very technology that enabled us to win our previous battles. What better option for us, then, than to blend with our artifacts and coevolve with them? Those are the best peace and survival terms that we can expect at this point.

So what remains of our quest for meaning and purpose in life? Dawkins unflinchingly observes, "In a universe of physical forces and genetic replication, some people are going to get hurt, other people are going to get lucky, and you won't find any rhyme or reason in it, nor any justice. The universe we observe has precisely the properties we should expect if there is, at bottom, no design, no purpose, no evil and no good, nothing but blind pitiless indifference."[22]

An existence that is as endless as it is purposeless: this seems to be a good working definition of Hell. What bitter irony that such a fate should be prescribed by a group I have named the Party of Yeah. But Dawkins and his followers have simply taken the materialist doctrine to its logical conclusion. This conclusion should give everyone in the Party of Yeah pause. To see its full force, recall that a few centuries ago modern science and America were both constructed on the foundation of conquering nature so that, by harvesting nature's bounty, man would be free to choose a better life for himself. But the materialist view holds that this freedom is an illusion. Our choices, even our technology, simply reflect the mindless operations of the genetic code that is built into our bodies and over which we have effectively no control. Far from us prevailing over the laws of evolution, those laws remain in firm control, and we are their helpless subjects. The stunning conclusion is that modern science is a failure and America is a failure. Far from man conquering nature, it is nature that continues to reign tyrannically over man.

CHAPTER TEN

THE GIFT

The Things That Matter the Most

Wealth is evidently not the good we are seeking, for it is merely useful and for the sake of something else.

—Aristotle, *Nicomachean Ethics*

We are living in an astonishing moment in history in which the problem of scarcity, which has plagued our species from the dawn of mankind, is vanishing before our eyes. Wealth has exploded and spread beyond the confines of a narrow caste; suddenly, it has become accessible to a large segment of society. Mass affluence, once a philosopher's dream, is now a social reality. What could be more exhilarating than for people—and entire societies—to relish the victory over necessity! This victory is deserved, it is the product of long struggle, and we should enjoy it to the fullest. At the same time, we should be alert to a new and grave danger that is concealed within the triumph itself. There is a serpent in the grass, beckoning us with an alluring temptation—to eat of the tree of knowledge and become like gods. If we succumb to this temptation, we will throw away our opportunity to make good on the promise of wealth and undo the American experiment at the very moment of its supreme triumph.

Let us take a moment to understand our current predicament. We are living in a new millennium, and it seems clear that the challenges of the future are going to be quite different from those in the past. The twentieth century, for example, was the century of collectivism, characterized by a welfare state at home and socialism and communism abroad. Collectivism was a doctrine for coping with scarcity. Its premise was that there is not enough to go around; how can we go about sharing the pie so that everybody has a decent slice? Coping with scarcity has been the political problem for governments, and the personal struggle of individuals and families, since the time of the Babylonians.

But now that age has passed, and America has a new problem: coping with prosperity. If the old problem was about how to acquire wealth, the new debate is over how to use it. We live in a time and place where wealth has become abundant. In 1958, John Kenneth Galbraith published *The Affluent Society,* in which he asserted that America had become a rich country. At that time this was not strictly true: many Americans still went to bed hungry, many shivered in winter, many didn't have cars or indoor plumbing. Moreover, while in 1958 most people were middle class, very few could be called rich.

Today the United States truly is an affluent society. Not only do we have a billionaires' club, but this is a country where more than 5 million households, which is to say 15 million people, are millionaires. America has created the first overclass, the first mass affluent class, in world history, and similar classes will soon form in other countries as well. For the members of this overclass, it seems safe to say that they can pretty much do whatever they want for the rest of their lives. If leisure can be defined as doing what you want to do, as opposed to doing nothing, the overclass is the new leisure class. It may work harder than any other group, but that is because it chooses to spend its time in this way rather than on the beach or the golf course.

So what about the Americans who don't belong to the mass affluent class? By any historical standard, by comparison with most other countries, they are rich too! A family that subsists at the poverty line, as defined by the U.S. government, has a standard of living that is higher than 80 percent of the world's population. So if you live in America you've already won the lottery. You have to grow up in another country, as I did, to fully understand this. In the middle-class family in which I was raised in Bombay, I didn't lack for necessities, but I grew up without many things that ordinary Americans take for granted: a telephone, a television, air-conditioning, hot water in the shower. It didn't occur to me to complain, because compared to everyone else in our area, we were well off. My background gives me a special vantage point from which to see America, and I am constantly stupefied at how blessed Americans are. I recognize, of course, that Americans have problems, but those problems are quite different from those of a family in San Salvador or Calcutta where there isn't enough to eat, where your children run about in tattered rags, where the rain comes streaming through the roof of your hut, and where those sly cousins, disease and death, are constantly lurking about your door.

The events of the past two and a half decades—the collapse of the Berlin Wall, the discrediting of socialism, the explosion of technology, and the juggernaut of noninflationary growth—have all worked together to suggest a single conclusion: that the economic problem has been solved. We know how to create wealth. We know how to make people, and countries, rich. It doesn't follow, of course, that everyone is rich already. But America has already achieved mass affluence, and other countries are following its lead and moving in the same direction. This recipe for prosperity and the freedom to shape the rest of your life is America's gift to the world. And there is no reason to believe that any country, whatever its natural resources, cannot achieve prosperity. But there is only one way to do it, and that is the American way of technological capitalism.

Capitalism has won the economic war, but it has not yet won the moral war. This is the basis of the new politics that is emerging in America. The old debate—over the size and role of government—is largely obsolete. Government has become a spectator and an occasional nuisance, but by and large, nobody cares what the government does. Policy pundits will continue to argue about what to do with this surplus or how to make up that shortfall, but the government has ceased to be central to the fate of the economy. Perhaps the only way the government can have an impact today is to screw things up. What is needed, therefore, is for a government to have low tax rates and stable monetary policy and to preserve free trade. Apart from this there is no reason for it to interfere in the economy. If the new president changed into his pajamas every afternoon and took a long nap, like Calvin Coolidge, this would probably be good for the market and good for the country.

*   *   *

The new debate is over the moral legitimacy of the new economy powered by technology and capitalism. As we have seen, there are basically two arguments against capitalism: the left-wing claim that it leaves many people poor and the right-wing claim that it makes many people rich. Let me note at the outset that poor countries cannot afford to have either argument. In a place such as India or Rwanda, where the vast majority of people are poor, there is no use in pointing fingers of blame at the few people who are rich, because all their wealth could do little to relieve the situation of the masses. If the left-wing critique seems irrelevant to people in the Third World, they are likely to find the right-wing argument mystifying. At a time when people in poor countries are desperately trying to better their condition, you cannot lecture them about the moral and social perils of affluence; they would surely think you were joking. It's not that they would disagree with you; they simply wouldn't know what you were talking about.

Even so, this is not India or Rwanda, and here, in the prosperous West, we have the luxury of debating the critiques offered on the left and the right. And we should debate them, because the concerns being raised are entirely appropriate for a wealthy society. The left-wing argument is no longer about absolute poverty, which is no longer a significant problem in America or most of Europe. Rather, the argument is over relative poverty, and the urgency and force of the egalitarian critique is due to the magnitude of income and wealth differences. Is it right that a workingman who plays by the rules should struggle to live comfortably while a thirty-two-year-old with an idea for a software company has a net worth that exceeds the gross national product of Sri Lanka? Is it fair that a nurse makes an annual salary of $36,000 while celebrities such as Ricky Martin make $36 million?

More broadly, the middle class, which is generally the stabilizing force in a society, has now bifurcated into an upper middle class that has money in the market and benefits from free trade and technology, and a lower middle class that feels threatened by immigration, free trade, and technology, and whose incomes have stagnated. The first group has been called the bourgeois bohemians; the second, we could call the bourgeois peasants. This doesn't mean that the bourgeois peasants are worse off. Very few Americans are worse off in terms of their standard of living than, say, a decade or two ago. But they are worse off relative to the enormous gains made by those who are ahead of them. The sting of inequality persists because the relative gaps between people have become larger and show no sign of closing. What makes this debate especially poignant is that inequality today is largely the consequence of merit. By "merit" I do not mean IQ or intrinsic moral worth; I mean the ability to supply goods that other people are willing to pay for. In a capitalist economy, the outstanding software programmer who is five times as good as the mediocre programmer may well find a company that is willing to pay him five times as much. How do stars such as Ricky Martin get rich? Through the nurse and innumerable other ordinary folk who dip into their pockets and pay $80 apiece to buy tickets to his concerts. Given these voluntary actions, it is easy to see that even if incomes were completely equalized by edict, in short order the inequalities that we see today would reemerge.

Today's market is more meritocratic than ever before. This is not to say that nepotism has been completely eradicated. Every society is characterized by a combination of nepotism or favoritism and merit or earned reward. (Racial discrimination, for instance, is one form of nepotism. Hiring your lazy nephew to work for your company is another.) America has moved dramatically in the direction of merit and is likely to continue to do so. What this means is that most people who are well off today weren't born to their money; they earned it. This doesn't mean they weren't lucky. But luck tends to favor the prepared mind. As author Randy Komisar puts it, successful people don't enjoy "dumb luck"; rather, they enjoy "smart luck." These are people who start companies and professional practices, take risks, and put themselves in a position where the gods of the market can smile upon them. In this sense, they deserve their good fortune. The question therefore arises, What is their debt to those who have less?

Traditionally, rich people got their wealth through inheritance. Inherited wealth tends to produce an accompanying sense of social obligation or noblesse oblige. It makes sense for a person who didn't do anything to deserve his fortune to presume that the poor too are victims of fate. In the past there were obligations, both of law and of sentiment, that arose between the upper and lower classes. The most extreme example of this was feudalism, with its intricate set of social and legal bonds. But some version of this hierarchy has existed in every society. It arises out of the shared sense that one's place in life is the product of circumstances beyond one's choosing.

Today's rich, by contrast, have risen to the top in the most open, mobile, and entrepreneurial society that has ever existed. As we have seen, most of them have not come from wealthy families. They are well-educated people who have developed marketable skills or come up with new ideas. They have seized the opportunities that are there to be taken. In short, they have engaged in market competition and prevailed. They are in the position of a runner who has won a race that is open for anyone to enter. What do they owe to the contestants who came in behind them? Nothing. Meritocratic societies tend to produce a diminished sense of social obligation. So what do the winners in such a society say if confronted by the plight of the embittered working class? Not "Let them eat cake," but perhaps "Let them watch big-screen TVs."

Whether this consolation prize—I can buy Sri Lanka, but you get to have cool new gadgets every year—will appease the lower classes and keep their spirits up remains to be seen. I don't think it will. The danger, as I see it, is not revolution but despair. As sociologist Michael Young argued in *The Rise of the Meritocracy*, the inequalities produced by a merit-based regime are very hard to bear, because the person who loses under a system whose legitimacy he accepts is forced into the recognition that he is a loser.[1] The winner didn't collect his reward because he was born into the aristocracy or had a rich uncle; by the terms set by the free market, he deserved to win. And it follows that the loser didn't fail because of the vagaries of circumstance: by those same rules, he deserved to lose and has only himself to blame for his inferiority.

The humane solution, therefore, is to soften the blow for the losers. One way to do this is to give them a long-term stake in the market. Proposals to permit a portion of Social Security funds to be invested in stocks and mutual funds are a step in this direction. Despite the recent volatility in the market, such a move is neither risky nor destabilizing. Historical experience and the logic of economic growth both dictate that markets always go up in the long term. Can anyone doubt that the Dow Jones Industrial Average in 2025 will be substantially higher than it is now? Even if stocks continue to yield 7 percent a year, their historical average, that means in a quarter of a century the Dow will be over

50,000. The historic antagonism between the laboring class and the investor class would be greatly mitigated if the size of the investor class were increased from 50 percent to 100 percent of the population. That way, every citizen would have a profitable stake in the system.

Another preferred solution is to focus on equal educational opportunity. The notion of giving every child equal access to education through high school is a noble goal, and it enjoys widespread support in the tech world. I would go further: it would be a great achievement for this affluent society to be able to offer all young people the chance to go to the best college or university to which they can be admitted. When I first came to this country as an exchange student in the late 1970s, I was astonished to discover that Ivy League colleges had a policy that said if you can get in, no matter what your means, we will make available a package of grants and loans so that you can attend. The only reason I was able to attend Dartmouth was the existence of such a need-based financial aid program. And it would be a glorious thing to be able to offer such an incentive to every student at every institution of higher education.

The question is not whether such schemes of educational opportunity are affordable—America has the resources—but whether they should be set up by government or by the private sector. Many people insist that equal opportunity is the government's responsibility. Even people who normally consider the government ignorant, incompetent, and out of it are willing to concede that here is a grand project for public policy: we must give the children of the poor the same chance to succeed as the children of the rich.

Equal opportunity seems like a logical fulfillment of the equality principle in the Declaration of Independence. Yet it is an ideal that cannot and should not be realized through the actions of the government. Indeed, for the state to enforce equal opportunity would be to contravene the true meaning of the Declaration and to subvert the principle of a free society. Let me illustrate. I have a five-year-old daughter. Since she was born—actually, since she was conceived—my wife and I have gone to great lengths in the Great Yuppie Parenting Race. At one time we even played classical music while she was in the womb. Crazy us. Currently the little rogue is taking ballet lessons and swim lessons. My wife goes over her workbooks. I am teaching her chess.

Why are we doing these things? We are, of course, trying to develop her abilities so that she can get the most out of life. The practical effect of our actions, however, is that we are working to give our daughter an edge—that is, a better chance to succeed than everybody else's children. Even though we might be embarrassed to think of it this way, we are doing our utmost to undermine equal opportunity. So are all the other parents who are trying to get their children into the best schools, the best colleges, and in general give them the best possible upbringing and education. None of them believes in equal opportunity either! Now, to enforce equal opportunity, the government could do one of two things: it could try to pull my daughter down, or it could work to raise other people's children up. The first is clearly destructive and immoral, but the second is also unfair. The government is obliged to treat all citizens equally. Why should it work to undo the benefits that my wife and I have labored so hard to provide? Why should it offer more to children whose parents have not taken the trouble?

Let me be clear: the government is certainly entitled to provide all children with a baseline access to education. I would like to see this baseline set pretty high, so that everybody has a chance to develop his or her basic skills. This expansion of opportunity, however, does not necessarily promote equality. After all, if every child is taught chess in school and my daughter gets an hour of additional instruction every day at home, the chances are that she will remain well ahead of the others. So what I am challenging here is the prevalent and wrongheaded notion that the government should seek to *equalize* opportunities and life chances. There is simply no way that all children can be given the same benefits as, say, Michael Dell's children. So the venture is unfeasible. But it's also unethical because it undermines the scope of parents to invest in their children's betterment that is an essential part of their exercise of freedom. What the government can guarantee is not equality of outcomes, not even equality of opportunity, only equality of rights.

Of course, if Michael Dell wants to promote equal opportunity, he could donate money to give other people's children some of the same benefits that his children enjoy. This is a legitimate goal for philanthropy: to go beyond equality of rights and provide, insofar as this is possible, something resembling equality of life chances. As I said earlier, I would like to see educational access for young people expanded

beyond elementary and secondary education to include college education as well. It is a goal both noble and affordable for the private sector.

At one time only the government could afford to pay for an ambitious social enterprise like this one. Today Bill Gates, with $21 billion
in his philanthropic foundation, is a small government unto himself,
and so are many other American tycoons. In New York a group of rich
businessmen has put up a large pot of money so that thousands of poor
and lower-middle-class parents can afford to send their children to private schools. The scholarship fund puts in $3,000, and the parents pay
the rest. I don't know which is more impressive: that parents are willing
to pay the extra money to forgo public education and send their children to better schools, or that wealthy businessmen are willing to pay
$3,000 to educate the kids of complete strangers. These are the gifts of
sacrifice and generosity that are a testament to loving parents and a caring community.

So much for the issue of inequality. The egalitarian left-wing critique is
complemented by, and over time is likely to merge with, the right-wing
critique based on community and morality. The right-wing critique is
no less broadly felt, and in some ways it is more powerful, because it
cuts deeper and engages more visceral passions. Let me put it in its
sharpest form. There used to be an old world and an old neighborhood
where people lived in close relationship with God, with nature, and
with one another. Using the term of the social theorist Ferdinand Ton-
nies, let us call this old world *Gemeinschaft. Gemeinschaft* means community, and its defining relationship is solidarity. Here people were part
of a natural and moral order. The world was "enchanted," which is to
say that man was at the mercy of forces larger than himself. There was
a sense of awe and vulnerability in our dealing with nature. There was
a sense of closeness with one's fellowman. Relationships were based on
love and friendship. Happiness, in this world, was defined as fulfilling
one's role in this larger framework. In the old world, the good life and
the happy life were seen as largely identical.

The problem, in the right-wing view, is that we have given up this
world of virtue, happiness, and wholeness. It is no answer to this charge
to say that the old world never really existed, that it was only a "city in
speech," and so on. Even if it was never realized, it was the governing

ideal. The best thinkers in the old world made an attempt to move their communities, to make asymptotic progress, toward this ideal. And some of them thought that in certain times and places—say Periclean Athens—the ideal had been very nearly realized. The force of the right-wing argument is that we have given up trying to achieve the good society. We have sold our souls for money.

Tragically, in this view, *Gemeinschaft* has been replaced by *Gesellschaft*. The community based on solidarity has been replaced by the society based on commerce. No longer do we feel one with nature; we now try to conquer nature. Relationships are no longer based on affection; rather, they are based on contract. Even the old sacramental understanding of the family is lost; even our spouse and children become instruments of our self-gratification. In this view, society is now held together by the shared selfishness and greed of its citizens. What could be more shameful than the naked pursuit of wealth and material possessions that is characteristic of the new economy? "My neighbor is a millionaire, I have to be a millionaire." Every human value—a just regard for nature, the obligations of family, the sense of shared community—seems to be trampled in this mad stampede for riches.

I have to admit that I feel the force of this critique. I grew up in a community largely defined by *Gemeinschaft*, and I now live in a society mostly based on *Gesellschaft*. But I also realize that once a society has moved from *Gemeinschaft* to *Gesellschaft* there is no way of going back. And as in my case, most people would not want to go back. They come to realize that what held the old community together was three things: ethnic identity, economic necessity, and the threat of conflict with the outside world. Homogeneity, scarcity, and war create bonds of kinship and mutual dependence between people; they are the cement that holds the tribe together. This was true of the ancient tribe of Israel, it was true of the Puritans who first came to America, and it is still true of the small subculture in which I grew up on the outskirts of Bombay. The virtues of what Tom Brokaw calls the "greatest generation" were also the product of homogeneity, scarcity, and war, and when the country became more diverse, peaceful, and prosperous, those virtues became harder to find.

The problem with the right-wing critique is that the principle of solidarity works only when a community is small, poor, and threatened. Communism, which is one version of the principle of solidarity, works quite well in the smallest of human communities, the family. The traditional family, after all, is based on the Marxist principle: from each according to his ability, to each according to his need. But Adam Smith was right to recognize that this principle cannot be applied on the large scale. We cannot feel toward people we don't know the same attachment that we feel for those who are closely related to us. Even our circle of friends is going to be limited; our dealings with the rest of the world must be governed by civility and contract.

So are we condemned to living in a society based on self-interest and greed? When I hear the familiar charge of "greed" launched against entrepreneurs and capitalists, I ask myself: Is it reasonable to ask that a farmer in Kansas get up at four o'clock in the morning to plant potatoes so that New Yorkers can have steak and potatoes for dinner? Does justice require that you and I stop working for gain and labor only for the good of society? Such notions are utterly fanciful and absurd. The desire of people to support themselves and their families is not a wicked impulse, it is a decent impulse. It is rooted in self-interest, but it is self-interest ennobled by filial attachment and responsibility. Historically, selfishness and greed have been in the same abundant supply that they are now. But they have had a different outlet: conquest. If the people in your tribe wanted more possessions, you simply seized them. Sometimes this principle extended to human beings: the woman taken in captivity became a concubine, the man who surrendered in battle became a slave.

The modern philosophers who advocated technological capitalism rejected conquest and enslavement as providing a right to possession. The new social and economic system they advocated was based on recognizing the motivating power of selfishness and greed, but also on limiting the sphere in which those passions operate. As Tocqueville put it, "Men cannot be cured of the love of riches, but they may be persuaded to enrich themselves by none but honest means."[2] Greed and selfishness are part of our human nature; it would be futile to try to root them out. What capitalism does is to channel them in such a way that their destructive power is minimized and they actually work to promote the common good. Capitalism civilizes greed in much the same way that marriage civilizes lust. Indeed, the actual workings of capitalism do more than steer greed into a socially beneficial outlet; in a positive sense, capitalism encourages empathy, consideration, and fair dealing with others. The reason is that to be successful, a businessman must anticipate the wants and needs of his customers, and if he wants his business to prosper he has to keep treating the customer relationship as special.

A good example of how capitalism makes bad boys behave themselves was given to me by T. J. Rodgers, CEO of Cypress Semiconductor. Rodgers loves to present himself as an outlaw figure who wouldn't mind—and might actually enjoy—giving people the shaft. But he confesses that on most occasions when he gets the chance to do it, he doesn't. He recalls a recent case: "I know this chip supplier of mine who was in a financial crunch. Now, I could screw the guy and pay him way below the market value for this stuff. I'd get it too, because the guy was in trouble. But I paid him the market price, because I've been in this business a while, and I know there will come a time when the demand for chips is very heavy and the supply is running behind. So that's when this guy is in a position to screw me. I don't want that, so I treat the guy fairly even when I can afford to take advantage of him."

The moral argument for capitalism is that it makes us better people because it puts our imagination and our efforts at the behest of others. Success is defined as the ability to serve the needs and desires of others, and the most successful entrepreneurs are those who do this best. There is no reason whatsoever for businessmen and businesswomen to feel guilty about being successful, because their success is the proof that they have effectively met the wants of their fellow human beings and thus earned a just reward. More than any social type, except perhaps the clergy, the capitalist is, in his everyday conduct, oriented to the task of helping and serving others.

Moreover, the capitalist has this over the politician and the clergyman: he has in practice done more to raise the standard of living of the poor than all the government and church programs in history. Using techniques of high-yield agriculture, multinational corporations such as Monsanto and the Archer Daniels Midland Company have fed more hungry people than all the state-sponsored and clergy-operated soup kitchens combined. Continuing in this tradition, the companies that are setting up electric power grids and Internet services from Karachi to Mexico City are empowering the disenfranchised and giving them the means to be self-reliant in a way that no government and church handouts can possibly do. This is the justification for the Party of Yeah's triumphant claim that in the new millennium, it will be the scientist and the entrepreneur who will lead the world. I believe this claim is fully justified.

Nevertheless, the Party of Nah is right that the gains of techno-capitalism have come at a price. I agree with Schumpeter and others that capitalism unleashes a gale of creative destruction that transforms mores, morals, and social institutions, and not always for the better. The moral and social changes caused by the Industrial Revolution were, in retrospect, as significant as the economic changes. And it seems safe to assume that equally far-reaching changes are under way because of the Information Revolution. The good news is that the new economy may help undo some of the damage inflicted on social institutions by the old economy.

This is not to say that we can recover the *Gemeinschaft* that characterized the old world. We cannot restore the enchanted relationship to nature that our ancestors enjoyed. The extended family, in which old people stay with, and are looked after by, their children, is unlikely to return. Nor is the patriarchal family, in its biblical or Victorian form, going to come back. As long as people move around, community attachments will be transitory. In a sense, voluntary communities have permanently replaced inherited ones. But the impossibility of a complete return to the old world does not mean that we cannot strengthen our relationships to nature, family, and community.

Wealth and technology can give us the means, and the knowledge, to preserve beaches, mountain ranges, wetlands, and rain forests. As families become more affluent, they can make more choices: Mom can opt to stay home if she wants to. Technology is making it possible for both parents to work from the house, restoring the preindustrial notion of the family as a united social and economic unit. Finally, wealth and technology are giving more people unprecedented opportunities to travel, to meet people, and to establish real and virtual relationships that were simply impossible in the past. A cyberspace community of fly-fishing enthusiasts, Verdi aficionados, or Goan Indian expatriates is quite different from the community in which I grew up. But it too is based on shared experiences and interpersonal relationships, and it makes possible profound satisfactions that can strengthen and supplement our real-world ties.

The greatest loss in the movement from *Gemeinschaft* to *Gesellschaft* has been the obliteration of the horizon of significance that gave people in the old world a deep conviction of life's purpose as part of a moral order embedded in the cosmos. Today it is virtually impossible for people to accept such an order, and what has made the problem worse is that its partial replacement is also losing its importance. By "partial replacement" what I mean is that until recently, all over the world, most people derived a strong sense of satisfaction and purpose from providing for their families and sheltering their children from the ravages of necessity. I know my parents took great pride in the fact that they were able to keep a roof over our heads, to provide us with three meals a day, and to care for us when we were sick.

But now there are millions of people all over the world—most of them in the West, and the greatest proportion in America—for whom the struggle for existence has effectively ended. They are rich enough, and their societies provide a sufficient infrastructure, that they don't have to worry about such mundane matters as survival. Software entrepreneur Ann Winblad says, "When I was growing up, talk about money in my family was all about making ends meet. I think of my five nieces and nephews. If they need something, I can just write a check."[3] It is wonderful to be in this position, and the rest of the world is trying to get there as fast as it can, but the strange consequence is that this group can no longer expect to find its source of meaning in the same place that Winblad's parents and mine did. They are able to ask, as only a handful of people in any given society have been able to in the past, What do I want to do with the rest of my life? What is my life for?

As affluence spreads, I believe that tens and eventually hundreds of millions of people will be asking just this question. That they can ask it is in and of itself a great moral achievement, because it opens up to innumerable ordinary people avenues of human fulfillment that were previously open only to aristocrats. Yet at the same time it is a strangely disquieting question, because there is no complete answer to it within the modern techno-capitalist framework. As we have seen, America is a country based on the notion of giving people the means to triumph over necessity so that they could pursue happiness. But the founders didn't say much about how this was to be achieved.

In Silicon Valley and other tech cities, some people are so unsure about how to pursue happiness that even when they can afford a great deal of leisure, they continue to work, work, work. The reason they don't stop, Paul Argenti of the Amos Tuck Business School told me, "is because they don't know what else to do. They don't have any other interests. I once told one of my former students who had made a lot of money to take six months off, go to Martha's Vineyard, and read *Great Expectations* and *Death of a Salesman*. He looked at me as if I was crazy. He said he hadn't read books like that since high school. His life outside his work was totally empty."

A second strategy for pursuing happiness, employed not just by rich people but by people in virtually every segment of society, is to engage in a riot of consumerism. In going berserk and buying a lot of stuff, they expose themselves to the scolding of the intellectuals, who are contemptuous of what Walter Benjamin once termed "the fetishism of merchandise." This condescension, however, fails to take into account the genuine fascination, charm, and delight that new acquisitions and toys give us. Wouldn't you like to have a Jacuzzi with a built-in music system in your bathroom? How about a St. John outfit that makes you the very definition of elegance? Or a TV screen that drops out of your ceiling? Or a computer system for your car talks to you and gives you street directions? These are all fairly cool items. An acquaintance of mine, upon hearing one too many admonitions from the Party of Nah, finally blurted out, "The people who say that money doesn't buy happiness simply don't know where to shop!"

At the same time, many people discover that material possessions, however abundant and engaging, do not satisfy their deepest longings. Without a sense of larger perspective, the pursuit of possessions can assume a tedious and even futile aspect, becoming in the end a "joyless quest for joy." I can hear the ordinary guy's retort: "Oh yeah? I'd love to have that problem." Such a person is so obsessed with improving his lifestyle that you cannot convince him that there is more to life than that. He is so busy huffing and puffing his way up the hill that he is oblivious to the fact that there are greater peaks to climb. His incomprehension testifies to the truth of Michael Novak's observation: only the man who has bread understands that "man does not live by bread alone."

Today more and more successful people are fully cognizant of the limits of materialism. They are searching everywhere for a sense of meaning, of purpose, of something higher to which they can devote themselves. Many of them are trying to find meaning in the workplace: "the life that works." Those who have the means are trying to find it in philanthropy: "getting by giving." Some invest in "socially conscious" mutual funds. Others are joining movements aimed at teaching them how to simplify their life. A good number are trying to find virtue by buying old Shaker furniture and eating organic food. Still others are chasing after spiritual gurus from Tibet and India. A few Silicon Valley entrepreneurs are beginning to sound like spiritual gurus themselves.

The Party of Nah is sure to scorn such efforts on the grounds that there is much in this "new spirituality" that is trendy and silly. I admit that this is sometimes so. It is also the case that these spiritual strivings are less concerned with obligation and more with self-fulfillment, less oriented to the afterlife and more focused on this one. Even so, I suspect that the quest for something higher is going to become a mass pursuit in affluent societies, and in general it is a trend that should be welcomed. However clumsy and faltering, such efforts are thoroughly consistent with the American Dream, which is more than a dream of materialist delights. Indeed the American Dream is based on a deep faith in the power of prosperity to better the human condition.

Although the founders did not spell out the content of morality or happiness, some of them, such as John Adams, were determined to provide their progeny with the prerequisites for their fulfillment. Adams famously said that his generation would devote itself to war and commerce in the hope that succeeding generations could devote themselves to art and contemplation.

Here is where the Party of Nah has a vital contribution to make. It is the ancient thinkers, from Homer to Plato to Aristotle to Epicurus to Marcus Aurelius to Cicero to Dante, who have thought hardest about the content of the good life and the virtues that make it possible. Aristotle, for example, argued that a certain amount of material comfort is necessary for the good life but beyond this happiness comes not from the pursuit of more but from the practice of the classical virtues such as courage, magnanimity, temperance, and justice. Epicurus was a hedonist in principle but not a wild party guy; he believed that a more practical strategy for increasing happiness was to avoid pain rather than pursue pleasure. Marcus Aurelius and the Stoics sought to make themselves indifferent to both pleasure and pain so that they could endure anything, even death, with serenity. And Dante had a vision of a spiritual journey that would provide, even in this life, a foretaste of Heaven.

These visions cannot be recovered in the way they were advocated—as conceptions or blueprints for society as a whole—but they can supply us with personal horizons of understanding and significance. By reading good books, by taking them seriously as advancing claims about the good life, we can let the great thoughts of the ancient world speak to us and transform us from within. Through such pursuits we can test the claim of the ancient philosophers that contemplation is the highest and most satisfying activity for a free human being.

I believe that this claim is correct, but there are other views of the good life—the life devoted to great and heroic action, the life devoted to the private joys of family and relaxation, the life dedicated to teaching, the life charged with political involvement, the life devoted to the service of others, the life devoted to prayer—that were seriously offered, and seriously considered, in the ancient world. One of the wonderful things about the wide orbit of freedom that our society offers today is that we can forge our own conception of the good life, and pursue it, within what Hayek called "a framework of competing utopias." Helping us understand which path to take: this is the gift the old world can give us.

In this context, I have been disturbed to see more and more of our educational institutions move away from the liberal arts and focus on "high-tech education." Courses in computing and programming are replacing courses in literature, political science, and history. The goal is to educate young people to function better in a technological society. But it is a terribly shortsighted strategy. The reason is that knowing about computers is going to become less important in the near future.

Right now computers are still fairly complicated. Every now and then something breaks down and wipes out all your files. The manual appears to be written in an alien script. Mastering the Sphinx-like contraption seems like a fundamental educational challenge. But computers are becoming simpler to use. Some techno-geeks are unhappy about this; they like being Gnostics of the software universe. But consumers want simplification, and so it is coming fast. Pretty soon the computer will function like electricity or the radio: turn it on, and it will do what you want it to do. As computing power becomes embedded in our everyday appliances and integrated into the infrastructure of our lives, we will rely on computers, but we won't spend much time thinking about them. I don't turn on the light and then marvel about electricity; I take it for granted. So too we will take the power to compute and communicate for granted. It is a law of economics that as things become cheaper and more abundant, their value in human terms declines to zero. Air, for instance, is indispensable to life, but since it is so plentiful it costs nothing and we don't spend time thinking about it. Computers, cell phones, and the rest of the paraphernalia of the Information Revolution are headed for the same fate.

All of this means that the best education for the future is not an education in software programming or in how computers operate but an education in the liberal arts. What our children most need to learn is the argument between Socrates and Thrasymachus, whether the Renaissance preceded the Reformation, what the Copernican revolution accomplished, and why the American founders preferred representative democracy to the direct democracy that the Athenians practiced. As some of the most insightful members of the tech world recognize, we are in a transitional phase in which computer literacy seems of paramount importance; that phase will soon pass. The next, more enduring, phase will be one in which "pipes" will decline in importance and "content" will become supreme. By content I don't mean just "information"; rather, I mean knowledge, understanding, and wisdom. In an age where the facts are easily accessible, knowledge, understanding, and wisdom have become premium goods.

Indeed knowledge, understanding, and wisdom have never been more needed than they are now. The reason is that our society is getting ready to take a plunge into completely uncharted territory, and great benefits, but also grave dangers, lie ahead. The benefits as well as the dangers arise because of the power supplied by biotechnology. It is entirely legitimate that we expand our consideration of the moral implications of wealth to include the moral implications of technology. Indeed, we cannot postpone this debate, because the newest technologies are coming fast, and they offer us a most awesome power: the power to remake human beings, the power to alter human nature. The moral conundrum of technology is simply this: Should we impose any limits on this power?

There are many in the Party of Yeah who say no. They welcome the new power as a further chapter in the history of human liberation. They point out that nanoengineering and biotechnology will allow us to manipulate atoms and genes and create things that have never existed before. We will be able to "grow" oil, metals, and buildings and "make" vegetables and animals with medicinal properties. Already we are demonstrating the power to remake human beings: gene therapy has been successfully employed to treat diseases at the genetic level, and the next logical steps are cloning, germ-line cures for disease, and genetic enhancement of our children. With each step, say the techno-utopians, who are the most gung-ho activists in the Party of Yeah, we will continue the upward march of progress toward living longer, developing greater capacities, and ultimately evolving into a higher form of being.

These are grandiose ideas, suffused, as Mark Helprin warns, with hubris, but it is justifiable hubris because the powers of technology are truly amazing. In most respects, I welcome the advent of the new technologies, which are likely to further reduce scarcity, eliminate suffering, and cure previously intractable diseases. I am in favor of bioengineering that provides high-yield, pest-resistant crops to help feed the world's hungry. Xenotransplantation may feel funny, but surely a pig's liver is better than no liver at all. I have no problem with genetic therapy to cure disease; I am even willing to endorse germ-line therapy that not only cures illness but also prevents it from being transmitted to the next generation. Under certain circumstances, I can see the benefits of cloning. The cloning of animals can provide organs for transplant as well as animals with medicinal properties ("drugstores on the hoof"). Even human cloning seems defensible when it offers the prospect of a biological child to people who might not otherwise be able to have one.

But there is a temptation contained in these exercises in humanitarianism. The seduction is to keep going, to take the next step. And when we take that step, when we start designing our children, when we start remaking human beings, then I think we have crossed a new and perilous frontier. Even cloning does not cross this frontier, because it merely replicates an existing genetic palette. It is unconvincing to argue, as some techno-utopians do, that giving a child a heightened genetic capacity for music or athletics or intelligence is no different from what my wife and I are attempting, namely, to improve our child's artistic and athletic and intellectual skills. But there is a big difference: it is one thing to take a person's given nature and given capacity and seek to develop it, quite another to seek to shape that person's nature and innate abilities in accordance with one's will.

Perhaps the renovation of genetic traits constitutes a new level in the engineering of human beings, some techno-utopians concede, but they insist that the bridge has already been crossed. There is no distinction, they contend, between gene therapy and gene enhancement. If we allow parents to cure retardation, we have to permit them to try to make their children into Albert Einstein. If we let people give their kids gene therapy to eliminate dwarfism, we have to let people employ enhancements so that their offspring can all become six feet tall. This argument is completely bogus, because it presumes that there is no valid distinction between health and sickness.

By contrast, every doctor understands this distinction, which is the basis for having a medical profession in the first place. Hard cases will no doubt arise, such as the child who is genetically disposed to fall a few inches below the normal height or ten points below the mean IQ, but these are degrees of abnormality that do not undermine the standard of normality; indeed, they rely on it. Hard cases such as these no more disprove the difference between health and sickness than the existence of twilight disproves the difference between day and night. Most of the time, it will be very easy to tell if genetic engineering is being solicited to cure a disease or deformity or to enhance, improve, or perfect a human being.

I do not object to people attempting brain implants and somatic gene enhancements on themselves. Perhaps in some cases these will do some good; others may end up doing themselves injury, wiping out their left brain, or, as neurobiologist Fred Gage put it, selecting themselves out of the gene pool. But at least these people have, through their free choice, done it to themselves. The problem arises when people seek to use enhancement technologies to shape the destiny of other people, including and especially their children.

Biologist Lee Silver argues that we have the right to terminate pregnancy and control our children's lives in every other way, so why shouldn't parents, in the exercise of free-market eugenics, be permitted to alter their child's genetic constitution?[4] In the single instance of gene therapy to cure disease, I admit that they can. The reason for this is that in this one limited case we can trust the parents to make a decision that there is every rational reason to believe their offspring would decide in the identical manner, were he or she in a position to make the choice. One cannot take seriously someone who says, "I can't believe my parents did that to me. I would have chosen to have Parkinson's disease."

But in every other case, people have no right to bend the genetic constitution of their children—or anyone else—to their will. That they might in good conscience seek to do so is the temptation that must be resisted. Indeed, it must be outlawed. But such a ban will not come by itself; it will come only as a result of a united effort on the part of thoughtful and decent members of the Parties of Nah and Yeah who jointly mobilize against the schemes of the techno-utopians. The reason is that what the techno-utopians want—namely to remake other human beings and to redesign human nature—represents a fundamental attack on the integrity of humanity, the value of human life, and the principle of the American Revolution.

To understand why this is so, let us recall that the scientific-capitalist project at the heart of the American experiment arose as a project for the "conquest of nature." Francis Bacon was a man with a fertile imagination, but never did he conceive that the enterprise to conquer nature would eventually seek to conquer human nature. Nor did the American founders. Their goal was to take human nature as a given, as something less elevated than the angels and thus requiring a government characterized by separation of offices, checks and balances, and limited power. At the same time, the founders saw human nature as more elevated than that of other animals. They held that human beings have claims to dignity and rights that do not extend to animals: in particular, human beings cannot be killed for sport or rightfully governed without their consent.

The principles of the founders were extremely far-reaching. They called into question the legitimacy of every existing government, because at the time of the American founding, no government in the world was based entirely on the consent of the governed. The ideals of the founders even called into question their own practices, such as slavery. It took the genius of Abraham Lincoln and the tragedy of the Civil War to compel the enforcement of the central principle of the Declaration of Independence: that each of us has an inalienable right to life, liberty, and the pursuit of happiness, and that these rights shall not be abrogated without our consent.

The attempt to enhance and redesign other human beings represents a flagrant denial of this principle, which is the basis of our dignity and rights. Indeed, it represents a restoration of the principle of slavery, and the argument between the defenders and critics of genetic enhancement is identical in principle, and very nearly in form, to the argument between Stephen Douglas and Abraham Lincoln on the issue of human enslavement.[5]

In this tempestuous exchange, which laid the groundwork for the Civil War, Douglas argued for the prochoice position. He wanted to let each new territory decide for itself whether it wanted to keep slavery or not. Douglas argued that it was wrong for the federal government to impose its morality on the new territories; they should be able to determine their own futures. A champion of moral diversity, Douglas wanted the American people to agree to disagree on slavery. Douglas advocated for each community a very high value: the right to self-determination, the freedom to choose.

But Abraham Lincoln challenged him on the ground that choice cannot be exercised without reference to the content of the choice. How can it make sense to permit a person to choose to enslave another human being? How can self-determination be invoked to deny others self-determination? How can choice be used to negate choice? A free people may disagree on many things, but it cannot disagree on the distinction between freedom and despotism itself. Lincoln summarized Douglas's argument in this way: "That if any one man choose to enslave another, no third man shall be allowed to object."

Lincoln's argument was based on a simple premise: "As I would not be a slave, so I would not be a master." Lincoln rejects in principle the subordination implied in the master-slave relationship. Those who want freedom for themselves, he insists, must also show themselves willing to extend it to others. At its deepest level, Lincoln's argument is that the legitimacy of popular consent is itself dependent on a doctrine of natural rights that arises out of a specific understanding of human nature and human dignity. If Negroes are like hogs, Lincoln said, then Douglas is right: there is no problem with choosing to own them. Of course they may be governed without their consent. But if Negroes are human beings, then it is grotesquely evil to treat them like hogs, to buy and sell and treat them as objects of merchandise.

"Slavery," Lincoln said, "is founded in the selfishness of man's nature—opposition to it, in his love of justice. These principles are in eternal antagonism; and when brought into collision so fiercely... convulsions must ceaselessly follow." What Lincoln is saying is that self-interest by itself is too base a foundation for the new experiment called America. Selfishness is part of our nature, but it is not the best part of our nature. It should be subordinated to a nobler ideal. Lincoln is making a case for America on the highest ground claimed by the ancients. He does this by seeking to dedicate America to a higher proposition: that all men are created equal. It is the denial of this truth, Lincoln warns, that will bring on the cataclysm.

Let me restate Lincoln's position in the context of the debate over designing other human beings. We speak of "our children," but they are not really ours: we do not own them. At most, we own ourselves. It is true that *Roe v. Wade* gives us the right to kill our unborn in the womb. The right to abortion has been defended, both by its advocates and by the Supreme Court, as the right of a woman to control her own body. This is not the same as saying the woman has ownership of the fetus, that the fetus is the woman's property. The Supreme Court has said that as long as the fetus is occupying her womb, she can treat it as an unwelcome intruder and get rid of it. (Even here, technology is changing the debate by moving up the period when the fetus can survive outside the womb.) But once a woman decides to carry the pregnancy to term, she has already *exercised* her choice. She has chosen to give birth to the child, which is in the process of becoming an independent human being with its own dignity and rights.

As parents, we have been entrusted with our children, and it is our privilege and responsibility to raise them as best we can. Undoubtedly we will infuse them with our values and expectations, but even so, the good parent will respect the child's right to follow his or her own path in life. There is something perversely restrictive about parents who pressure their children to follow the same professional path that they did or to become the "first doctor in the family." These efforts, however well meaning, are a betrayal of the true meaning of parenthood. Indeed, American culture encourages a certain measure of adolescent rebellion against parental expectations precisely so that young people making the transition to independence can "find themselves" and discover their own identity and voice.

Consequently, no one, not even parents, has the right to treat their children as chattel. This is the enterprise that is being championed by the techno-utopians, who are trying to convert everyone within the Party of Yeah to their wicked scheme. Some of these people even profess to be libertarians, but in fact they are totalitarians. They speak about freedom and choice, although what they advocate is despotism and human bondage. They want to be "good Nazis," who have a responsible strategy for producing a master race. Their ridiculous premise is that we are the wisest generation that has ever existed or ever will exist. Thus they urge us to break completely from the past and shape all future generations according to our wills. While they present this project as consistent with the scientific quest for progress, the crossing of the final frontier in the "conquest of nature," this rhetoric reveals itself to be a chilling example of Orwellian doublespeak. The power they seek to exercise is not over "nature" but over *other human beings*.

No form of rule is more barbarous than the one that seeks to convert another person into merchandise and make him or her in the image of one's own will. Parents who try to design their children are in some ways more tyrannical than slave owners, who merely sought to steal the labor of their slaves. Undoubtedly some people, such as Gregory Pence, will protest and say that they wish only the best for their children, they are doing this only for their own good. But this is just what the slave owners said! They too used the excuse of the welfare of their slaves to justify ruling them without their consent. "We look after our slaves when they are sick," these scoundrels said. "We've got a health care plan for them that the free laborers in the North don't have." Then, as now, the argument is self-serving. What makes us think that in designing our children it will be their objective good—rather than our desires, our preferences, and our will—that has the final say?

Unable to argue on the basis of justice, the techno-utopians finally resort to a raw assertion of power. "We are going to do this," they say, "and nobody can stop us. If we can't do it in the United States, we'll do it in the Bahamas." I suspect that something like this is going to happen, either in the islands or somewhere else, and we should treat it in exactly the manner that we treat the slave trading that now exists in the Sudan and other parts of Africa. Our response to the argument from power should be a very simple one: "Go ahead and do it in the Bahamas. You'll be arrested when you land in Florida." This may sound like an unduly severe reaction, but it is duly severe. What is at stake, now as in Lincoln's day, is the viability of the American experiment in ordered liberty, indeed the viability of the human race itself.

The argument against slavery is that you may not tyrannize over the life and freedom of another person *for any reason whatsoever*. Even that individual's consent cannot overturn this "inalienable" right: one does not have the right to sell oneself into slavery. This is the clear meaning of the central American proposition. The object of the American Revolution that is now spreading throughout the world has always been the affirmation, not the repudiation, of human nature. The founders envisioned technology and capitalism as providing the framework and the tools for human beings to live richer, fuller lives. They would have abhorred, as we should, the heinous materialist doctrine that reduces our humanity to protein-based computers. They would have scorned, as we should, the preposterous view that we are the servants of our technology. They would have strenuously opposed, as we should, the efforts on the part of the techno-utopians to design their offspring; to alter, improve, and perfect human nature; or to relinquish our humanity in pursuit of some posthuman ideal.

Mary Shelley's novel *Frankenstein*, written in 1818, describes a monster that is the laboratory creation of a doctor who refuses to accept the natural limits of humanity. He wants to appropriate to himself the traditional prerogatives of the gods, such as control over human mortality. He even talks about making "a new species" with "me as its creator and source." In his rhetoric Frankenstein sounds very much like today's techno-utopians and techno-Nietzscheans. And contrary to what most people think, the real monster in the novel isn't the lumbering, tragic creature; it is the doctor who creates him. This is the prophetic message of Shelley's work: in seeking to become gods, we are going to make monsters of ourselves.

Instead of taking this dangerous and evil path, let us recognize, and be grateful for, the gift of life. Our life, and our human nature, are precious things that have been gratuitously given to us. Nature is a gift that is entrusted to us for safekeeping. So are love and friendship, neither of which we deserve or earn. Even our creativity isn't so much something we do, it is something we are open to—the light of inspiration flashes through us. Therefore the authentic stance of the creative person is one of humble and thankful receptivity. Finally we should celebrate the gift of America to the world. We are ridiculously fortunate to be living in this country at this time in history. Moreover, the American Dream has become a global dream that is spreading hope to other nations as well.

Let us resist the temptation to arrogance, the oldest temptation in the world, which in its current form whispers into our ear that we are omniscient enough to remake our children and our species. Instead of succumbing to such folly, let us appreciate the wondrous freedom and abundance that we enjoy. Let us use them well, to find meaning and happiness in our lives and to extend the same chance to our children and grandchildren. In living both the good life and the life that is good, we can demonstrate the virtue of prosperity, vindicate the American experiment, and augment the happiness of mankind.

NOTES

In general, where a source of a quote is not specified, the quote comes from an interview by the author.

Introduction: Geek Chic

1. Cited in George Gilder, *Wealth and Poverty* (New York: Basic Books, 1980), p. 236.

2. Peter Drucker, reply to letters, *The Atlantic Monthly*, February 2000, p. 13.

1: A World Without Limits

1. David Denby, "The Quarter of Living Dangerously," *The New Yorker*, April 24 & May 1, 2000.

2. Michael Weiss, "Trader Moms," *Ladies' Home Journal*, October 1999.

3. "Everybody's an Expert," *Red Herring*, April 2000.

4. Dyan Machan, "An Edison for a New Age," *Forbes*, May 17, 1999, p. 181.

5. Geoff Cook, "Hey, I Just Work Here," *Wired*, March 2000, p. 232.

6. "Who Wants to Be a Venture Capitalist?" *Red Herring*, May 2000.

7. "It's Your Choice," *Fast Company*, January–February 2000, p. 202.

8. "The Internet Economy: The World's Next Growth Engine," *Business Week*, October 4, 1999, p. 72.

9. Louis Auchincloss, "The Persistence of the WASP," *Forbes ASAP*, November 30, 1998, p. 262.

10. "The Ninth Zero," *Worth*, June 1999, p. 144.

11. U.S. Bureau of the Census, *Statistical Abstract of the United States* (Washington, D.C.: U.S. Government Printing Office, 1999), p. 462.

12. Ronald Alsop, ed., *Wall Street Journal Almanac 1999* (New York: Ballantine, 1999), pp. 386–462; see also Mark Sauer, "In Bill Gates's Pocket Is the Wealth of Nations," *San Diego Union-Tribune*, January 20, 2000, p. E1.

13. Evan Marcus, "The World's First Trillionaire," *Wired*, September 1999, p. 163.

14. "America's 400 Richest People," *Forbes*, 1999 edition, special issue [October 1999], pp. 414–18.

15. "America's 400 Richest People," *Forbes*, September 13, 1982.

16. "America's 400 Richest People," *Forbes*, 1999, pp. 414–18.

17. Sue Zesiger, "Silicon Speed," *Fortune,* September 27, 1999, p. 120.

18. Andrew Feinberg, "Buccaneer Collector," *Forbes ASAP,* February 24, 1997, p. 43.

19. David Campbell and Michael Parisi, "Individual Income Tax Returns, 1997," *SOIS Bulletin,* Winter 1998–99, p. 13, Fig. F.

20. Arthur Kennickell, "An Examination of Changes in the Distribution of Wealth from 1989 to 1998" (Washington, D.C.: Federal Reserve Board, 2000), Table 4-B; see also Ashley Dunn, "Fairy Tale Falls Short for Rich," *Los Angeles Times,* March 14, 2000.

21. U.S. Bureau of the Census, *Statistical Abstract of the United States* (Washington, D.C.: U.S. Government Printing Office, 1994), p. 482.

22. See, e.g., Stan Davis and Christopher Meyer, "The Future of Wealth," *World Link,* January–February 1999, p. 62; Kevin Kelly, "The Roaring Zeros," *Wired,* September 1999, p. 152.

23. Tom Wolfe, "Aspirations of an American Century," speech to the American Association of Advertising Agencies, reprinted in *Advertising Age,* June 12, 1989.

24. Thomas Stanley and William Danko, *The Millionaire Next Door* (New York: Pocket Books, 1996), p. 12.

25. U.S. Bureau of the Census, *Statistical Abstract of the United States* (Washington, D.C.: U.S. Government Printing Office, 1999), p. 474.

26. "Family Net Worth by Selected Characteristics, 1989, 1992, 1995 and 1998 Surveys," *Survey of Consumer Finances* (Washington, D.C.: U.S. Federal Reserve Board, January 2000).

27. U.S. Bureau of the Census, "Historical Income Tables," Table F-1, www.census.gov.

28. Kennickell, "An Examination of Changes in the Distribution of Wealth," Table 4-B.

29. Andrew Hacker, *Money* (New York: Simon & Schuster, 1998), p. 73.

30. Bruce Horovitz, "'90s Luxury Beyond Top of the Line," *USA Today,* July 6, 1999, p. 2A.

31. Michael Lewis, "The Speculator," *The New Republic,* January 10 & 24, 1994, p. 22.

32. Joanne Meschery, "Horowitz Family Values," *San Francisco,* November 1999, pp. 19–20.

33. U.S. Bureau of the Census, *Statistical Abstract of the United States* (Washington, D.C.: U.S. Government Printing Office, 1999), p. 481.

34. Harry Dent, Jr., *The Roaring 2000s* (New York: Simon & Schuster, 1998), p. 201.

35. James Watson, "The Road Ahead," in *Engineering the Human Germline,* ed. Gregory Stock and John Campbell (New York: Oxford University Press, 2000), pp. 35, 78–79, 85.

36. Lee Silver, *Remaking Eden* (New York: Avon Books, 1998), pp. 70, 292.

37. Peter Cochrane, "Borg in the Mirror," *Forbes ASAP,* October 4, 1999, p. 42.

38. Ray Kurzweil, *The Age of Spiritual Machines* (New York: Penguin, 1999), pp. 35, 130.

39. Leroy Hood, "The Human Genome Project—Launch Pad for Human Genetic Engineering," in Stock and Campbell, eds., *Engineering the Human Germline,* p. 18.

2: The Gathering Storm

1. Robert Schiller, *Irrational Exuberance* (Princeton, N.J.: Princeton University Press, 2000); see also *Fast Company,* June 2000, p. 198.

2. Alan Abelson, "The Wages of Fun," *Barron's,* April 24, 2000, p. 3; Alan Abelson, "Bye, Bye, Bubble," *Barron's,* May 22, 2000, p. 5.

3. Jim Cramer, "Thud," *The New Republic,* May 1, 2000, p. 42.

4. Jeremy Grantham, "Investment Guide," *Forbes,* June 12, 2000, pp. 316, 320.

5. Chris Farrell, "Death of the Dot-Coms?" *Business Week,* May 22, 2000.

6. Tom Peters, "The Wired Diaries 2000," *Wired,* January 2000, p. 82.

7. Harry Dent, *The Roaring 2000s* (New York: Simon & Schuster, 1998), p. 21.

8. Michael Malone, "The Gildered Age," *Forbes ASAP,* February 21, 2000, p. 130.

9. George Gilder, "Life Span vs. Life Spam," *Forbes ASAP,* April 6, 1998, p. 78.

10. George Gilder, "The Materialist Superstition," lecture sponsored by the Acton Institute, Rome, Italy, 1998.

11. George Gilder, "Political Principles of the Telecosm," speech to the Manhattan Institute, New York, October 21, 1999.

12. George Gilder, "The Soul of Silicon," *Forbes ASAP,* June 1, 1998, pp. 111–12.

13. "Apple's Core Employee," *Business Week,* January 17, 2000, p. 44.

14. Brent Schlender, "The Three Faces of Steve," *Fortune,* November 9, 1998, p. 104.

15. David Kaplan, *The Silicon Boys* (New York: HarperPerennial: 1999), p. 330.

16. Otis Port, "Customers Move into the Driver's Seat," *Business Week,* October 4, 1999, p. 103.

17. "Riding High," special issue on entrepreneurs, *Newsweek,* 2000, p. 32.

18. Virginia Postrel, *The Future and Its Enemies* (New York: Free Press, 1998), pp. xv, 15.

19. Todd Buchholz, "A World of Good," *Worth,* December 1999–January 2000, p. 97.

20. Melanie Warner, "The Young and the Loaded," *Fortune,* September 27, 1999, p. 88.

21. Larissa MacFarquhar, "Caesar.com," *The New Yorker,* April 3, 2000, p. 35.

22. Freeman Dyson, *The Sun, the Genome, and the Internet* (New York: Oxford University Press, 1999), pp. 61, 72.

23. Rick Tetzeli, "What It's Really Like to Be Marc Andreessen," *Fortune,* December 9, 1996, p. 156.

24. "George Yeo," *Wall Street Journal,* January 1, 2000, p. R39.

25. Cited in Roderick Simpson, "Cloning. Problem? No Problem," *Wired,* September 1997.

26. Studs Terkel, "The Last Human Voice," *Forbes ASAP,* December 1, 1997, p. 222.

27. U.S. Census Bureau, Current Population Reports, *Money Income in the United States: 1998* (Washington, D.C.: U.S. Government Printing Office, 1999), p. 5.

28. Jared Bernstein, Elizabeth McNichol, Robert Zahradnik, and Lawrence Mishel, *Pulling Apart* (Washington, D.C.: Center for Budget and Policy Priorities, 2000), p. 56.

29. Walter Mead, "How America Got Rich," *Worth,* September 1999.

30. United Nations, *Human Development Report* (New York: Oxford University Press, 1999).

31. Amartya Sen, "Will There Be Any Hope for the Poor?" *Time,* May 22, 2000, p. 94.

32. Richard Rorty, *Achieving Our Country* (Cambridge, Mass.: Harvard University Press, 1998), p. 56.

33. Paul Krugman, "Who Knew? The Swedish Model Is Working," *Fortune,* October 25, 1999, pp. 48, 50.

34. Bruce Ackerman and Anne Alstott, *The Stakeholder Society* (New Haven, Conn.: Yale University Press, 1999).

35. James Tobin, "A Liberal Agenda," in *The New Inequality,* ed. Richard Freeman (Boston: Beacon Press, 1999), p. 58.

36. James Boswell, *The Life of Samuel Johnson* (Chicago: University of Chicago Press, 1952), p. 182.

37. Cited in James Lardner, "The Rich Get Richer," *U.S. News & World Report,* February 21, 2000, p. 43.

38. Dyson, *The Sun, the Genome, and the Internet,* p. 58.

39. For an analysis of "deep ecology," see Luc Ferry, *The New Ecological Order* (Chicago: University of Chicago Press, 1995).

40. Cited in Paul Raeburn, "Home Wreckers," *Popular Science,* January 2000, p. 50.

41. George Will, *The Pursuit of Virtue and Other Tory Notions* (New York: Simon & Schuster, 1982), p. 36.

42. Hilton Kramer, "Knitting of the Brow," *Forbes ASAP,* October 4, 1999, pp. 189–90.

43. Richard John Neuhaus, "The Internet Produces a Global Village of Village Idiots," *Forbes ASAP,* December 2, 1996.

44. See, e.g., Glenn Stanton, "Don't Blame the Generation of 1968," and Kenneth Myers, "The Cultural Context of the Sexual Revolution," *Family Policy,* January–February 1999.

45. Cited in E. J. Dionne, "Why Civil Society? Why Now?" *The Brookings Review,* Fall 1997, p. 7.

46. Cited in Paul Starobin, "Rethinking Capitalism," *National Journal,* January 18, 1997, p. 107.

47. Rich Miller, "Does Anybody Love the IMF or World Bank?" *Business Week,* April 24, 2000, p. 47.

48. "Jose Bove," *Business Week,* June 19, 2000, p. 176.

49. Bill Joy, "Why the Future Doesn't Need Us," *Wired,* April 2000.

50. Jonathan Kaufman, "Even Leftists Have Servants Now," *Wall Street Journal,* June 23, 1999, p. B1.

51. "Timothy Andrew Koogle," *Business Week,* September 7, 1998, p. 75.

52. Janet Lowe, *Bill Gates Speaks* (New York: John Wiley and Sons, 1998), p. 156.

53. Susan Moran, "The Unknown," *Business 2.0,* June 1999, p. 71.

54. John Cassidy, "The Woman in the Bubble," *The New Yorker,* April 26 & May 3, 1999, p. 65.

55. "Silicon Valley: How It Really Works," *Business Week,* August 25, 1997, p. 70.

56. John Gorham, "If He Builds It, Will They Come?" *Forbes,* October 12, 1998.

57. David Brooks, *Bobos in Paradise* (New York: Simon & Schuster, 2000).

58. Thorstein Veblen, *The Theory of the Leisure Class* (New York: Penguin, 1994), p. 137.

59. Bill Gates, *The Road Ahead* (New York: Penguin, 1995), pp. 248, 252.

60. "Why He Wears Those Sweaters," *Business Week,* February 7, 2000, p. 25.

61. Paul Fussell, *Class* (New York: Summit, 1983), p. 67.

62. Michael Patrick Allen, *The Founding Fortunes* (New York: Dutton, 1987), p. 252.

63. Cited in Diana Henriques, "Determined to Share the Wealth," *New York Times,* November 29, 1998, p. B13.

3: Created Unequal

1. "Turn On, Type In and Drop Out," *Forbes ASAP,* December 1, 1997, p. 51.

2. Edward Wolff, "Reconciling Alternative Estimates of Wealth Inequality from the Survey of Consumer Finances," American Enterprise Institute Seminar Series on Understanding Economic Inequality, Washington, D.C., February 9, 2000.

3. John Weicher, "Wealth in America: Increasing Inequality?" American Enterprise Institute Seminar Series on Understanding Economic Inequality, Washington, D.C., February 9, 2000.

4. Wolff, "Reconciling Alternative Estimates of Wealth Inequality," Table 7, p. 13.

5. Arthur Kennickell, "An Examination of Changes in the Distribution of Wealth from 1989 to 1998: Evidence from the Survey of Consumer Finances," American Enterprise Institute Seminar Series on Understanding Economic Inequality, Washington, D.C., February 9, 2000, Tables 1, 3.

6. Jared Bernstein, Elizabeth McNichol, Robert Zahradnik, and Lawrence Mishel, *Pulling Apart* (Washington, D.C.: Center for Budget and Policy Priorities, January 2000), p. 72.

7. "Executive Pay," *Business Week,* April 17, 2000, pp. 100–101.

8. U.S. Bureau of the Census, *Statistical Abstract of the United States* (Washington, D.C.: U.S. Government Printing Office, 1999), Table 761.

9. "Inside the Forty Richest," *Fortune,* September 27, 1999.

10. Rick Hampson, "What Would $1 Million Buy?" *USA Today,* December 22, 1999, pp. A1–2.

11. For his column detailing these views, see Rich Karlgaard, "Wealth Gap Follies," *Forbes,* October 11, 1999, p. 45.

12. Thorstein Veblen, *The Theory of the Leisure Class* (New York: Penguin, 1994), p. 204.

13. Peter Huber, "Wealth and Poverty," *Forbes,* December 27, 1999, p. 110.

14. Steve Fishman, "The Intensive Pet Care Unit," *New York,* January 17, 2000.

15. Michael Cox and Richard Alm, *Myths of Rich and Poor* (New York: Basic Books, 1999).

16. Robert Frank, *Luxury Fever* (New York: Free Press, 1999), pp. 3–4.

17. Data obtained from the Federal Aviation Administration.

18. Jonathan Kaufman, "Even Leftists Have Servants Now," *Wall Street Journal,* June 23, 1999, p. B1.

19. Cox and Alm, *Myths of Rich and Poor,* p. 15; see also Liz Spayd, "In Excess We Trust," *Washington Post,* May 26, 1996, p. C1; Robert Rector, "Not So Poor," *National Review,* October 25, 1999, p. 28.

20. Cited in Louis Uchitelle, "Devising New Math to Define Poverty," *New York Times*, February 23, 2000.

21. Thomas Jefferson, letter to Roger C. Weightman, June 24, 1826, in *The Portable Thomas Jefferson*, Merrill D. Peterson, ed. (New York: Penguin, 1985), p. 585.

22. Dirk Johnson, "When Money Is Everything, Except Hers," *New York Times*, October 14, 1998, p. A1.

23. Thomas Jefferson, letter to John Adams, October 28, 1813, in *The Portable Thomas Jefferson*, pp. 534–35.

24. See Robert Frank and Philip Cook, *The Winner-Take-All Society* (New York: Free Press, 1995).

25. U.S. Bureau of the Census, *Statistical Abstract of the United States* (Washington, D.C.: U.S. Government Printing Office, 1999), Table 753, p. 480.

26. Dora Costa, *The Evolution of Retirement* (Chicago: University of Chicago Press, 1998).

27. Sarah Lyall, "Murdoch Blood, Murdoch Empire," *Vanity Fair*, July 1997, p. 16.

4: The Lottery of Success

1. Thorstein Veblen, *The Theory of the Leisure Class* (New York: Penguin, 1994), p. 23.

2. "Voices of the Revolution," *Forbes ASAP*, February 21, 2000, p. 84.

3. "America's 400 Richest People," *Forbes*, 1999 edition, special issue [October 1999], p. 50.

4. Thomas Stanley and William Danko, *The Millionaire Next Door* (New York: Pocket Books, 1996), p. 3.

5. Ibid., p. 9.

6. Gary Becker, "Global Silicon Valleys? First, Kill All the Subsidies," *Business Week*, March 27, 2000, p. 26.

7. Patricia Sellers, "These Women Rule," *Fortune*, October 25, 1999, p. 94.

8. "Kim Polese," *Wall Street Journal*, January 1, 2000, p. R24.

9. National Science Foundation, *Science and Engineering Doctorate Awards: 1998* (Arlington, Va: NSF, 2000), pp. 1–3, 15–18.

10. *Red Herring*, February 2000, p. 35.

11. Scott Thurm, "Asian Immigrants Are Reshaping Silicon Valley," *Wall Street Journal*, June 24, 1999, p. B6; Alex Salkever, "The Curry Network," *The Industry Standard*, January 24, 2000, p. 289.

12. Andrew Hacker, *Money* (New York: Touchstone, 1998), pp. 159–65; U.S. Bureau of the Census, *Statistical Abstract of the United States* (Washington, D.C.: U.S. Government Printing Office, 1999), Table 759, p. 482.

13. "How to Bridge America's Digital Divide," *Business Week,* May 8, 2000, p. 56.

14. *Fast Company,* March 2000, p. 215.

15. Janet Lowe, *Ted Turner Speaks* (New York: John Wiley and Sons, 1999), p. 195; Howard Fineman, "Why Ted Gave It Away," *Newsweek,* November 29, 1997, p. 31.

16. "The Bill and Warren Show," *Fortune,* July 20, 1998, p. 64.

17. "The Godfather of Broadband," *Fortune,* January 24, 2000, p. 108.

18. Larissa MacFarquhar, "Looking for Trouble," *The New Yorker,* December 6, 1999, p. 78.

19. "Frederick W. Smith," *Fast Company,* April 2000, p. 98.

20. Laurence Zuckerman, "Private Jets for (More of) the People," *New York Times,* June 27, 1999, sec. 3, p. 2.

21. "Ted Turner," *Millionaire Magazine,* July 1999, p. 26.

22. "The Cisco Grown Up," *Business Week,* January 10, 2000, p. 62.

23. "Amazon.com and Beyond," *Wired,* July 2000, p. 254.

24. "Please, I'm Surfing," *Forbes,* March 22, 1999, p. 182.

25. "The Bill and Warren Show," p. 62.

26. Ibid., pp. 62, 64.

27. John Rawls, *A Theory of Justice* (Cambridge, Mass.: Harvard University Press, 1999), pp. 7, 11, 13–14, 89.

28. Ibid., pp. 90, 230.

29. Ibid., p. 252.

30. Joseph Schumpeter, *Capitalism, Socialism and Democracy* (New York: HarperPerennial, 1976), p. 67.

31. Michael Cox and Richard Alm, *Myths of Rich and Poor* (New York: Basic Books, 1999), pp. 48–50; Michael Cox and Richard Alm, "The Accidental Philanthropist," *Philanthropy,* November–December 1998.

32. Michael Walzer, *Radical Principles* (New York: Basic Books, 1980), pp. 240, 248; Michael Walzer, *Spheres of Justice* (New York: Basic Books, 1983), pp. 106, 107–8.

33. Robert Fogel, *The Fourth Great Awakening and the Future of Egalitarianism* (Chicago: University of Chicago Press, 2000).

34. Lowe, *Ted Turner Speaks,* pp. 15–16, 28.

35. Michael Lewis, *The New New Thing* (New York: Norton, 2000), pp. 260–61.

36. Adam Smith, *A Theory of Moral Sentiments* (Indianapolis: Liberty Fund, 1982), pp. 181–83.

37. Sports fans please note: From the fact that losers derive important psychological gains from rooting for sports teams, it does not follow that all those who root for sports teams are losers.

5: Eye of the Needle

1. "Craig Speaks," *Forbes*, June 12, 2000, p. 77.

2. Jim Collins, "Built to Flip," *Fast Company*, March 2000.

3. "Kim Polese," *Wall Street Journal*, January 1, 2000, p. R24.

4. Eric Ransdell, "The Nike Story? Just Tell It!" *Fast Company*, January–February 2000, pp. 44–46.

5. "Greed," ABC special report by John Stossel, February 3, 1998.

6. Richard M. DeVos, *Compassionate Capitalism* (New York: Dutton, 1993), p. 242.

7. Mark 10:25–27; Matt. 19:24; Luke 18:25.

8. Adam Smith, *The Wealth of Nations* (Chicago: University of Chicago Press, 1976), vol. 1, p. 18.

9. Justin Hibbard, "For Love or Money," *Red Herring*, January 2000.

10. George Gilder, *Wealth and Poverty* (New York: Basic Books, 1981), pp. 21–27; George Gilder, "The Soul of Silicon," *Forbes ASAP*, June 1, 1998, pp. 116, 118.

11. Gilder, "The Soul of Silicon," p. 118.

12. Ayn Rand, *The Virtue of Selfishness* (New York: Signet, 1964), pp. vii–xi, 17, 27, 31.

13. Adam Smith, *A Theory of Moral Sentiments* (Indianapolis: Liberty Fund, 1982), p. 25.

14. Smith, *The Wealth of Nations*, vol. 1, pp. 362–63.

15. Cited in Scott Kirsner, "The Customer Experience," *Net Company*, Fall 1999, p. 23.

16. Cited in *Fortune*, September 27, 1999, p. 88.

17. 1 Tim. 6:10

18. Jim Wallis, *Faith Works* (New York: Random House, 2000), pp. 71–72.

19. Randy Alcorn, *Money, Possessions and Eternity* (Wheaton, Ill.: Tyndale House, 1989).

20. Mark 12:42–44.

21. Luke 12:16–21.

22. Luke 16:19–31.

23. Luke 6:24–25.

24. Mark 10:17–22; Matt. 19:16–22; Luke 18:18–27.

25. Matt. 25:14–30.

26. Robert Sirico, "The Parable of the Talents," *The Freeman,* July 1994.

27. Some of the quotations in the discussion are taken from "T. J. Rodgers," *The American Enterprise,* July–August 1997, pp. 21–25.

28. Greg Easterbrook, "Run-on Sentencing," *The New Republic,* April 26 & May 3, 1999, p. 60.

29. See, e.g., Amy Bayer, "Always Willing to Start at Top, Trump Mulls Run for President," *San Diego Union-Tribune,* September 25, 1999, p. A18.

30. George Soros, *Soros on Soros* (New York: John Wiley and Sons, 1995), p. 248.

31. Melanie Warner, "The Young and the Loaded," *Fortune,* September 27, 1999, p. 79.

32. James 1:12.

33. For an overview of these studies, see Philip Hilts, "In Forecasting Their Emotions, Most People Flunk Out," *New York Times,* February 16, 1996.

34. Robert Lane, "Does Money Buy Happiness?" *The Public Interest,* Fall 1993.

35. Richard Easterlin, *Growth Triumphant* (Ann Arbor: University of Michigan Press, 1996).

36. Richard Sennett, *The Corrosion of Character* (New York: Norton, 1998).

6: *The World We Have Lost*

1. Jordan Fisher-Smith, "Field Observations: An Interview with Wendell Berry," *Orion,* Autumn 1993; Wendell Berry, "Why I Am Not Going to Buy a Computer," and "Rules for a Local Economy," *Resurgence,* May 1995; Wendell Berry, *The Unsettling of America* (San Francisco: Sierra Club Books, 1977), p. 21.

2. Joseph Schumpeter, *Capitalism, Socialism and Democracy* (New York: HarperPerennial, 1976), p. 84.

3. Daniel Bell, *The Cultural Contradictions of Capitalism* (New York: Basic Books, 1996), pp. xxx, 19, 37–38.

4. Francis Fukuyama, *The Great Disruption* (New York: Free Press, 1999).

5. David Bosworth, "The Spirit of Capitalism, 2000," *The Public Interest,* Winter 2000, pp. 3–28.

6. Gertrude Himmelfarb, *Marriage and Morals Among the Victorians* (New York: Knopf, 1985), p. 21; Gertrude Himmelfarb, *The De-Moralization of Society* (New York: Knopf, 1995), pp. 13–14.

7. Paul Hawken, Amory Lovins, and Hunter Lovins, *Natural Capitalism* (Boston: Little, Brown, 2000).

8. Peter Huber, *Hard Green* (New York: Basic Books, 1999), pp. 149–53.

9. Mark Arax, "Packard Foundation Puts Its Faith, Funds in the Central Valley," *Los Angeles Times*, October 24, 1999, p. A30.

10. Huber, *Hard Green*, pp. 73, 107.

11. Adam Smith, *The Wealth of Nations* (Chicago: University of Chicago Press, 1976), vol. 2, pp. 302–3.

12. Cited in Katharine Mieszkowski, "Clued In? Sign On!" *Fast Company*, March 2000, p. 46.

13. Jeff Skoll, "New Town Square," *Forbes ASAP*, October 4, 1999, pp. 65–66.

14. Howard Rheingold, *The Virtual Community* (New York: HarperCollins, 1993), p. 26.

15. See, e.g., Peter de Jonge, "Amazon.com," *New York Times Magazine*, March 14, 1999, p. 41; Evan Schwartz, "Linking the Information Superhighway to Main Street," *New York Times*, October 9, 1994.

16. Virginia Postrel, "Alone but Not Lonely," *Forbes ASAP*, February 22, 1999, p. 95.

17. Freeman Dyson, *The Sun, the Genome, and the Internet* (New York: Oxford University Press, 1999), pp. 64–65; see also Stewart Brand, "Freeman Dyson's Brain," *Wired*, February 1998.

18. Richard Sennett, *The Corrosion of Character* (New York: Norton, 1999), pp. 9–10, 44, 98, 133.

19. "Scott McNealy's Rising Sun," *Business Week*, January 22, 1996, p. 71.

20. Justin Hibbard, "Branching Out," *Red Herring*, September 1999, p. 66.

21. Eryn Brown, "Valley of the Dollars," *Fortune*, September 27, 1999, p. 103.

22. Ann Morse, "Modern Mamas," *Citizen*, January 1999, p. 20.

23. Robert Putnam, *Bowling Alone* (New York: Simon & Schuster, 2000).

24. Seymour Martin Lipset, *American Exceptionalism* (New York: Norton, 1997).

25. Stephen Doheny-Farina, *The Wired Neighborhood* (New Haven, Conn.: Yale University Press, 1996), pp. 7–8.

26. Rheingold, *The Virtual Community*, p. 2.

27. "Blurbage," *Business 2.0*, February 2000, p. 257.

7: A Future That Works

1. Kevin Kelly, "Interview with the Luddite," *Wired*, June 1995.

2. Benjamin Franklin, *The Autobiography of Benjamin Franklin*, ed. Leonard Labaree (New Haven, Conn.: Yale University Press, 1964), pp. 127–29.

3. Max Weber, *The Protestant Ethic and the Spirit of Capitalism* (New York: Charles Scribner's Sons, 1976).

4. Alfred Zimmern, *The Greek Commonwealth* (New York: Oxford University Press, 1931), p. 215.

5. Hannah Arendt, *The Human Condition* (Chicago: University of Chicago Press, 1998), p. 157.

6. Confucius, *The Analects*, trans. D. C. Lau (New York: Penguin, 1986), p. 74.

7. Paul Rahe, *Republics Ancient and Modern* (Chapel Hill: University of North Carolina Press, 1994), vol. 1, p. 44.

8. *Plutarch on Sparta*, trans. Richard J. A. Talbert (New York: Penguin, 1988), p. 132.

9. Alexis de Tocqueville *Democracy in America* (New York: Vintage, 1990), vol. 2, p. 121.

10. Jacob Viner, "Early Attitudes Towards Trade and the Merchant," in *Essays on the Intellectual History of Economics*, ed. Douglas Irwin (Princeton, N.J.: Princeton University Press, 1991), pp. 39–40.

11. Joel Mokyr, *The Lever of Riches* (New York: Oxford University Press, 1990), pp. 29, 195.

12. Jacques Ellul, *The Technological Society* (New York: Vintage, 1964).

13. Leo Strauss, *On Tyranny* (Ithaca, N.Y.: Cornell University Press, 1975), p. 190.

14. René Descartes, *Discourse on Method*, in *The Philosophical Works of Descartes*, ed. Elizabeth Haldane and G. R. T. Ross (Cambridge, England: Cambridge University Press, 1981), p. 119.

15. James Boswell, *The Life of Johnson* (New York: Oxford University Press, 1933), vol. 1, p. 567.

16. Machiavelli, *The Prince* (New York: Penguin, 1981), pp. 91, 97, 133.

17. Ibid., pp. 90–91.

18. Thomas Hobbes, *Leviathan* (Cambridge, England: Great Britain University Press, 1996), pp. 70, 89, 120–21.

19. Cited in Gertrude Himmelfarb, *The Idea of Poverty* (New York: Knopf, 1984), p. 28.

20. James Spedding, Robert Ellis, and Douglas Heath, *The Works of Francis Bacon* (London: Longman, 1857), vol. 3, p. 222; vol. 4, p. 29. For an overview of Bacon's thought, see Markku Peltonen, *The Cambridge Companion to Bacon* (Cambridge, England: Cambridge University Press, 1996).

21. Virginia Postrel, *The Future and Its Enemies* (New York: Free Press, 1998), p. 97.

22. For this analysis I am indebted to Thomas Pangle, *The Spirit of Modern Republicanism* (Chicago: University of Chicago Press, 1988), p. 159.

23. John Locke, *Second Treatise*, in *Two Treatises on Government*, ed. Peter Laslett (Cambridge, England: Cambridge University Press, 1988), pp. 285–302.

24. Alexander Hamilton, James Madison, and John Jay, *The Federalist Papers*, ed. Clinton Rossiter (New York: Mentor, 1961), no. 14, p. 104.

25. This quotation is from John Adams in an 1818 letter to Hezekiah Niles; see Bernard Bailyn, *The Ideological Origins of the American Revolution* (Cambridge, Mass.: Harvard University Press, 1992), p. 160.

26. Thomas Jefferson, letter to Roger Weightman, June 24, 1826; Thomas Jefferson, *Notes on the State of Virginia* in *The Portable Thomas Jefferson*, ed. Merrill D. Peterson (New York: Penguin, 1985), pp. 210, 585.

27. Roy Basler, ed., *The Collected Works of Abraham Lincoln* (New Brunswick, N.J.: Rutgers University Press, 1953), vol. 2, pp. 405–6.

28. Hamilton, Madison, and Jay, *The Federalist Papers*, no. 12, p. 91.

29. Ibid., no. 10, p. 78.

30. Abraham Lincoln, "Lecture on Discoveries and Inventions," delivered in Jacksonville, Ill., February 1859; cited in Michael Novak, *The Fire of Invention* (Lanham, Md.: Rowman & Littlefield, 1997), pp. 53, 58–59.

8: The Conquest of Human Nature

1. Danny Hillis, "The Big Picture," *Wired*, January 1998.

2. Cited in Jeff Lyons and Peter Gorner, *Altered Fates* (New York: Norton, 1996), p. 537.

3. Cited in Ronald Bailey, "Liberation Biology," *Reason*, May 1999.

4. Michael Malone, "Pixie's Last Lesson," *Forbes ASAP*, October 4, 1999, p. 54.

5. Freeman Dyson, "The Ascent of Science," *Civilization*, February–March 2000, p. 63.

6. Cited in Lyons and Gorner, *Altered Fates*, p. 35.

7. Michael Rose, "Aging as a Target for Genetic Engineering," in *Engineering the Human Germline*, ed. Gregory Stock and John Campbell (New York: Oxford University Press, 2000), p. 51.

8. Cited in Brian Alexander, "Don't Die, Stay Pretty," *Wired*, January 2000, p. 185.

9. Jan Morris, "Herstory," *Forbes ASAP*, October 4, 1999, p. 84.

10. Lyons and Gorner, *Altered Fates*, p. 566.

11. Daniel Koshland, "Ethics and Safety," in Stock and Campbell, eds., *Engineering the Human Germline*, p. 29.

12. E. O. Wilson, *On Human Nature* (Cambridge, Mass.: Harvard University Press, 1978), p. 208.

13. www.isteve.com

14. Lee Silver, *Remaking Eden* (New York: Avon, 1998), pp. 9, 133–34, 136, 233–37, 292–93; see also Bailey, "Liberation Biology."

15. Ray Kurzweil, *The Age of Spiritual Machines* (New York: Penguin, 1999), pp. ix, 3, 5, 130, 153.

16. Kevin Warwick, "Cyborg 1.0," *Wired*, February 2000; Jay Bookman, "The Evolution of E-Man," *Atlanta Journal-Constitution*, March 19, 2000.

17. Mark Helprin, "Contrivance," *Forbes ASAP*, October 4, 1999, p. 250.

18. Charles Platt, "Clear the Line, I'm Sending Myself Right Now," *Wired*, January 2000, pp. 205–10.

19. Alexander, "Don't Die, Stay Pretty," p. 180.

20. Gary Kasparov, "Techmate," *Forbes ASAP*, February 22, 1999, p. 71.

21. John Searle, "Consciousness and the Philosophers," *New York Review of Books*, March 6, 1997; John Searle, "I Married a Computer," *New York Review of Books*, April 8, 1999.

22. Daniel Dennett, "Did HAL Commit Murder?" working paper, 1997.

23. John Maddox, "Implications of Cloning," *Nature* 380, 1996, p. 383.

24. French Anderson, "A New Front in the Battle Against Disease," in Stock and Campbell, eds., *Engineering the Human Germline*, p. 44.

25. Jeremy Rifkin, *The Biotech Century* (New York: Putnam, 1998), pp. xiii, 15, 101, 105, 138, 214.

26. Lyons and Gorner, *Altered Fates*, pp. 267-68.

9: The Seduction

1. Lee Silver, *Remaking Eden* (New York: Avon, 1998), pp. 10, 12.

2. John Campbell and Gregory Stock, "A Vision for Practical Human Germline Engineering," in *Engineering the Human Germline*, ed. Gregory Stock and John Campbell (New York: Oxford University Press, 2000), p. 11.

3. Freeman Dyson, *The Sun, the Genome, and the Internet* (New York: Oxford University Press, 1999), p. 110.

4. Cited in Michael Fox, *Beyond Evolution* (New York: Lyons Press, 1999), p. 27.

5. Gregory Pence, *Who's Afraid of Human Cloning?* (Lanham, Md.: Rowman & Littlefield, 1998), p. 168; Gregory Pence, "Maximize Parental Choice," in Stock and Campbell, eds., *Engineering the Human Germline*, p. 113.

6. Pence, "Maximize Parental Choice," ibid.

7. Silver, *Remaking Eden*, p. 257.

8. Virginia Postrel, *The Future and Its Enemies* (New York: Free Press, 1998), pp. 159, 162, 165; Virginia Postrel, "Do You Deserve to Live?" *Forbes*, April 17, 2000, p. 152.

9. Alexis de Tocqueville, *Democracy in America* (New York: Vintage, 1990), vol. 1, p. 244.

10. Cited in Ronald Bailey, "Liberation Biology," *Reason*, May 1999.

11. Cited in Fox, *Beyond Evolution*, p. 29.

12. Silver, *Remaking Eden*, pp. 27–28, 277; Bailey, "Liberation Biology."

13. Ronald Bailey, "Petri Dish Politics," *Reason*, December 1999.

14. Gregory Benford, "Biology: 2001," *Reason*, November 1995.

15. Herbert Stein, *What I Think* (Washington, D.C.: American Enterprise Institute Press, 1998), p. 225.

16. Kass's comments are based on a personal interview as well as the following sources: Leon Kass, *Toward a More Natural Science* (New York: Free Press, 1995), pp. xi, 8, 11, 79, 159, 278, 308–10, 314; Leon Kass, "The Wisdom of Repugnance," *The New Republic*, June 2, 1997; Leon Kass, "The Moral Meaning of Genetic Technology," *Commentary*, September 1999.

17. Statement by the International Academy of Humanism, 1997.

18. Richard Dawkins, *River out of Eden* (New York: Basic Books, 1995), pp. 17, 19.

19. Richard Dawkins, *The Selfish Gene* (New York: Oxford University Press, 1989), p. 2.

20. Richard Dawkins, *The Extended Phenotype* (New York: Oxford University Press, 1999).

21. Michael Schrage, "Revolutionary Evolutionist," *Wired*, July 1995.

22. Dawkins, *River out of Eden*, p. 133.

10: The Gift

1. Michael Young, *The Rise of the Meritocracy* (London: Thomas and Hudson, 1958).

2. Alexis de Tocqueville, *Democracy in America* (New York: Vintage, 1990), vol. 2, p. 26.

3. Robert Cringely, "High-Tech Wealth," *Forbes*, July 7, 1997, p. 304.

4. Lee Silver, *Remaking Eden* (New York: Avon Books, 1998), p. 277.

5. For the best in-depth analysis of these debates, see Harry Jaffa, *Crisis of the House Divided* (Chicago: University of Chicago Press, 1959).

INDEX

Printed in the United States
By Bookmasters